IMAGES
of America

SEATTLE'S SOUTH PARK

ON THE COVER: Cassell's Point, on the Duwamish River, located in what is now South Park, was a favorite family gathering place at the turn of the 20th century. The Eighth Avenue South Bridge is visible in the background. This photograph was taken in 1891. (Courtesy of University of Washington Libraries, Special Collections, La Roche 159.)

IMAGES
of America

SEATTLE'S SOUTH PARK

Amanda Zahler, Anna Marti,
and Gary Thomsen

ARCADIA
PUBLISHING

ISBN 978-0-7385-4863-0

Published by Arcadia Publishing
Charleston, South Carolina

Printed in the United States of America

Library of Congress Catalog Card Number: 2006930225

For all general information contact Arcadia Publishing at:
Telephone 843-853-2070
Fax 843-853-0044
E-mail sales@arcadiapublishing.com
For customer service and orders:
Toll-Free 1-888-313-2665

Visit us on the Internet at www.arcadiapublishing.com

This book is dedicated to the Duwamish River; stripped of her elegant curves, the Duwamish has provided a livelihood for its inhabitants for thousands of years. May we some day return the river's innocence back to her. In addition, we would also like to dedicate this book to John Beal, a man who gave life back to the river. He inspired many to dedicate time and energy restoring the Duwamish River and Hamm Creek, two of Seattle's forgotten waterways. We would also like to dedicate this book to the many families and residents that have over the years contributed to this small but very vibrant community.

After a series of suicides took place in Seattle, the Georgetown-South Seattle News *published an article on July 16, 1904, that stated, "During the month of June nine people in Seattle committed suicide. Persons who do not like Seattle should come to South Park where life is worth living."*

Contents

ACKNOWLEDGMENTS

Thanks to Gloria (Jacquie) Jaquemart, Theresa (Yellam Postel) Lytle, Lora Suggs, George and Barbara Criddle, Maria Desimone, Elizabeth Desimone, Patrick Stark, Richard Strong, SeaMar, Environmental Coalition of South Seattle (ECOSS), Deb and Tim McNeil, Dave and Alyshawndra Means, Maureen Carroll, Loretta Overen, Joseph Pasquarella-Smith, Nigel Day, Aaron and Alyssa Cone, University of Washington Libraries, Museum of History and Industry, Carolyn Marr, Wing Luke Asian Museum, John Fisher, Puget Sound Regional Archives, Phil Stairs, South Park Ladies Improvement Club, South Park Community Club, South Park Seniors, SPARC, *South Park News*, the *Seattle Times*, City of Seattle Municipal Archives, and Chief Sealth sports and events marketing class.

INTRODUCTION

Today South Park is an almost forgotten pioneer residential neighborhood in the city's Duwamish River area. Originally inhabited by Native Americans of the Duwamish tribe who fished the river, farmed potatoes, and found bulbs and berries along its meandering shores, the 16-mile Duwamish River provided some of the richest farmland in the area. Being navigable by canoe made it ideal for habitation and commerce, traits that would mark its later development.

In the early 1850s, South Park was settled by pioneers who found the land "fertile and easy to clear." Dallas Avenue was the first shopping area in South Park. Boasting a saloon, a barbershop, and a meat market, it was the early gathering place for South Park residents. South Park was growing, and its future was—and would be—tied to the Duwamish River.

The town of South Park quickly evolved into a civic-minded, forward-looking community of farmers, merchants, carpenters, and churchgoers. The little government oversaw bonds for liquor licenses, street and water improvements, and had its own town marshal and jail. The town's first mayor was S. J. Bevan, followed in office by Bud Brudenstein and George Lingenfelter.

At one point on the west side of South Park, there were seven small creeks that came together as McAllister Creek—which boasted a 60-foot base where it entered the Duwamish River. McAllister Creek was one of the largest feeder creeks to the Duwamish. Joe Desimone, a local farmer, put concrete dams on three of the seven creeks that formed McAllister Creek. He then diverted the water down to his farms. Martha Weir had another of the smaller creeks on her property. She sold her water rights to Georgetown because Georgetown did not have a fresh water supply. A pier went into the creek on her property and into Georgetown.

On October 19, 1903, a petition to the United States Congress was written as follows:

> Whereas the Duwamish River was formerly a navigable stream and whereas by reason of the formation of debris and sand bars where the said river empties into Elliott Bay, it is no longer possible for vessels to enter the said river as formerly and whereas the said obstructions have shut the Town of South Park out of an otherwise natural water connection with the commerce of Puget Sound thereby preventing the establishment in said Town of industries dependent upon water commerce. Now be it resolved by the Council of the Town of South Park Washington that the Congress of the United States be and it is hereby respectfully petitioned to cause said river to be dredged or said obstructions otherwise removed so as to restore the former navigability of the same. Attested by Henry B. Green, Clerk, and G. C. Lingenfelter, Mayor. (City of Seattle Municipal Archives.)

It is also clear that early city planners saw major potential for the river being developed into a major industrial area served by a straightened and deep channel.

The level ground in the Duwamish Valley, between Spokane Street and Black River Junction, is so located with relation to the center of the city, to the waterfront and to the railways, that it is especially adapted for industrial purposes. On of the greatest obstacles in the way of its development is the winding course of the Duwamish River, which swings from side to side. The straightening of this river, as planned by the Duwamish Waterway Commissioners, will accomplish two things at the same time. It will permit the laying out of highways for wagon and rail transportation, without interference by the river channel, and will lay the foundation for the creation of a great industrial harbor, at which factories and industries may be located and served by both rail and water facilities. The functions of this waterway will be quite distinct from that of the waterfront proper in the district above described. Generally speaking, it can be most advantageously used for purely industrial purposes. It will become a place where raw materials may be delivered and the finished product taken to and from industrial plants by lighters, barges, tram coasting steamer, etc. For that reason the bridges across this waterway should be at an elevation giving free passage to small boats, tugs and barges without opening of the draws. (Report of Municipal Plans Commission, Seattle, September 7, 1911.)

King County officials passed a resolution in 1914 calling for bids to construct a drawbridge at the location of the current Fourteenth Avenue South Bridge. Dallas Avenue South served as the approach to the Fourteenth Avenue South swing drawbridge. The first Fourteenth Avenue South Bridge was a wooden swing drawbridge design, with a center pivot pillar, which allowed the bridge to rotate around a pivot horizontally, and an asphalt roadbed. This bridge did not work out as well as intended, as the center pivot pillar allowed logs to collect on the pilings and choked the passage. A different type of bridge was needed.

The South Park Bridge was constructed in 1929–1931. Because it is the only operational example of a Scherzer rolling-lift bascule bridge in Washington, the bridge is listed on the National Register of Historic Places.

In 1936, when prominent farmer Joe Desimone learned that the Boeing Company was considering moving to California for expansion reasons, he donated (some claim that it was actually sold for $1) a portion of his land to Boeing, an act that led to the future success of Seattle's economy. In admiration of his generosity, Boeing officials presented Desimone with a plaque of appreciation. The portion that Desimone donated lies within the 107-acre lot that extends into Tukwila, Washington, and is known today as Plant Two.

The Boeing Company truly changed the way of life for South Park residents. There were men from the 63rd Coast Artillery positioned both at the foot and at the beginning of the bridge that crossed the Duwamish, and only Boeing workers with an identification badge were allowed to cross. If civilians needed to cross the bridge or wanted to go downtown, they had to board a bus once a week that was monitored. It took about four years before residents could cross the bridge again unescorted.

Having such an important cog in the war effort in the neighborhood created more than a few challenges for local residents. In total, there were three different types of military in South Park. Aside from the 63rd Coast Artillery, there was the "George Jordans," which were primarily made up of African American men from Georgetown. They were responsible for the "smudge pots" that were set up around South Park. If the military sent out a blackout alarm, the George Jordans would ignite the smudge pots, which sent up a dark cloud in the sky so that South Park was not visible from the sky.

South Park also had air raid wardens—men with flashlights and hard hats who would watch houses to make sure lights were off during blackouts. Therese Lytle recalls, "One evening my brother was changing in the bedroom closet and forgot to turn off the light. Sure enough, the air raid wardens came banging on our door and told my mother that all lights needed to be turned off.

For the last 150 years, South Park has been a portal of entry for many immigrants—Italian, Japanese, Polish, Belgian, and, more recently, Mexican, Guatemalan, Salvadoran, Cambodian,

Laotian, Samoan, and Vietnamese, to name a few. An article that appeared in the *Seattle Times* on April 25, 1988, entitled "House Headed for Japan Is Pillar of Past" details the story of one South Park immigrant—farmer Frank M. Kabuki.

> Before Frank Minoru Kabuki's farm disappears under the asphalt and warehouses that have taken over South Park, a small farmhouse from his place will be shipped to Japan to stand on a hill above Hiroshima as a reminder of the past. The 12 by 22 foot wood-frame house, a typical shelter for farm workers in the early part of this (the 20th) century, will become part of a museum of Japanese heritage, depicting part of the story of Japanese settlement on the West Coast of the U.S.

Frank Kabuki purchased his six-acre farm in 1952 and farmed his land with his wife. They grew cauliflower, lettuce, radishes, green onions, celery, and spinach, which he sold to Seattleites through Rosella's Fruit and Produce. In the last years of Kabuki's farm, he grew spinach for Rosella's and Uwajimaya, the local Japanese grocery chain and maintained a successful operation. Unfortunately, Kabuki lost several acres when a freeway was built and even more when Metro took a chunk for a huge sewer pipe. When just two acres were left, the Kabuki's little house—built around 1910 by an Italian family—was disassembled shingle by shingle, post by post, and sent to Japan on a container ship.

In 1993, on Hiroshima's 100th anniversary, the Hiroshima Museum opened, and the Kabuki's little white South Park farmhouse—complete with house furnishings, kitchen cabinets, wood-burning cook stove, and bed—were on display.

Over the years, the rezoning of South Park has created a unique and, at times, troublesome mix of industry and residential. Today South Park's residential area is less than a square mile. South Park, as a whole (residential and industrial), is bound on the east by the Duwamish River, on the west by the high ground of West Seattle and White Center, to the south by an expressway, and to the north by the First Avenue Bridge.

The *Seattle Post-Intelligencer*'s August 11, 1974, article titled "South Park: A Square Mile of Defiance" stated, "Rich black bottomland lies beneath the concrete shroud of factories and warehouses in this square mile ignored by the city planners."

This eclectic mix of residential and industrial zones makes life interesting in South Park. Jackie Jacquemart recalls running outside to retrieve her laundry from the outdoor clothing lines when the South Park Landfill was openly burning its trash. "If you didn't get it off the line fast enough, it was covered in soot and you'd have to wash it again!" Residents marched on city hall to protest the open burning of garbage at the South Park Landfill in 1962. Theresa Lytle recalls finding a bicycle in the trash heap. The bicycle required repairs beyond the means of her family (the Yellams), so she could not keep it. She did, however, find a cowbell tossed into the trash by a dairy farm going under. Theresa still uses that cowbell. When her husband, Richard, does not hear her calling him for dinner, she rings her South Park Landfill cowbell, and Richard comes running.

South Park is one of the oldest communities in Seattle. Although it has struggled with industrialization and urbanization, this little community is rich with history that few outside South Park know.

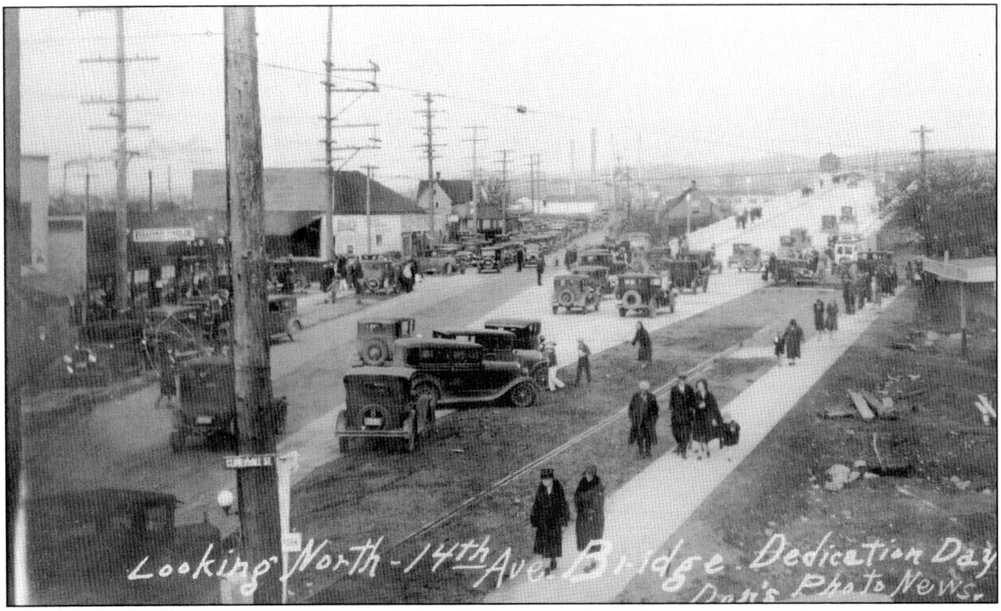

Pictured here is the 1931 South Park Bridge dedication. Note the presence of the original wooden Fourteenth Avenue South Bridge alongside the new concrete bascule South Park Bridge. The original, wooden Fourteenth Avenue Bridge was poorly designed, and debris regularly interfered with its ability to pivot, therefore interrupting efficient marine traffic passage up and down the Duwamish River. (Courtesy of Aaron and Alyssa Cone.)

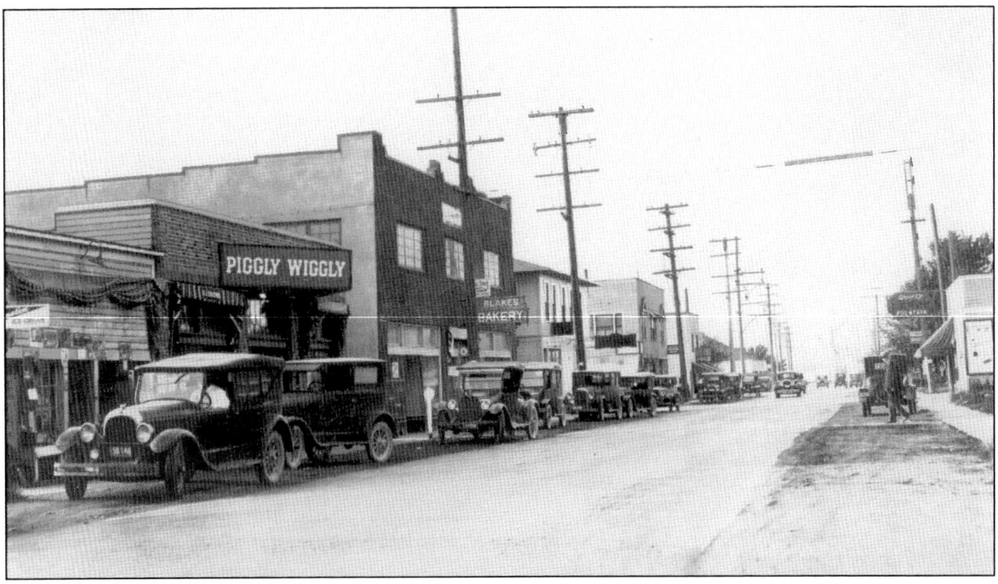

Fourteenth Avenue South is pictured here, with a car crossing the Fourteenth Avenue Bridge in the distance. When this photograph was taken *c.* 1931, both Fourteenth and Eighth Avenue South had bridges crossing the Duwamish River, which led to two major business cores along the Fourteenth and Eighth Avenue South arterials. Today Fourteenth Avenue South is the major commercial center of South Park, and its future is uncertain, as the 1931 South Park Bridge is on the verge of being closed due to multiple age-related failures. (Courtesy of Aaron and Alyssa Cone.)

One

EARLY FAMILIES

Realizing the vast opportunities that lay aside the Duwamish River, settlers began arriving in the area within months of the Denny party landing on Alki. In 1851, Eli Maple claimed land on what would later be known as South Park. During that same period, Luther Collins claimed land across the river and downstream from Maple, in what later became the neighboring community of Georgetown. In 1853, Daniel and Adam Schneider joined Maple. George Holt, Augustus Holgrave, William Ralston, Francis McNatt, and John Buckley also established farms in the area during this period.

In 1889, I. William Adams purchased the Donovan farm and platted the town of South Park. In 1891, the Grant Street Electric Railway extended a trolley line from Seattle to South Park, crossing the Duwamish River over a wooden drawbridge at Eighth Avenue South.

In 1900, August and Louise Ozar came to South Park from Belgium and Michigan, respectively. The Ozars owned and operated a blacksmith shop, popcorn and peanut store, and the South Park Bar (in the Ozar and Monteville Building at 110 Valley Road) with their five children. Their three boys attended school at Our Lady of Lourdes. Both of their daughters were married in the church. Albert and Irene La Franchi owned La Franchi dairy farm on a hillside south of the Duwamish River. The Paradottos owned La Cantina Saloon in the days of the gold rush. They later opened a grocery store.

In 1907, William Woolsey applied for a liquor license to operate the same bar, which he named Cloverdale Bar, at the corner of Eighth Avenue and Cloverdale Street. Family life involved taking the trolley down Eighth Avenue to Georgetown to get to Seattle. Prior to 1891 and the electric trolley, getting to Seattle and back could take a full day, as many people took a ferry to Georgetown and then had to get transportation to downtown.

Other early South Park families were the Burns, the Millers, the McCallisters, the Kellys, and the Alexander Prentice family. In the beginning, South Park was comprised of farms and the attendant businesses that supported that industry. This lifestyle changed dramatically with the influx of industry to the area, fueled partially by the advent of World War II. Even so, many descendents of these families stayed in South Park through the end of World War II.

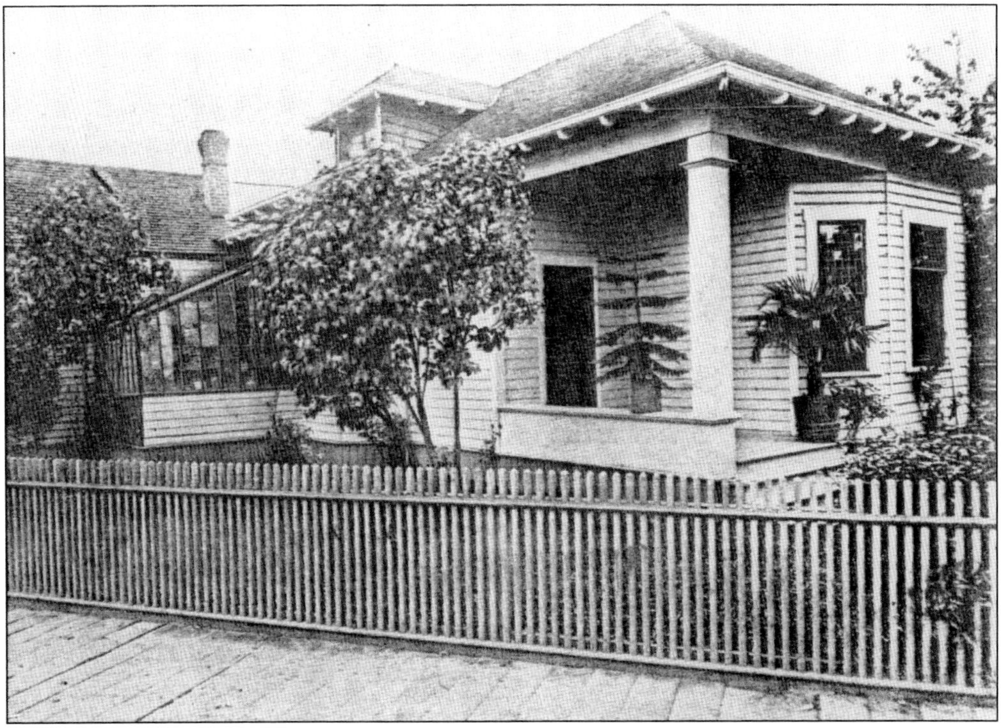

Pictured here is the B. F. Middleton home, which was built in 1894. It is located where Dallas and Tenth Avenues meet. This photograph was taken in the early 1900s. Middleton owned a grocery store on Dallas Avenue during the time when Dallas Avenue was the major retail core of South Park. (Courtesy of Theresa Lytle.)

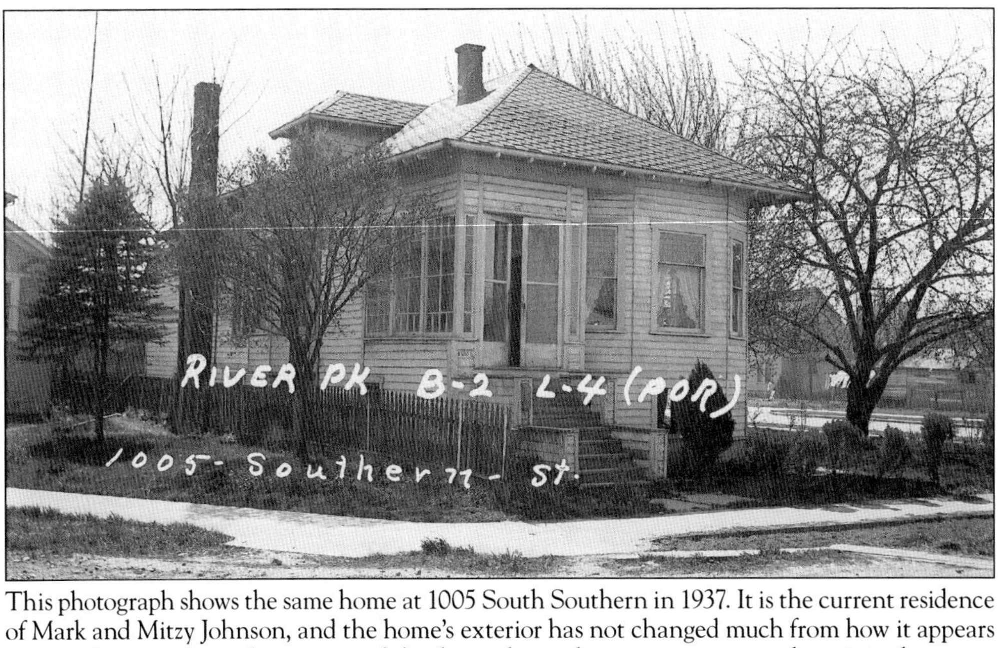

This photograph shows the same home at 1005 South Southern in 1937. It is the current residence of Mark and Mitzy Johnson, and the home's exterior has not changed much from how it appears in this photograph, as the owners of this home have chosen not to cover the original tongue-and-groove fir siding with aluminum or vinyl. (Courtesy of PSRA.)

Fred and Carl Marra are pictured outside of the Marra Farm located in South Park. The Marra family was part of the early Italian immigration into the South Park area, nearly all of whom were farmers. This photograph was taken in the early 1930s. (Courtesy of the George Criddle family.)

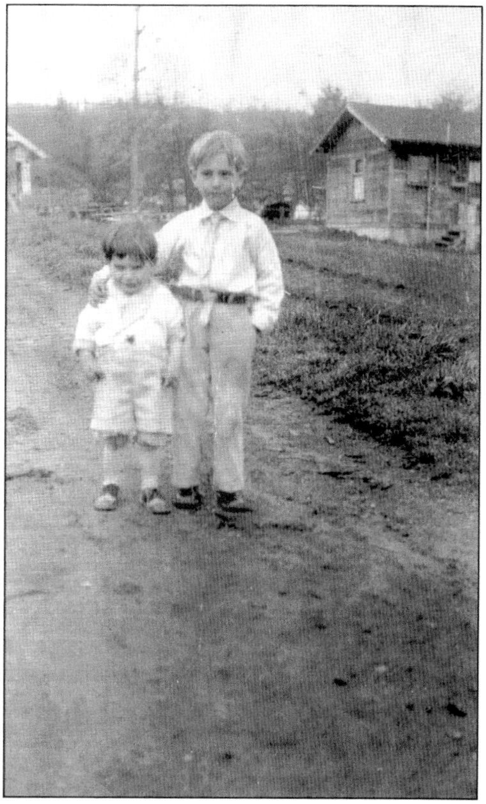

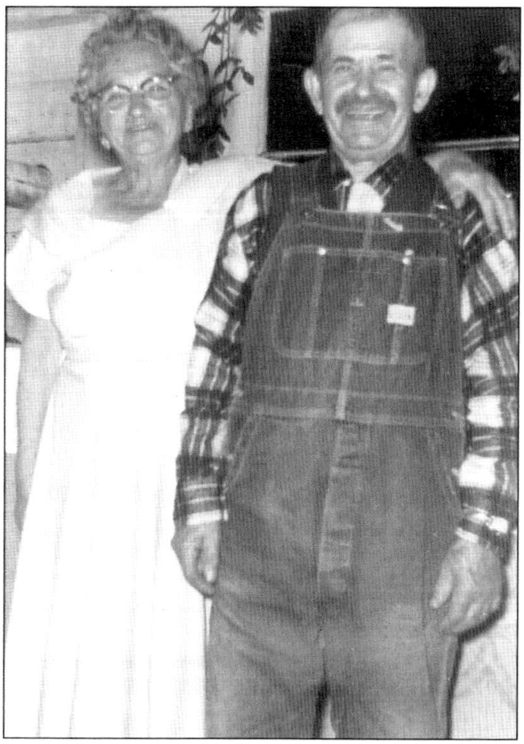

In 1962, Maria and Carmine Marra are pictured outside their South Park home. The Marra family played a very important role in the South Park farming community. Today the Marra Farm is a community garden located where the original farm once stood. (Courtesy of the George Criddle family.)

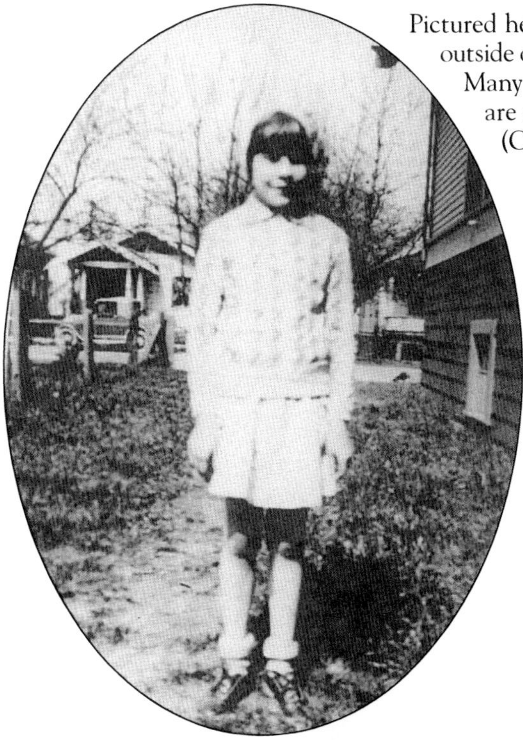

Pictured here around 1925 is one of the Anderson girls outside of her South Park home near Southern Street. Many of the homes that the Anderson family owned are still intact and have families living in them. (Courtesy of the Anderson family.)

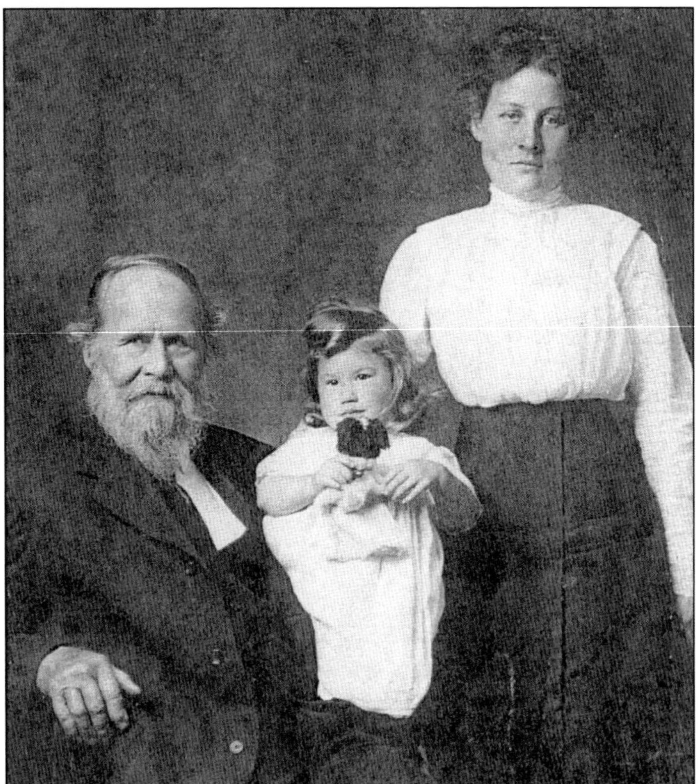

Like the Marra and Desimone families, the Andersons, pictured here, had much of their extended family within a few blocks inside South Park, with many homes along Southern and Rose Streets occupied by aunts, uncles, brothers, and sisters. The date this image was taken is unknown. (Courtesy of the Anderson family.)

Two of the young Anderson girls sit on a large roll of fencing outside of their South Park home on Southern Street, which still resembles much of the housing and landscape seen in this undated photograph. (Courtesy of the Anderson family.)

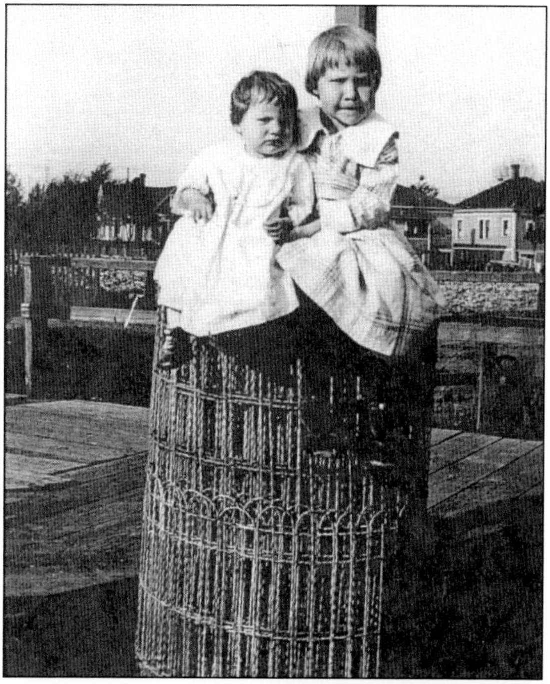

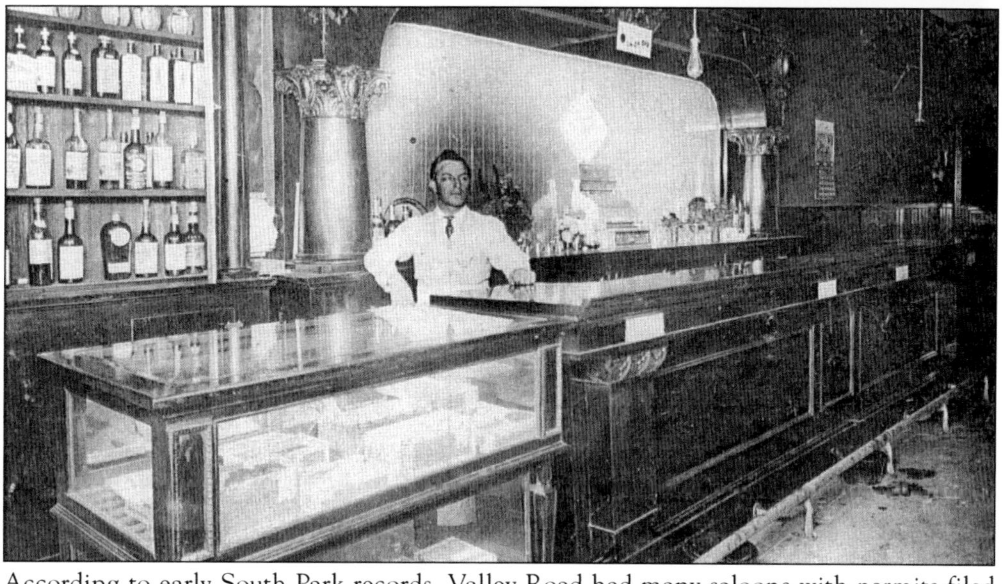

According to early South Park records, Valley Road had many saloons with permits filed with the South Park city clerk. Yellowstone Park Bar and the Turf Exchange (owned by J. H. Fitzgerald), the Union Bar (owned by Fred Schneider), the South Park Bar (in the Ozar and Monteville Building at 110 Valley Road), the Jacky Club (located at 115 Valley Road and owned by L. H. Keist), and the Duwamish Saloon (owned by Jules Maes on Valley Road) are a few of the bars that obtained permits from the town of South Park to sell alcohol. Valley Road had many salons yet that road no longer exists on any maps, as street names were changed when South Park annexed to Seattle. What is known from notes in the archives regarding the profile of Valley Road is that it intersected with South Eighth, Washington Boulevard, South Tenth, South Eleventh, Lookout Street, and McNatt Street. (Courtesy of the Anderson family.)

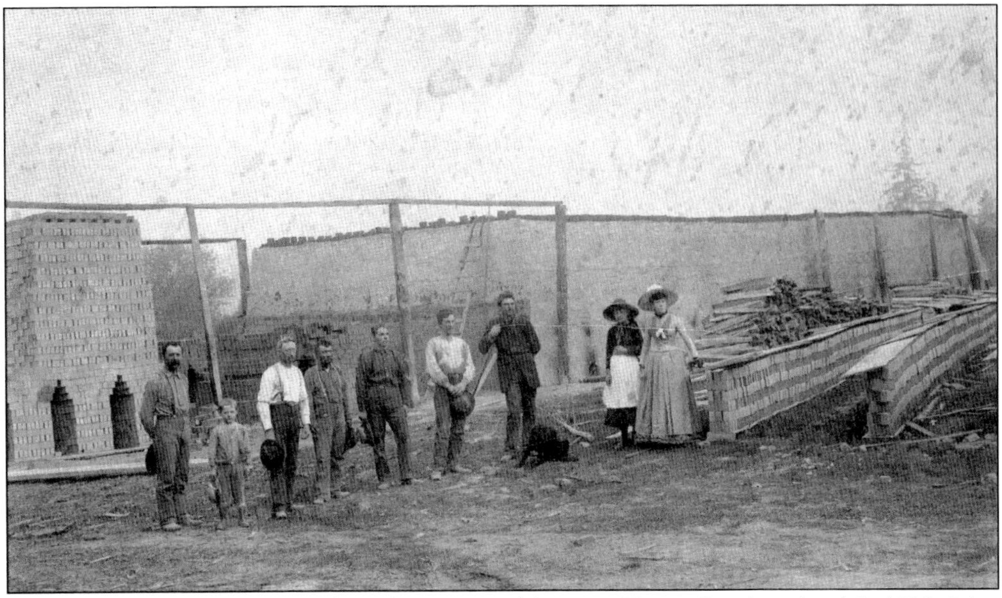

McAllister Brick Yard in South Park is pictured here on Easter Sunday, April 5, 1896. John McAllister and his family, while not early settlers, did settle along the banks of the Duwamish River in 1890. John and his family owned many acres in the northern part of South Park where Highway 99 and West Marginal Way now exist. The McAllister Brick Yard was a booming business, as builders liked the fireproof quality of brick construction over wood. (Courtesy of MOHAI, No. SHS8413.)

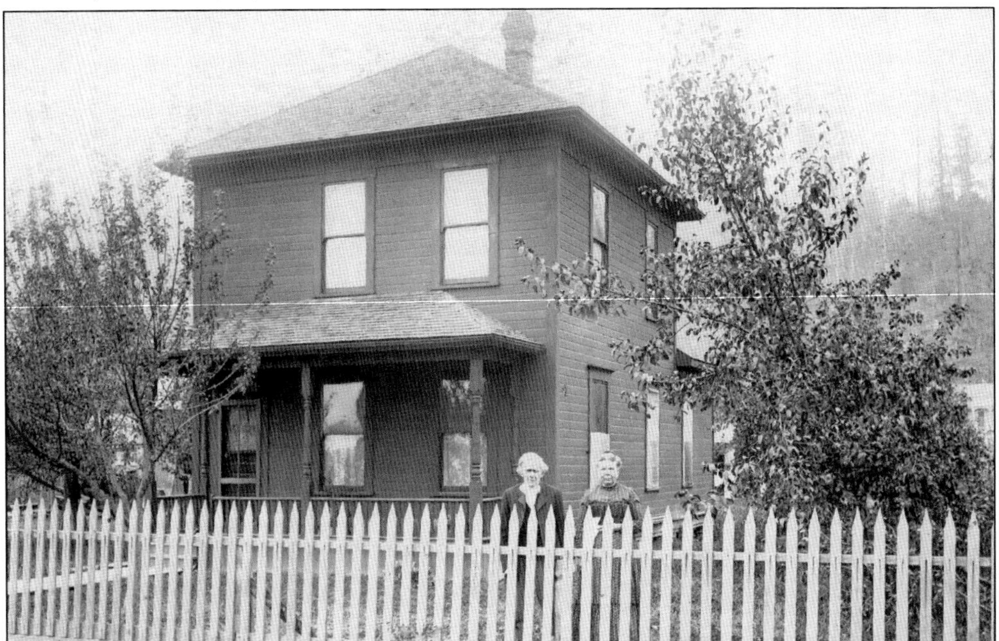

Aaron and Ann Mercer are pictured outside their home in South Park; no date is given. This home typifies many of the simple structures that existed throughout the residential areas of South Park in the late 1800s and early 1900s. There are a few homes with this simple architecture still standing in South Park today. (Courtesy of MOHAI, No. SHS8408)

Two

Our Lady of Lourdes and Churches

Before the Alaskan gold rush, when Seattle was still part of the Diocese of Nisqually, Father Prefontaine's parish, Our Lady of Good Help (constructed in 1869), was the only parish in Seattle. Father Prefontaine's assistant, Fr. Emmanuel Demanez, a young priest from Belgium, was aware of the number of Catholics in the outlying areas of Seattle and pushed for a parish to serve this ever-growing group. Father Demanez approached Bishop Aegidius Junger about starting a new parish in Seattle, though his idea was rejected several times. Finally, Father Demanez was able to persuade the Brothers of Our Lady of Lourdes from Oostakker, Belgium, to start a school in South Park.

In 1890, Brother Callixtus and Brother Henry came to Seattle, acquired land from I. W. Adams, and began building the College of Our Lady of Lourdes. In 1892, the school opened with Father Demanez as chaplain. Immediately after the school opened, its chapel was opened to all area Catholics. The school consisted of three large buildings and several smaller buildings. The largest building held a dormitory, a library, and a chapel. The second largest housed the refectory and a kitchen, and the third building had classrooms, a study hall, and a dormitory. On June 22, 1919, after a reception held in their honor, Brother Callixtus and Brother Henry left Seattle after 6:00 p.m. Mass to return to Belgium. Although their reason for parting is undocumented, some say that the brothers returned to Belgium in response to an announcement asking for aid with World War I orphans. Shortly after the brothers' departure, the school was closed and the larger buildings torn down. The school's chapel was then remodeled into what South Park residents remember as "the old church." The church was a small white building with a high steeple and was used until 1970.

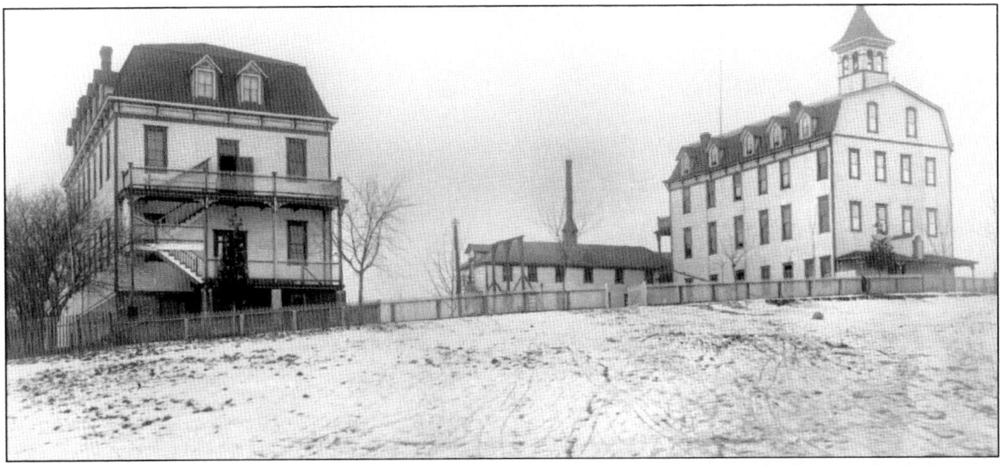

The Catholic church and school, living quarters, laundry, and eating hall were built by the Brethren of Our Lady of Lourdes of Ostaakes, Belgium, in 1892. There were 18 boarders and 40 day students. The building on the left held the study hall, playroom, classrooms, and chapel dormitory. The building in the center housed the kitchen and living quarters for the kitchen help. The building to the right was the chapel, dormitory, and library. The school closed in 1919 when the brethren returned to their homeland. The church continued to operate until the 1970s (in the remodeled chapel). It was torn down in 1983, and the property sold to Sea Mar in the 1990s. (Courtesy of Theresa Lytle.)

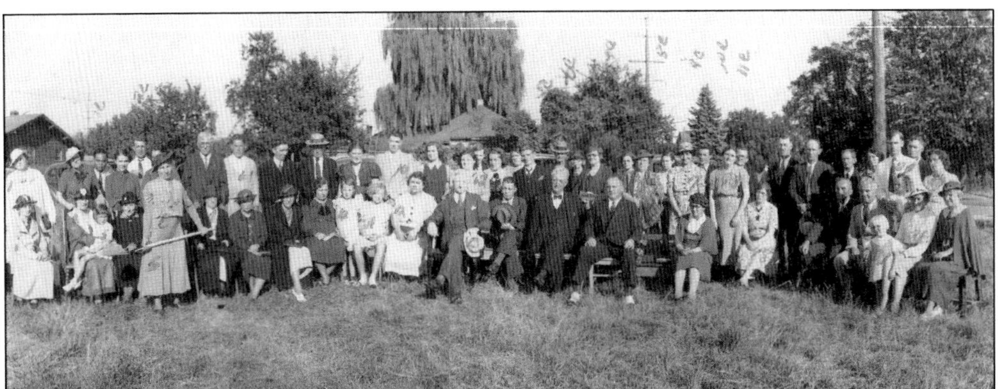

The groundbreaking ceremony in 1938 for the new Church of God is pictured here. The church opened for services in late 1940 under Reverend Christensen and is still located at the corner of Tenth and Cloverdale Street. (Courtesy of Theresa Lytle.)

Our Lady of Lourdes was one of the oldest churches in the entire Seattle area. The church no longer exists in South Park. It was torn down in 1992 to make way for several of the Sea Mar buildings located in the area. This photograph was taken sometime in the 1960s or 1970s. (Courtesy of Theresa Lytle.)

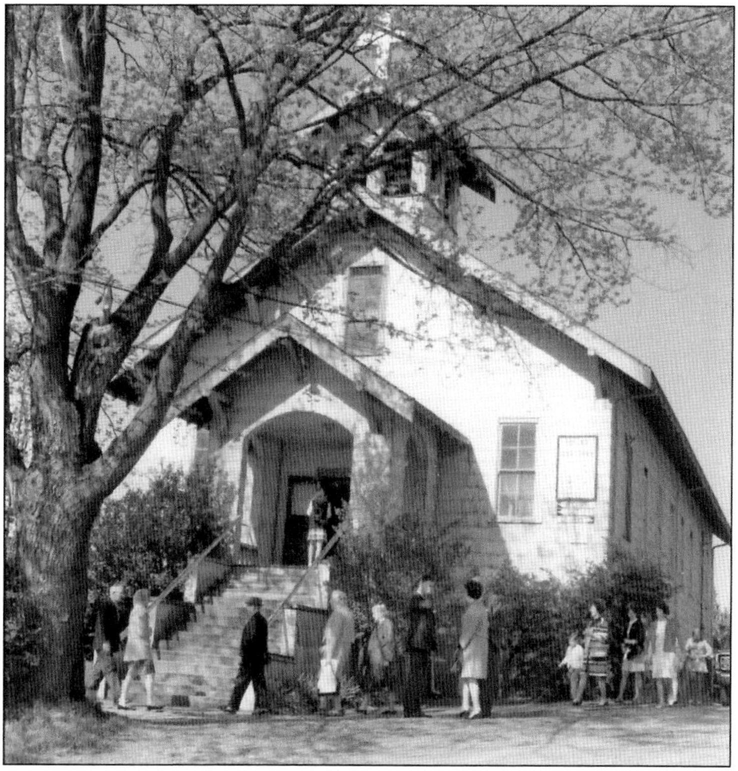

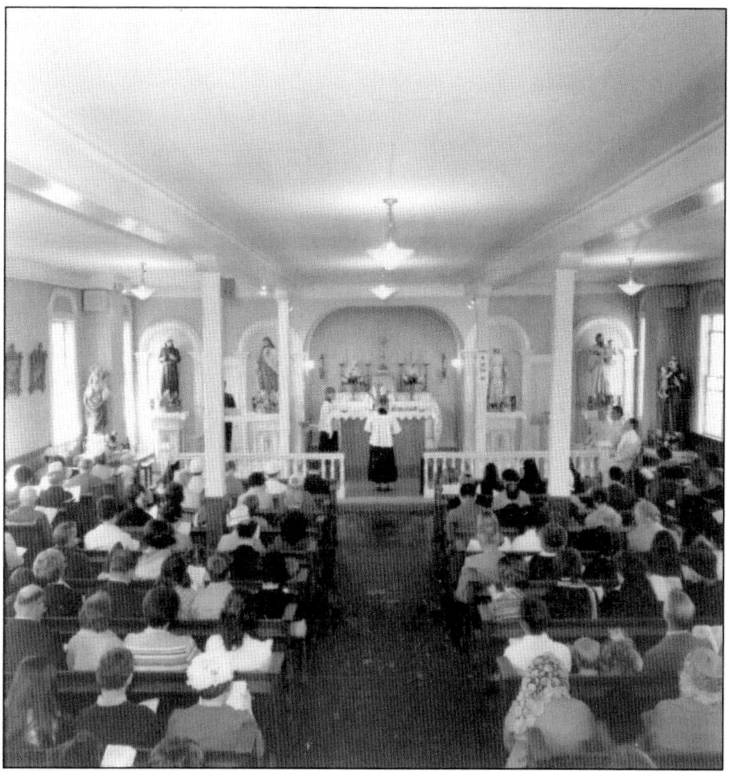

This is the interior of Our Lady of Lourdes, with Sunday mass in session. Our Lady of Lourdes held an annual event called St. Anthony's Festival, which involved a huge community parade and a dinner of spaghetti and ribs. (Courtesy of Theresa Lytle.)

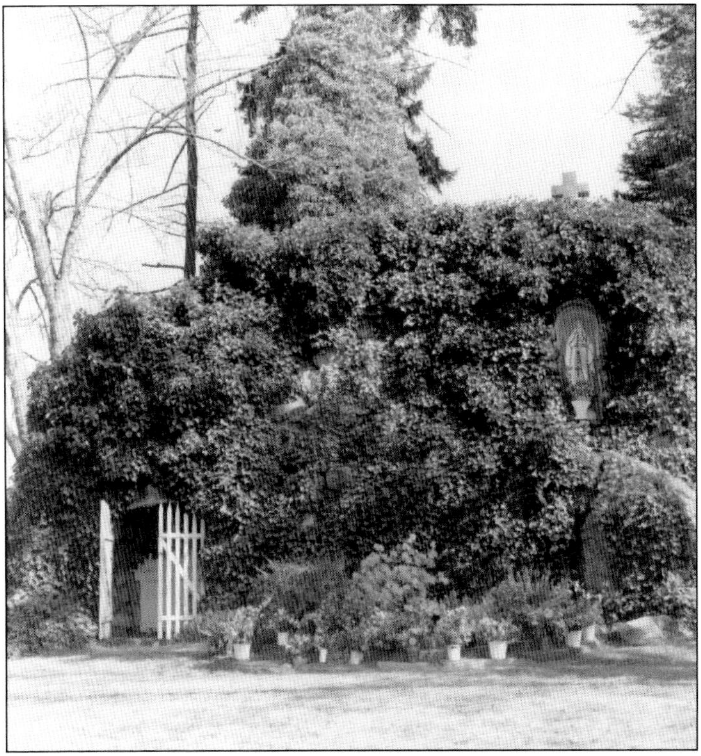

Pictured is the Grotto, which stood at Our Lady of Lourdes until 1992. According to parishioner and resident Theresa Lytle, the statue of Mary was stolen from its perch by the KKK. It was too heavy to carry far and was found in a nearby field. Parishioners repaired the statue and put it back in the Grotto. The exact date of this photograph is unknown but is likely from the 1960s or 1970s. (Courtesy of Theresa Lytle.)

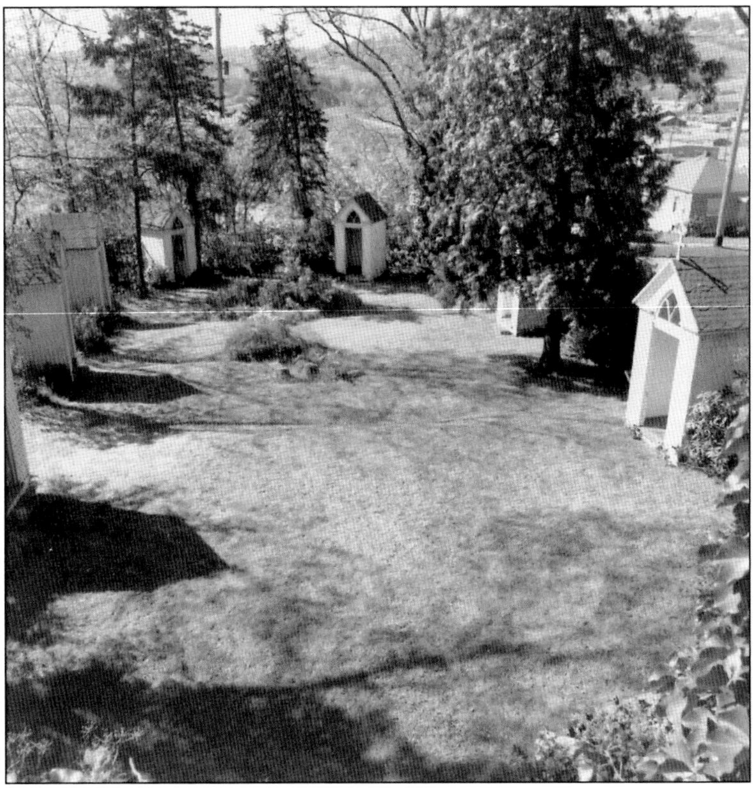

The grounds of Our Lady of Lourdes contained many prayer booths. Once a resident of the South Park Courts, Jackie Jaquemart recalls that when around the church "you couldn't help but be inspired because the grounds and setting were so beautiful." Jackie was an active member of Our Lady of Lourdes. (Courtesy of Theresa Lytle.)

Three

Community Schools

Since its beginnings, South Park has always had educational facilities for the local community. The first community school that South Park called its own was a small two-room shack that was constructed sometime around 1892 and was located on the corner of Twelfth and Sullivan. The small school boasted 60 pupils and one teacher. Albert M. Lingenfelter was the principal and brother to South Park's mayor—George. Its first commencement took place on May 23, 1900. It was not long before the school outgrew its building and the second South Park School was built. The new South Park School was constructed on the same location as the first, only it was a two-story wooden building that was able to house all eight grades, the most that were offered at that time, and continued to operate until 1932.

In 1909, the school board acquired land located on Concord Street between Seventh and Eighth Avenue South, and in 1912, they decided they would construct "a new modern, fireproof building." Construction for Concord School commenced in 1913 and was completed on January 21, 1914. On January 25, 1914, several hundred pupils came to the old South Park School for the last time. After roll call, the students removed all of the books, pads, and pencils from their desks and lined up in the hall with their materials. With a few last admonitions from teachers, a bell was rung and the students began to march through the wilderness to the new Concord School. "Before the group of students reached their destination they witnessed the streetcar making its first passage across the newly constructed bridge that crossed the Duwamish River on Eighth Avenue South, making it a truly memorable day" (Duwamish Diaries, Cleveland High School, 1949).

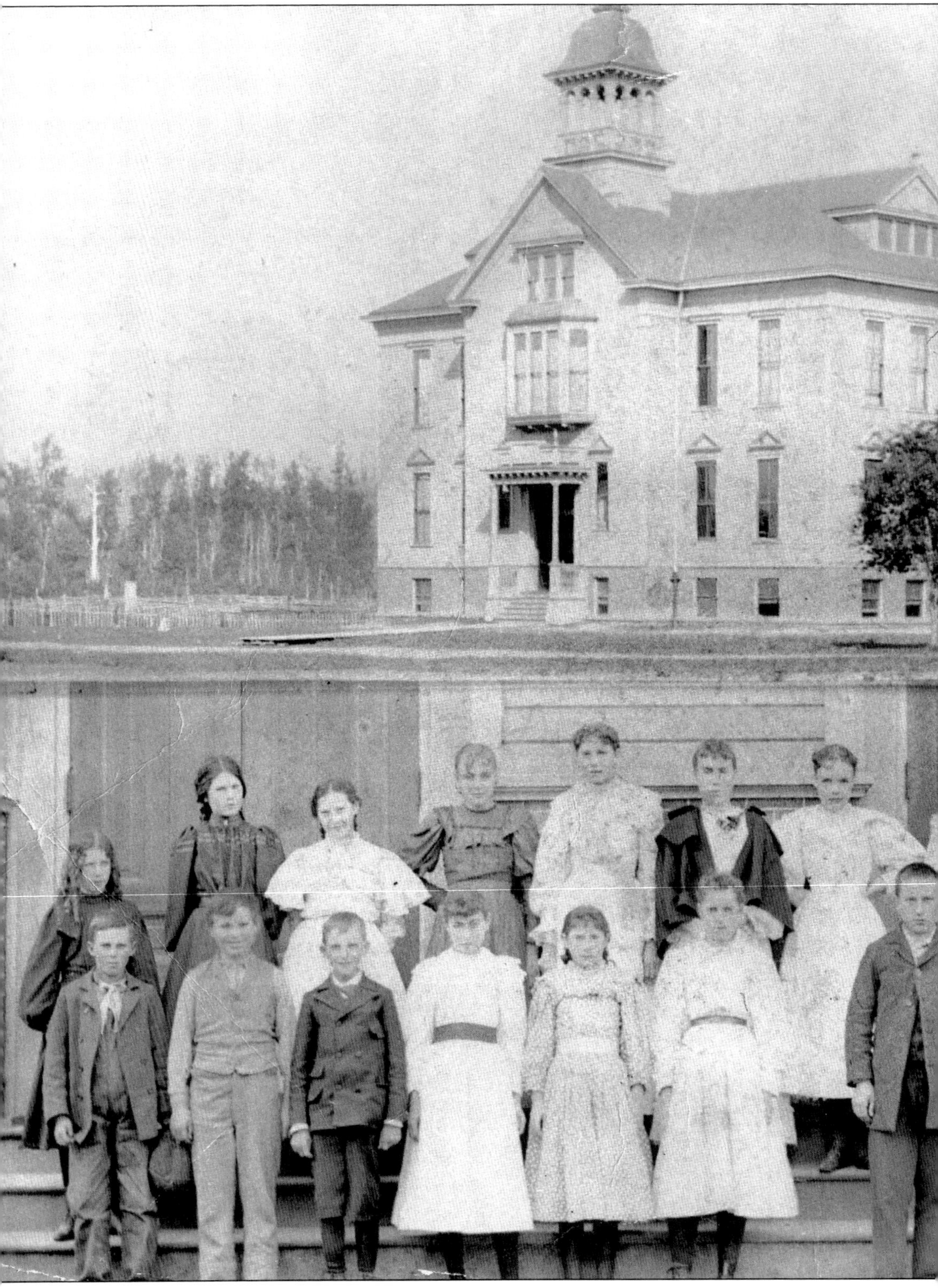

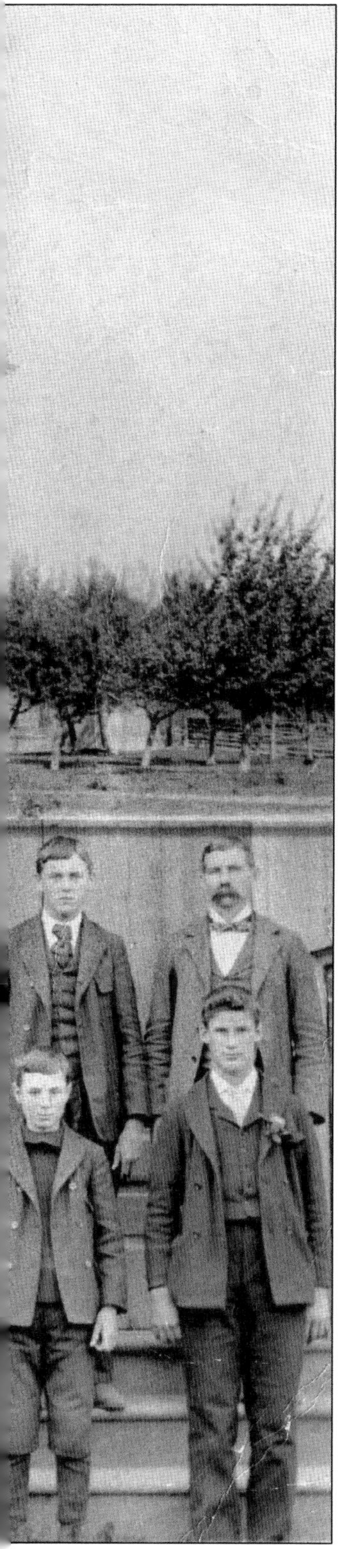

Here is a group of students outside the old South Park School, located on Twelfth and Sullivan, in the early 1900s. This building was torn down in the 1930s, and several small, single-story homes were built here to accommodate the many families moving to the area to support the war effort at Boeing. (Courtesy of George Criddle.)

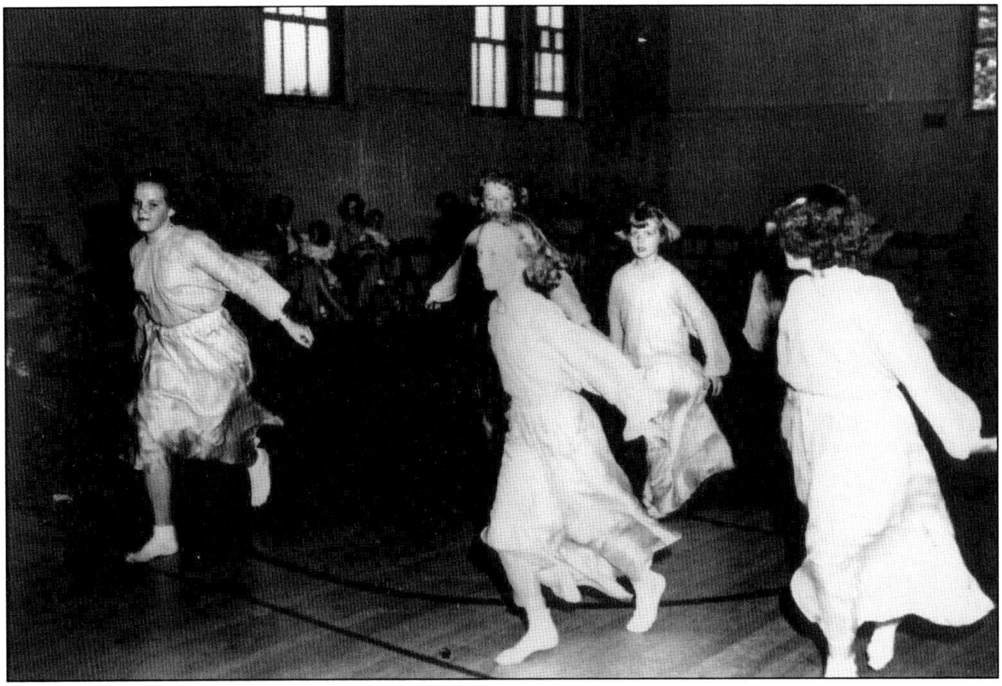

Pictured here are elementary students from South Park School at a grade-school dance at the South Park Field House. Grade-school dances were common in the early 1930s and 1940s. This photographed is believed to be from 1938. (Courtesy of George Criddle.)

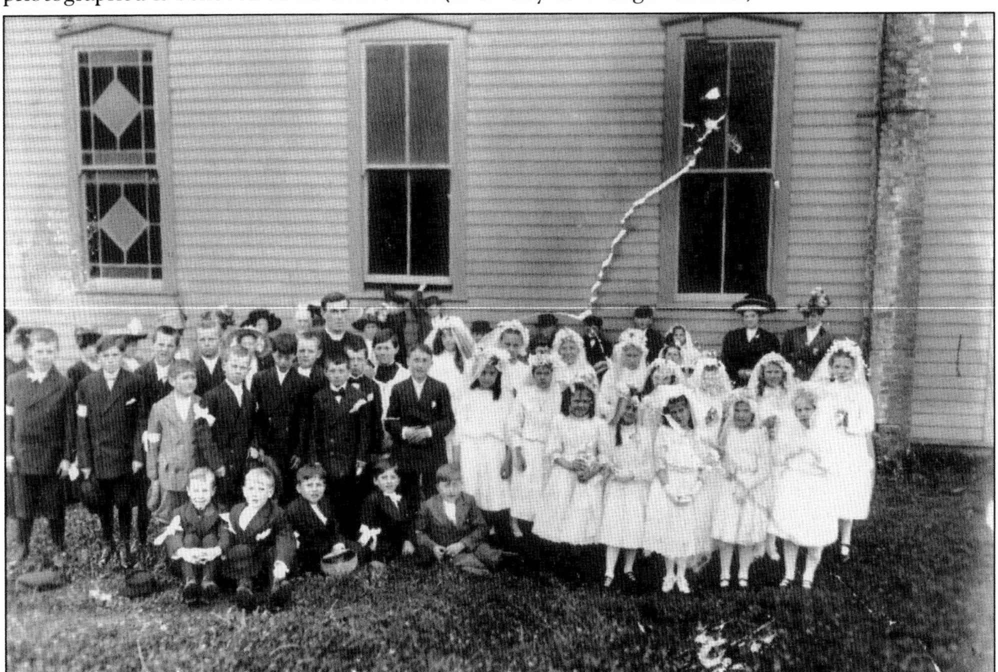

This early-1900s photograph, obtained by Mildred DeBerry from the Miller family, shows a fairly large group of children celebrating their first communion at our Our Lady of Lourdes Church. (Courtesy of George Criddle.)

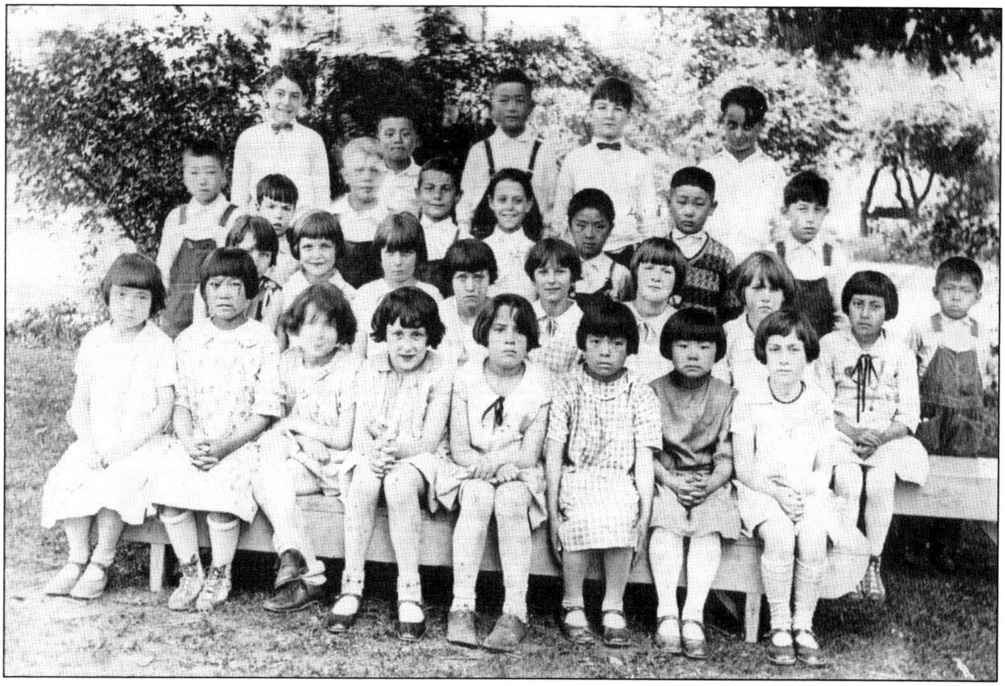

In 1928, the South Park community was very diverse, with a mix of Belgian, Italian, Japanese, and Latino farming families. Pictured here is a Concord School class photograph from 1928 that shows many of the various ethnicities. (Courtesy of Theresa Lytle.)

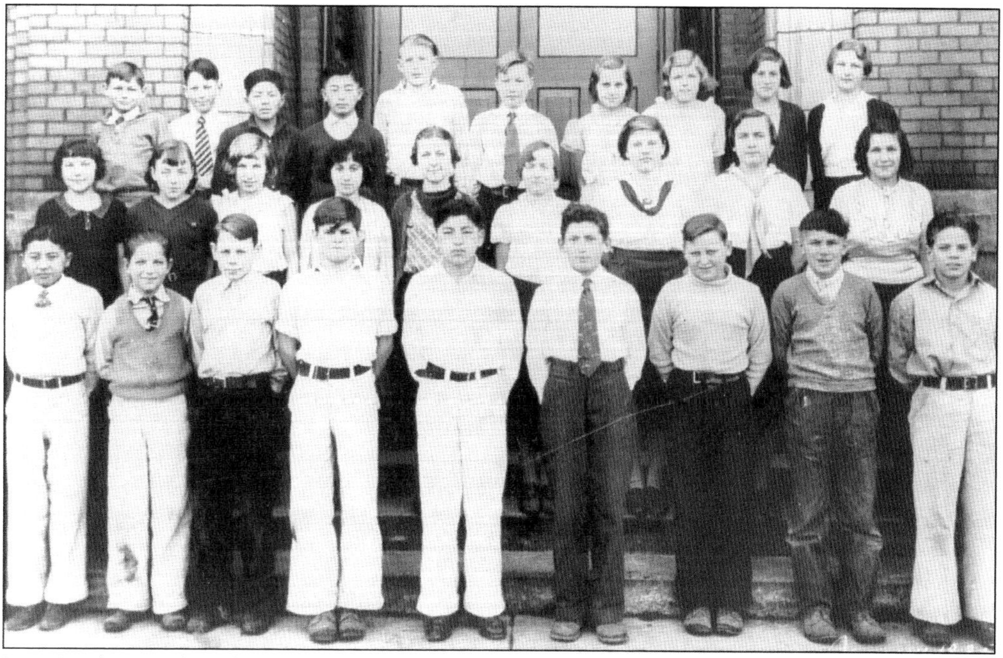

In 1932, the South Park neighborhood was still a very diverse community. This class photograph, taken in front of Concord School in 1932, shows just how diverse the area was. However, at the start of World War II, South Park lost a great deal of its diversity, as the majority of the Japanese farming families were sent to internment camps in California. (Courtesy of Theresa Lytle.)

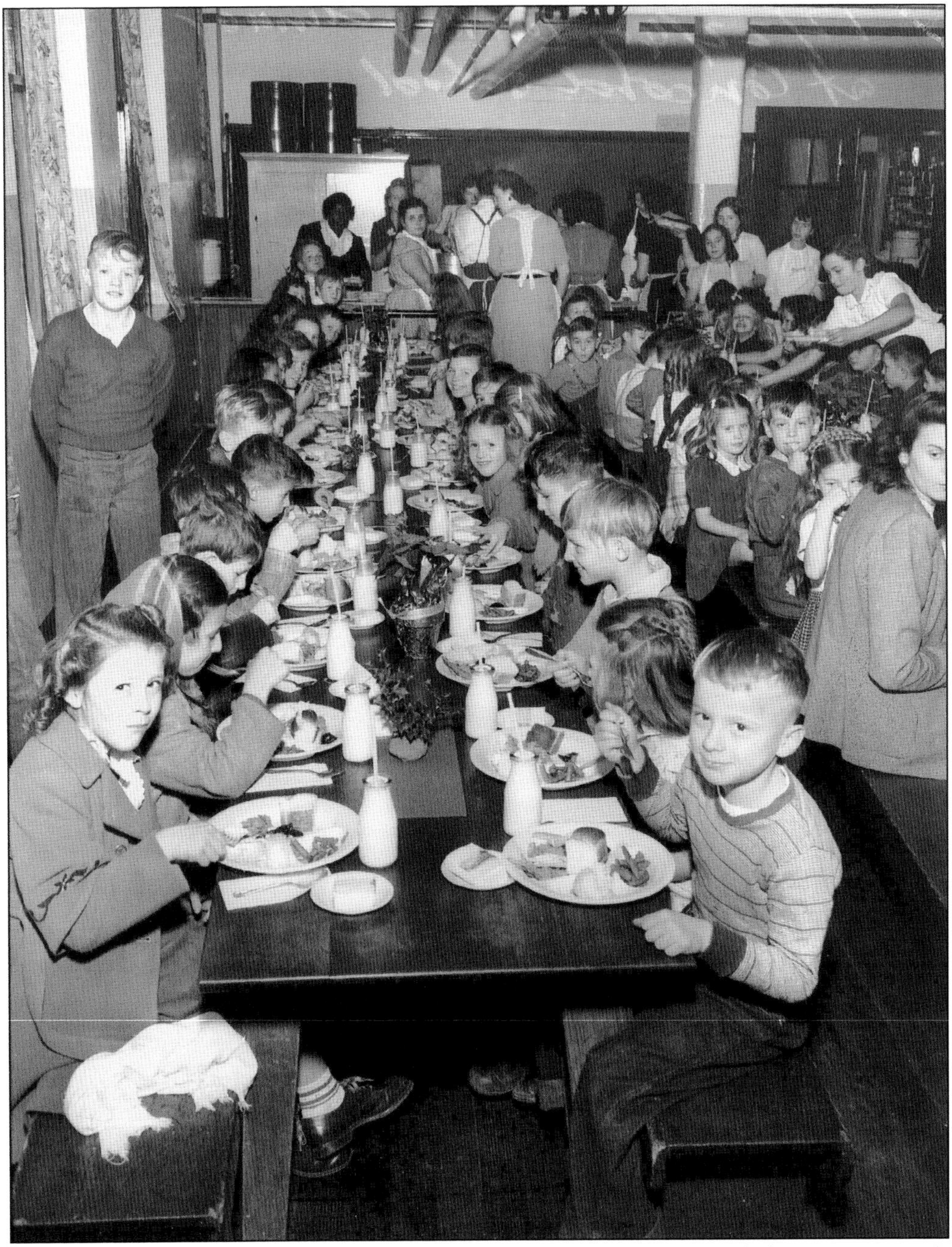

Children in this photograph are eating a holiday dinner hosted by Concord Elementary in 1947. Today Concord continues the holiday dinner event annually and also provides periodic family night dinners where anyone from the community is welcome to attend as long as they like lots of spaghetti. (Courtesy of MOHAI, No. PI25468.)

Four

FARMING

In the last half of the 19th century, the adjacent community of Georgetown experienced development and industry while South Park was left to the farmers. Immigrant farmers from Japan and Italy dominated South Park's truck farming community. They brought their produce to the Seattle Public Farmer's Market, which allowed farmers to sell directly to the public, bypassing middlemen and commission houses. The term "truck farm" refers to small farms where the farmer would load his truck with his bounty and truck it to local markets. Truck farms continued to operate in South Park up until the early 1960s.

John Ferrucci, a Pike Place Market pioneer, farmed his postage-stamp-sized, two-acre lot at 9145 Seventh Avenue South. For more than half a century, John sold radishes, spinach, corn, lettuce, turnips, peas, and mustard greens out of his worn wooden stall at the Pike Place Public Market. John's wife, Angela, was at his side.

Carmine and Maria Mara purchased a four-acre farm from Joe Desimone—a longtime resident and farmer and founder of the Pike Place Market—in 1920 on a handshake. The Italian families in South Park would work their farms seven days a week and spend Sunday afternoons relaxing and playing baseball at the South Park Field House. In the 1970s, the family sold the property to King County with the stipulation that it be preserved as farmland. Today the farm plays host to a variety of groups and functions including P-patch, Seattle Youth Garden Works, and Lettuce Link.

Giuseppe "Joe" Desimone was born on a farm in Avellino, Italy, in 1880. At the young age of 17, Joe arrived in America with half a dollar in his pocket. A few years later, he settled in South Park. By draining the Duwamish swamplands, the Desimones were able to bring up land bit by bit, and they ended up owning large tracts of some of the best farmlands in the area. At one point, Desimone amassed more than 70 acres of land in the South Park neighborhood and was the largest stockholder in the Pike Place Market.

The postwar years marked the end of many South Park farms. In 1935, there were 154,274 acres of farmland in King County. By 1967, less than 50,000 remained. The farms in South Park gave way to warehouses, manufacturing plants, businesses, freeways, and utilities, ending an era in Seattle's history.

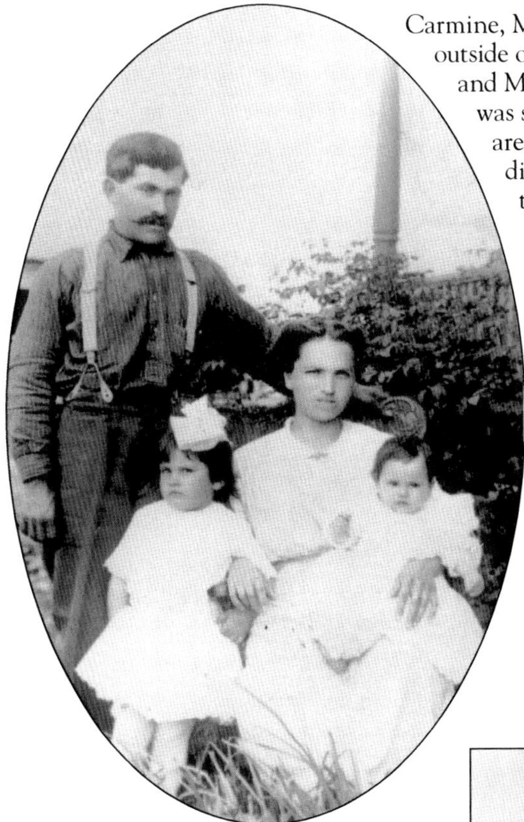

Carmine, Maria, Anna, and Minnie Marra are pictured outside of their South Park home in 1913. Carmine and Maria Marra had an arranged marriage that was set up by the Italian "godfather" of the area, Joe Desimone. At first, the Marra's had difficulty communicating because they spoke two very different Italian dialects. (Courtesy of George Criddle.)

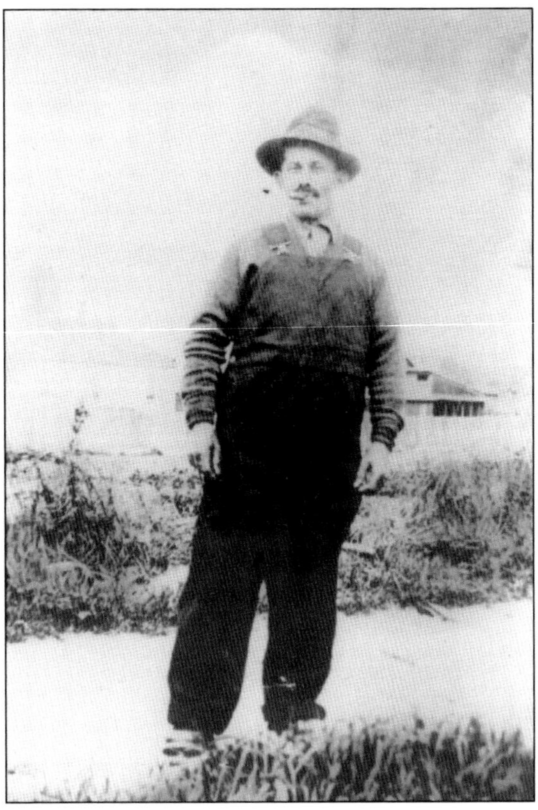

Carmine Marra stands proudly outside of his farm in South Park. His land today has been purchased by the city of Seattle and is known as Marra Farm. Seattle Youth Garden Works and Lettuce Links are just a few of the programs that now grow berries, fruits, and vegetables on his old farm. (Courtesy of George Criddle.)

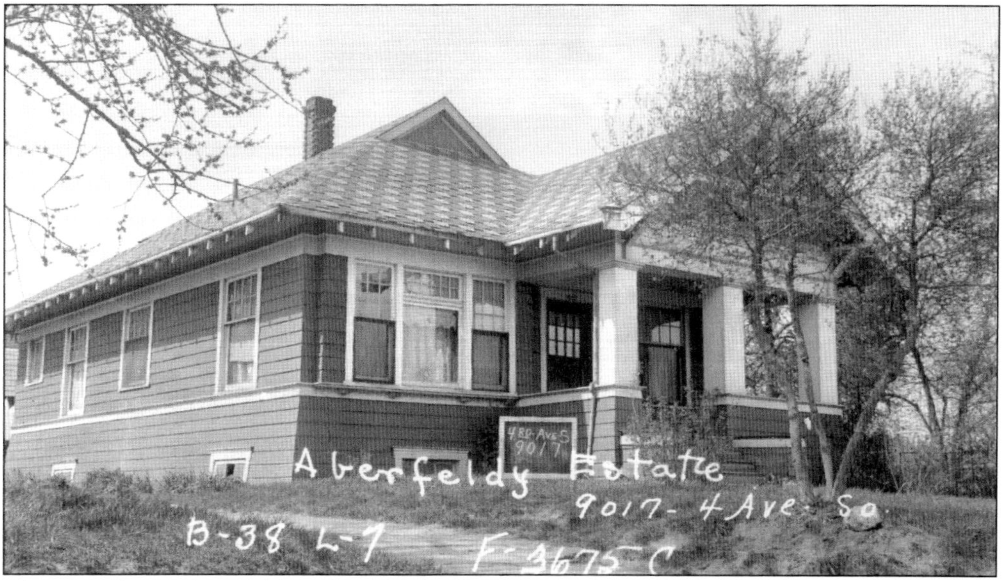

The Marra home, located in South Park, featured a "sitting porch," which was common on many of the local farming houses. The house sits up and across the street from the four-acre farming lot, providing an excellent view of the bounty. The photograph was taken in 1937. (Courtesy of PSRA.)

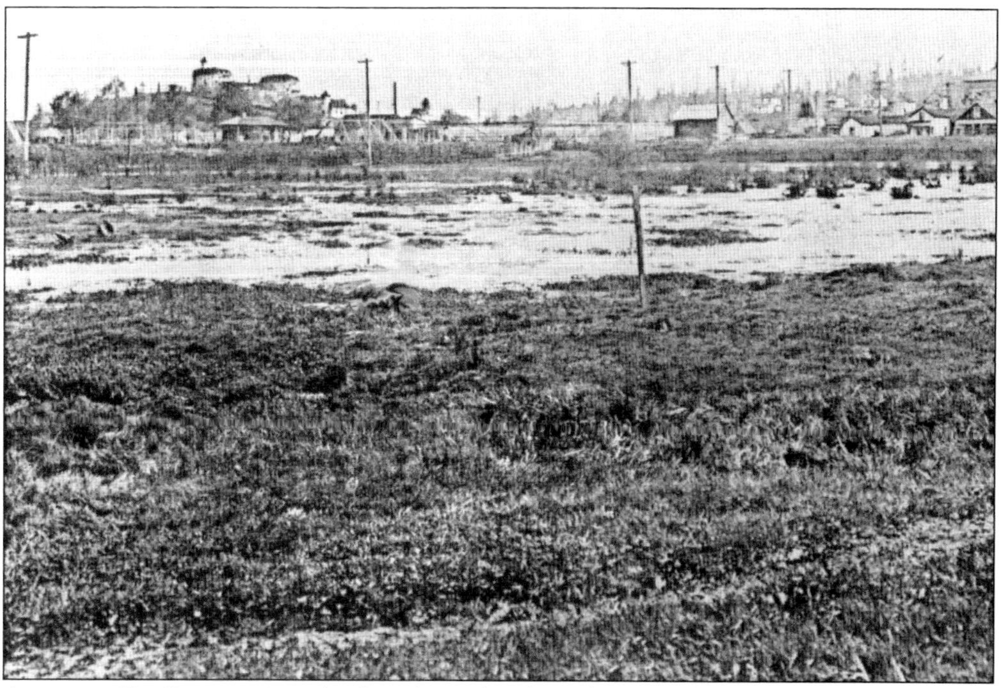

A section of Joe Desimone's garden farm, located at the end of Seventh Avenue, had been cultivated since 1899. At one point, Joe owned the majority of land in the South Park community, as well as a large portion in Georgetown. The three buildings of Our Lady of Lourdes can be seen in the upper left corner of this undated photograph. (Courtesy of Theresa Lytle.)

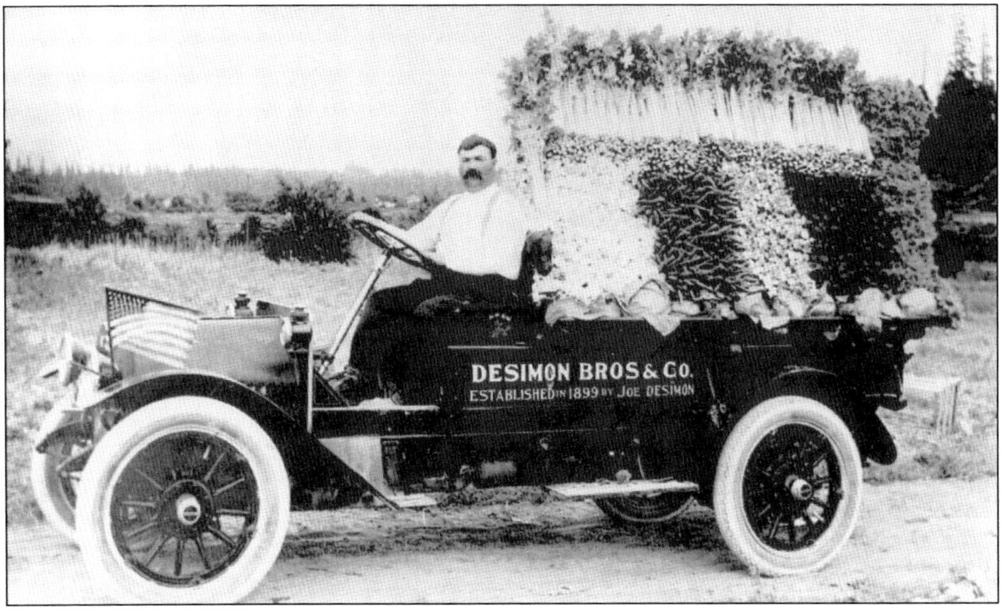

In this undated photograph, Joe Desimone sits proudly in his new produce truck, even though his last name appears misspelled. Joe was unaware because he was completely illiterate. Elizabeth and Maria Desimone recall that he signed his name with an "X." Desimone became an owner of the Pike Place Market. (Courtesy of Theresa Lytle.)

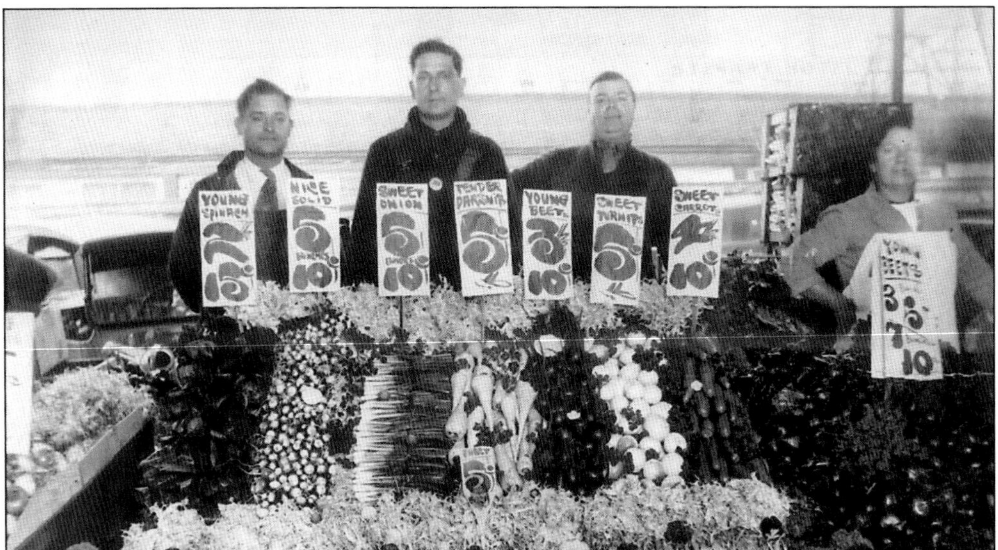

This photograph, taken in 1939 by Richard Desimone, Joe's son, celebrates the remodel of the Pike Place Farmer's Market. Joe was criticized for letting the market deteriorate, but the consensus is the market went downhill because of competition from supermarkets and the takeover of nearby farmlands by industries. By keeping maintenance costs to a minimum, though, Desimone was able to rent the farmers' stalls at very low rates and, in this way, made sure that the market survived. Desimone proprietorship continued until his health started failing in 1946. His son took over until the market came under public acquisition by the 1971 voters initiative. (Courtesy of the City of Seattle Municipal Archives.)

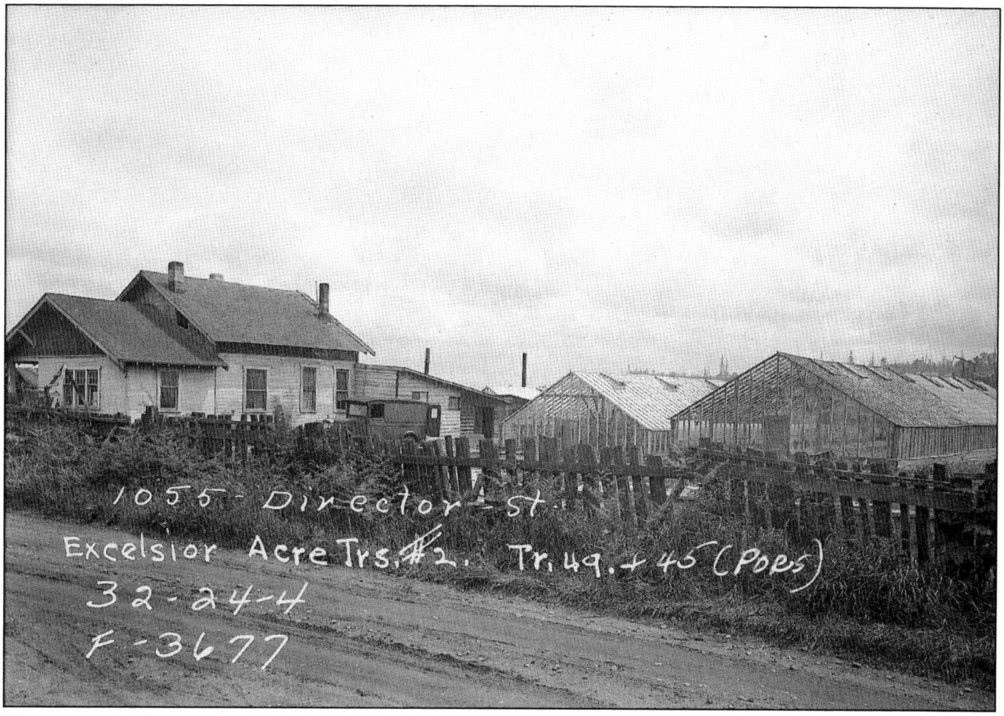

The quaint Shiomi family home, located in South Park on 1055 Director Street, is pictured in 1937. The family farmed for a living and owned several very large greenhouses in South Park for many years. Like other farmers in the area, the family sold their produce at the Pike Place Market. (Courtesy of PSRA.)

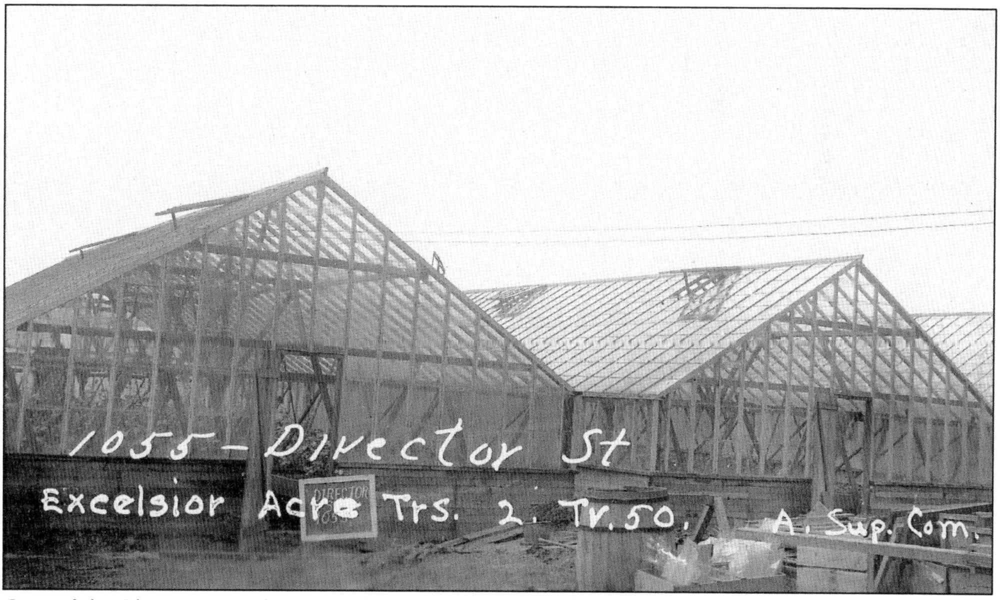

One of the Shiomi greenhouses, which was located in South Park, is picture here in 1937. Most greenhouses were equipped with water and oil heaters. While once a familiar sight all through the South Park area, there are no longer any greenhouses left in the community. (Courtesy of PSRA.)

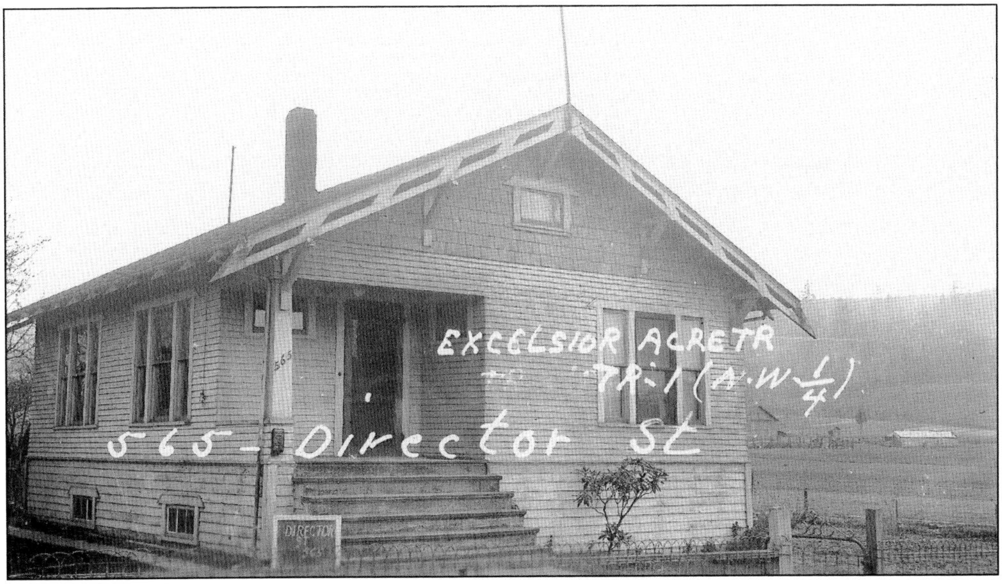

A typical South Park farm home, this one was located at 565 Director Street in 1937. Some of the early farmhouse architecture seen in South Park was influenced by those built in the Midwest. (Courtesy of PSRA.)

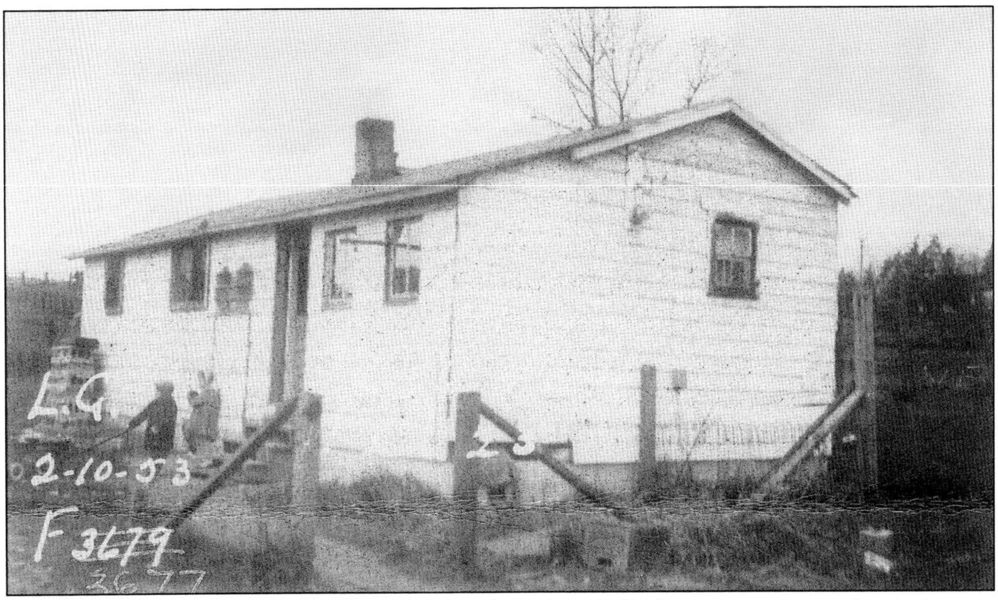

Here is a later model simple farmhouse in South Park in 1953. It was torn down after its lot was rezoned from agricultural and farming to industrial. (Courtesy of PSRA.)

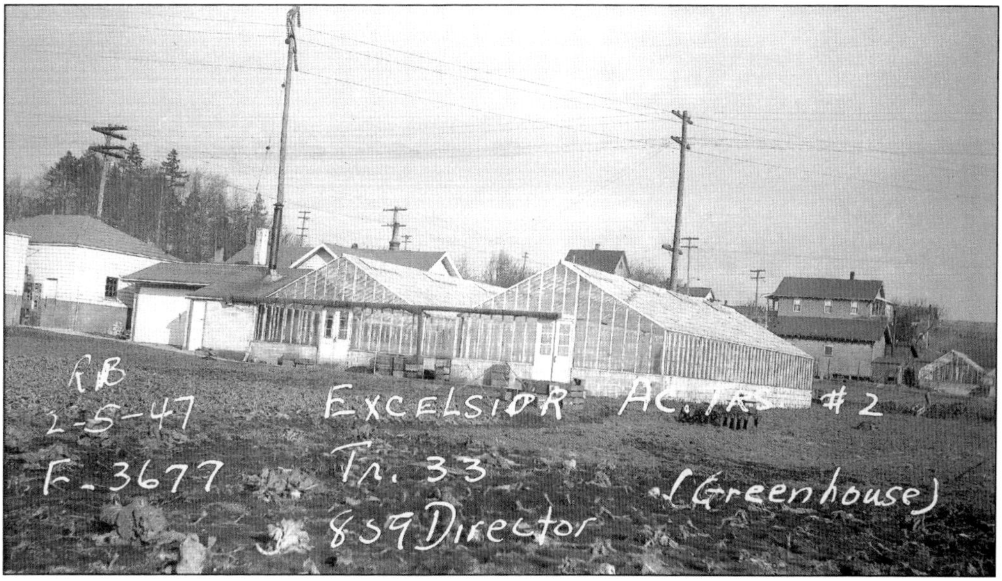

A set of greenhouses, seen here in 1947, was located in South Park at 859 Director Street. Today there are no greenhouses left in the community, despite the excellent soil. (Courtesy of PSRA.)

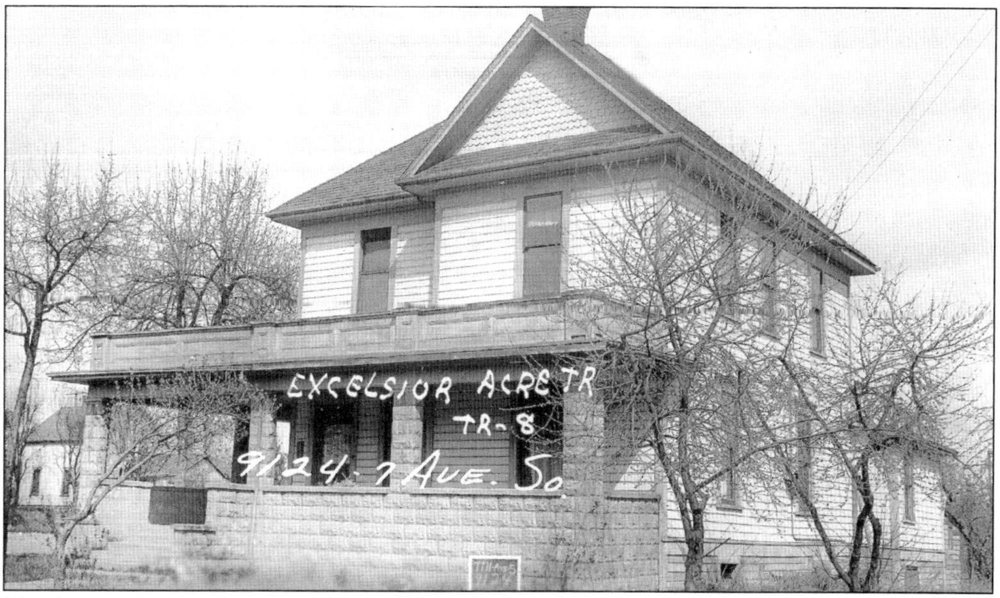

This large, two-story home was located at 9124 Seventh Avenue South in the middle of the truck farming district. Many of the early South Park homes like this one were torn down as large lots were rezoned from farming to industrial. This photograph was taken in 1937. (Courtesy of PSRA.)

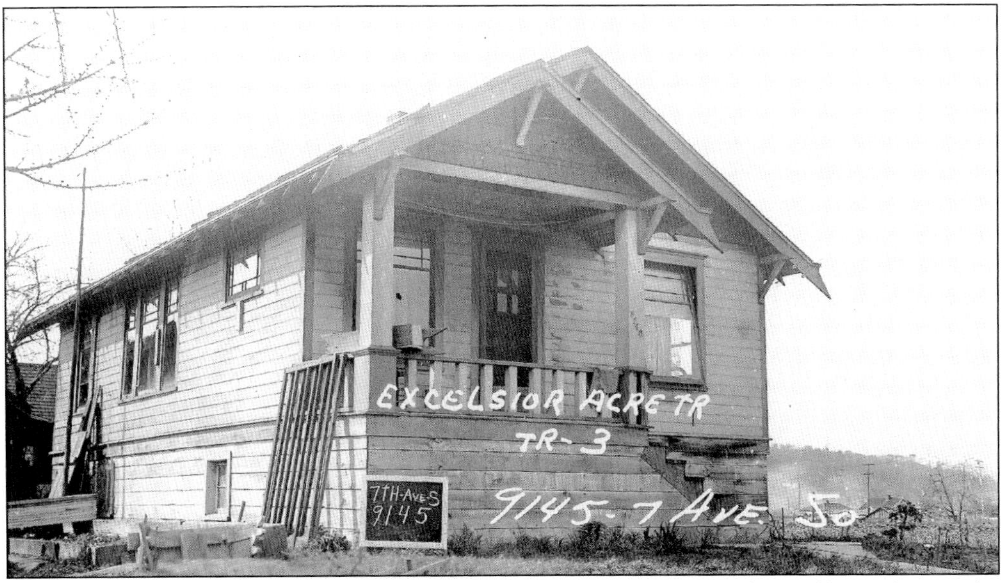

John Ferrucci built this home in 1916 at 9145 Seventh Avenue South. John and his wife, Angela, who were very active in the Italian farming community, sold the vegetables they grew on their lot in the Pike Place Market for many years. Angela was known for providing good recipes to anyone who purchased Ferrucci produce. This photograph was taken in 1937. (Courtesy of PSRA.)

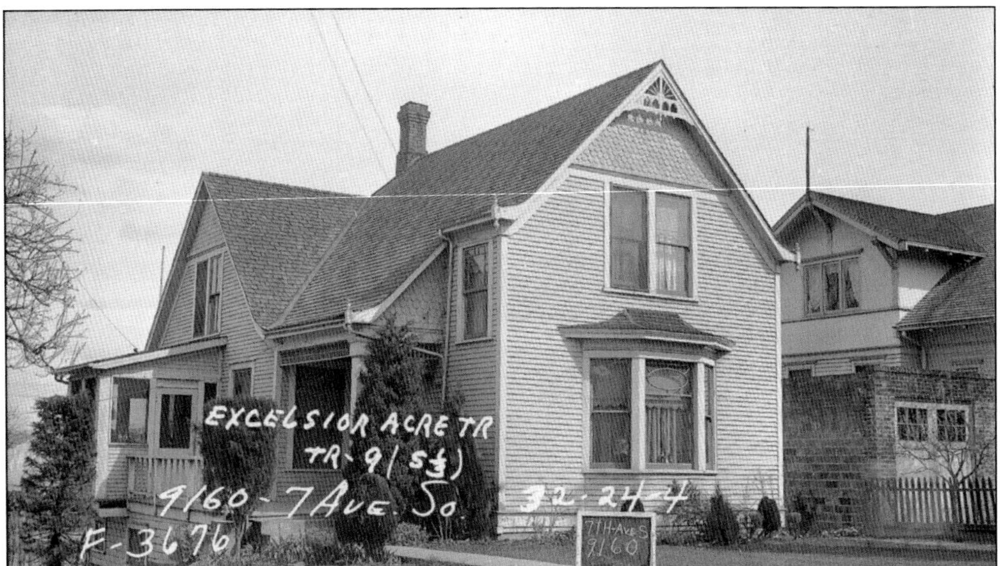

This stately South Park home was located at 9160 Seventh Avenue South in 1937. Currently this property is for sale, and plans are in place to subdivide the old truck farm lot into smaller lots to accommodate six to eight houses. (Courtesy of PSRA.)

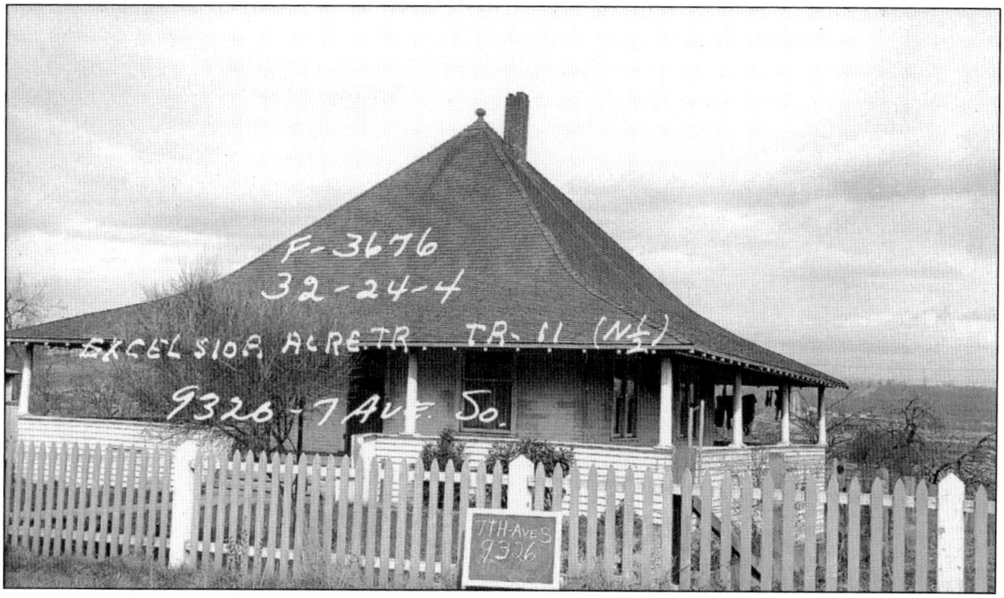

The Querio house, built in 1908, was owned by Peter Querio, a truck farmer who sold his fruits and produce at the Pike Place Market. The house was named a historical destination on November 3, 2004, after the Seattle Landmarks Preservation Board found the house to "embody the distinctive visible characteristics of an architectural style, period, or of a method of construction." It is the only known example of an Indian bungalow type in all of Washington State. After receiving historical designation saving it from demolition, the house was moved farther south on Seventh Avenue South to its current location. (Courtesy of PSRA.)

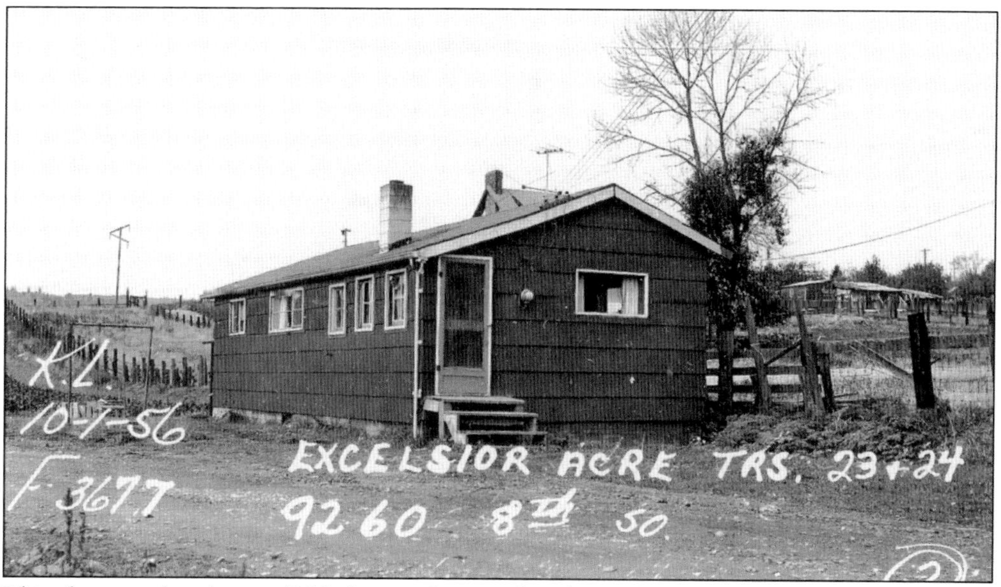

This photograph, taken in 1956, shows a Spartan farm home from the early 1900s. It was located at 9260 Eighth Avenue South. Note the expansive farmland surrounding the home. Even in the 1950s, South Park still had plenty of open space for farming. (Courtesy of PSRA.)

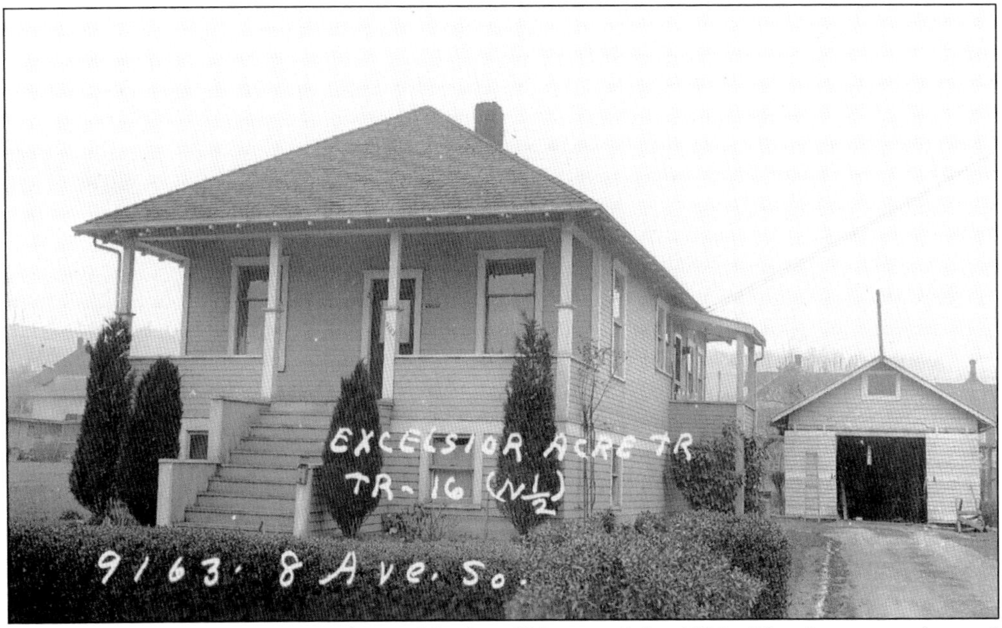

Pictured here in 1937 is a typical "neighborhood" home of the 1930s. This house was located at 9163 Eighth Avenue South but no longer exists in the South Park neighborhood. (Courtesy of PSRA.)

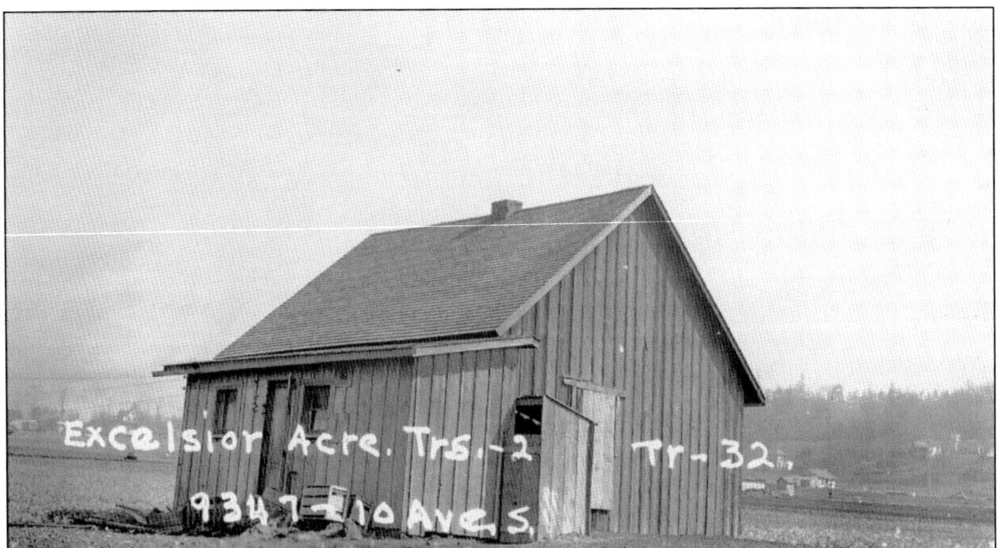

This home typifies the one-room houses that were lived in by many of the early farm workers, like Frank Kabuki. Photographed in 1937, the home was located at 9347 Tenth Avenue South and was surrounded by fields whose produce was sold in the Pike Place Farmers Market. In 1943, this structure was torn down. (Courtesy of PSRA.)

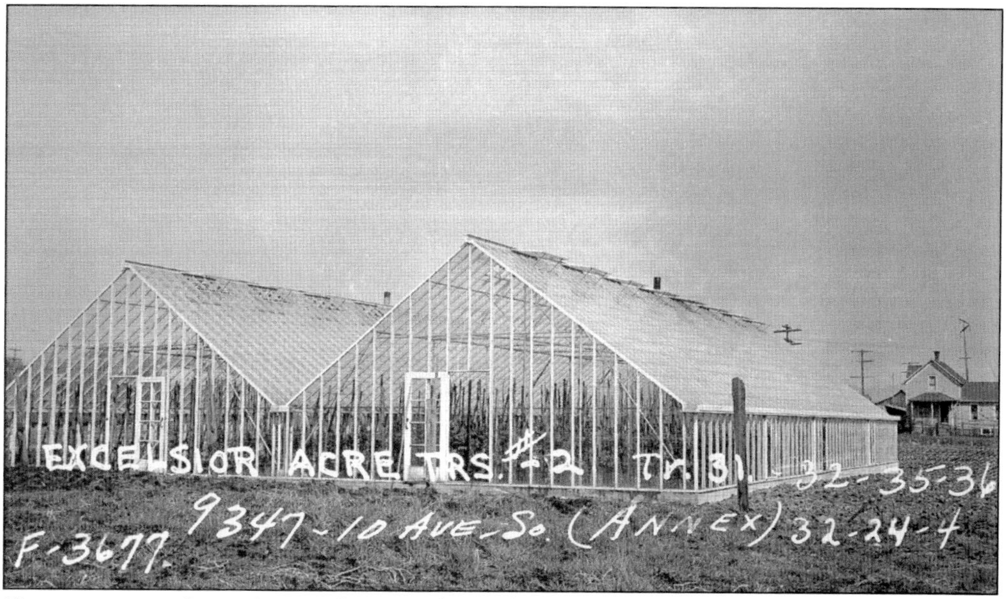

Here is a series of greenhouses that were located on 9347 Tenth Avenue South in 1937. These greenhouses are no longer in the South Park neighborhood. There is rich farmland underneath the pavement and industry that now occupies this location. (Courtesy of PSRA.)

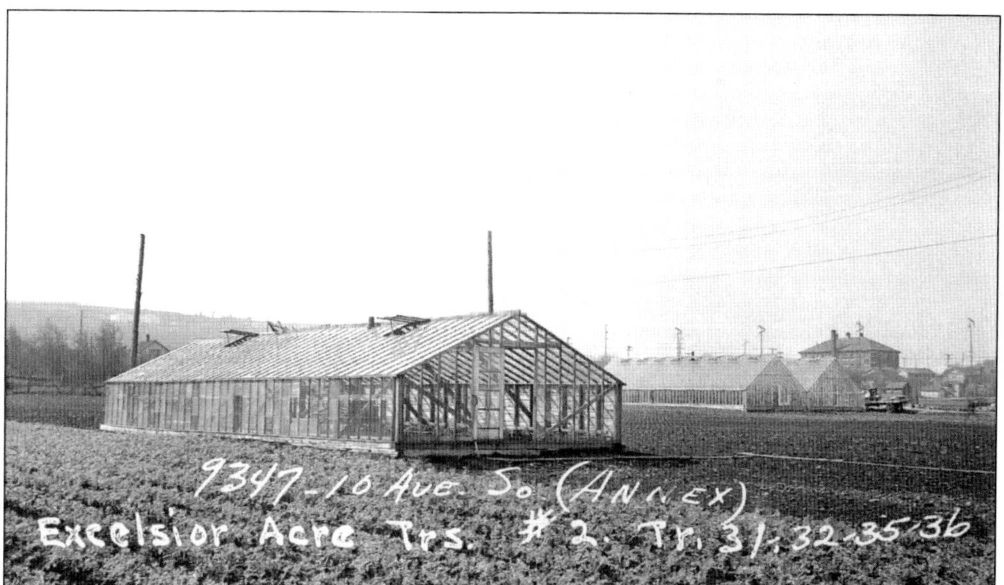

Here is another set of greenhouses that were once located in the South Park neighborhood in 1937. It has been estimated that during the 1930s, there were over 70 greenhouses spread throughout the South Park area. (Courtesy of PSRA.)

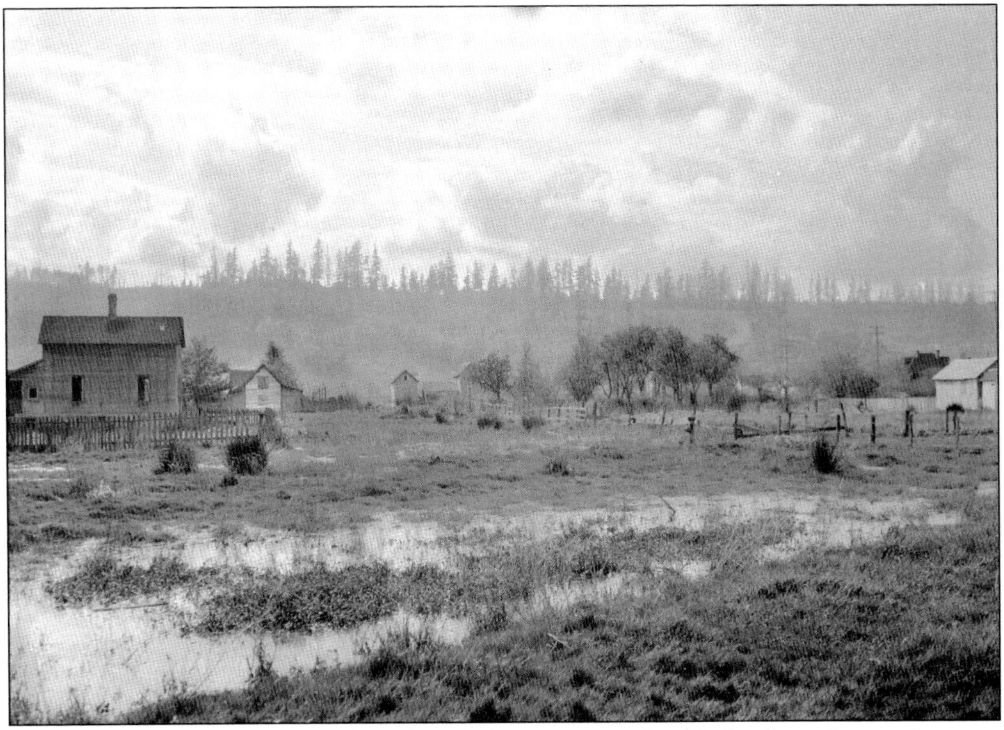

River Park Addition is the part of South Park that occupies a few blocks along the river between Fourteenth and Fifth Avenue South. This photograph was taken in 1914 before the completion of the straightening of the river, hence the standing water in this yard. After the straightening of the river, River Park Addition was converted into large farms with glass nurseries equipped with oil heaters to maximize the growing season. (Courtesy of the City of Seattle Municipal Archives.)

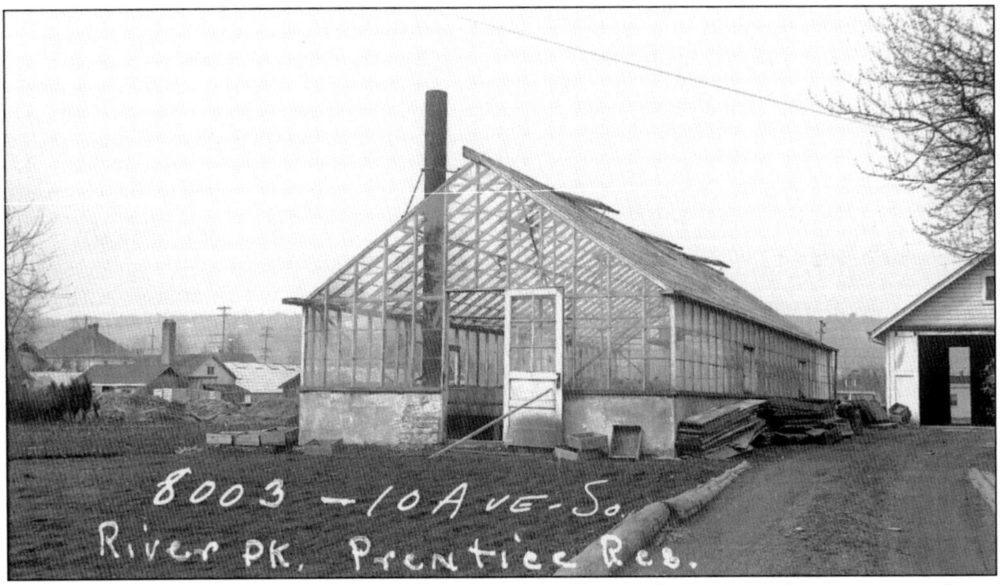

Built in 1920, this greenhouse was first owned by B. Tullo and then Carl Tullo. It was torn down in 1958 to make way for Ty Long, who wanted access to the river to move large jobs for his growing Long Paint Company. This photograph was taken in 1937. (Courtesy of PSRA.)

Five

Boeing and the War Years

Leaving Yale University in 1903 for the Northwest timber industry, William E. Boeing found himself in the forest trading areas around Grays Harbor, Washington. Five years later, in 1908, Boeing decided to move out of the Grays Harbor area and into Seattle, settling in a neighborhood near the Duwamish River. Living near the river, Boeing decided to have a custom yacht built by Heath's Shipyard, which was located near South Park on the Duwamish River. However, before the construction of his yacht was complete, Heath's Shipyard went into financial turmoil and was debating bankruptcy. On March 10, 1910, Boeing purchased the shipyard, saving it from its financial burden. After his completion of his yacht, Boeing's dream for being involved in aviation industry became a reality as Heath's Shipyard became the first home of the Boeing Company. The year was 1916.

The fledgling Boeing Company grew quickly. With government contracts and enterprising engineers, William Boeing steered the company to the forefront of American industry.

With the coming of World War II, South Park saw an increase in development. Many people were coming to the area to work at the Boeing Company and the numerous shipyards along the Duwamish. The housing situation became severe, and the King County Housing Authority Board arranged for the construction of the South Park Courts, a housing project similar to other developments that appeared during the same time around Seattle. South Park Courts consisted of 256 separate units. Each unit contained a living room, a bedroom, a bathroom, and a kitchen. In the beginning, the rent, which included light, heat, water, and garbage disposal, was $39 a month.

As was the case in many communities during World War II, South Park's Japanese families were sent to internment camps. Theresa Lytle, a South Park resident, recalls, "There was one family that lived close and had kids that I went to school with. They were sent to California to Tulle Lake. They did come back to South Park. When we were reunited with the kids at a class reunion, we were all very sad and cried for them because before they were sent away, they were on the verge of graduating from high school, and they wouldn't let them." The majority of Japanese farmers never came back to South Park. Their homes were shacks that were purchased by Joe Desimone when no one returned.

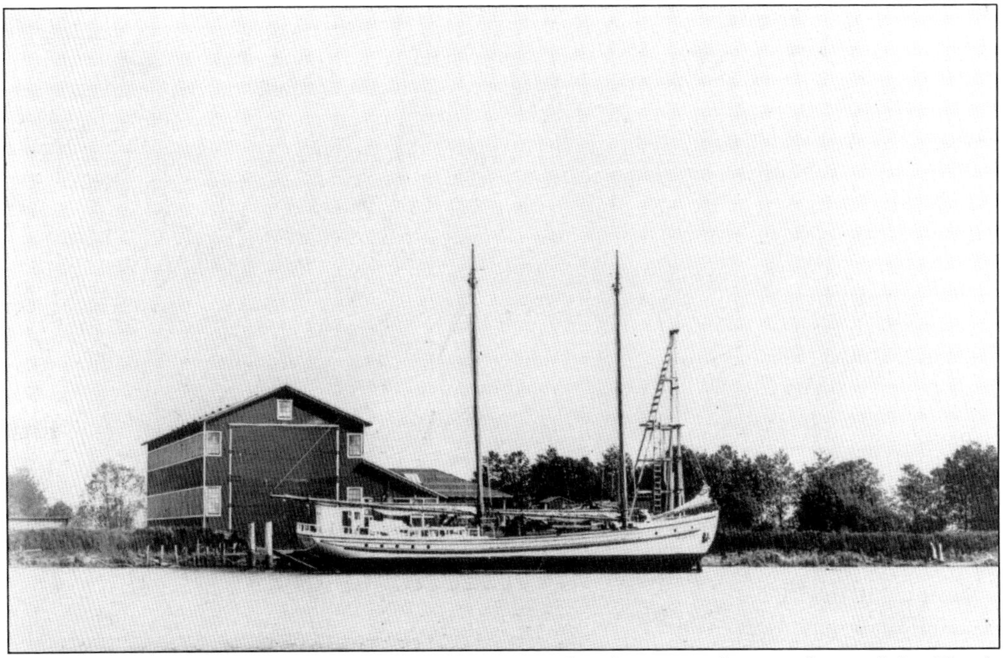

William Boeing's yacht, after construction was completed, appears here in front of the Heath Shipyard building where the Boeing Airplane Company got its start. Today the building is known as the Red Barn and has been relocated to the Museum of Flight. The Red Barn is where Boeing had his first airplane manufacturing plant. (Courtesy of Theresa Lytle.)

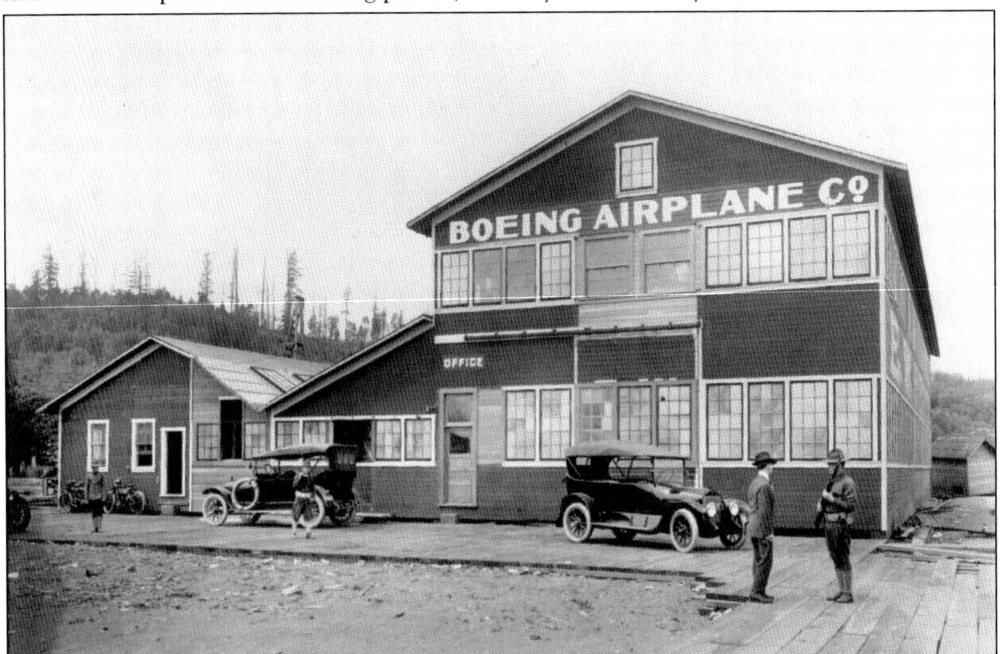

This photograph shows the Heath Shipyard building after its conversion into the Boeing Airplane Company. It is this building that is today known as the Red Barn and is located outside of the Museum of Flight. (Courtesy of Theresa Lytle.)

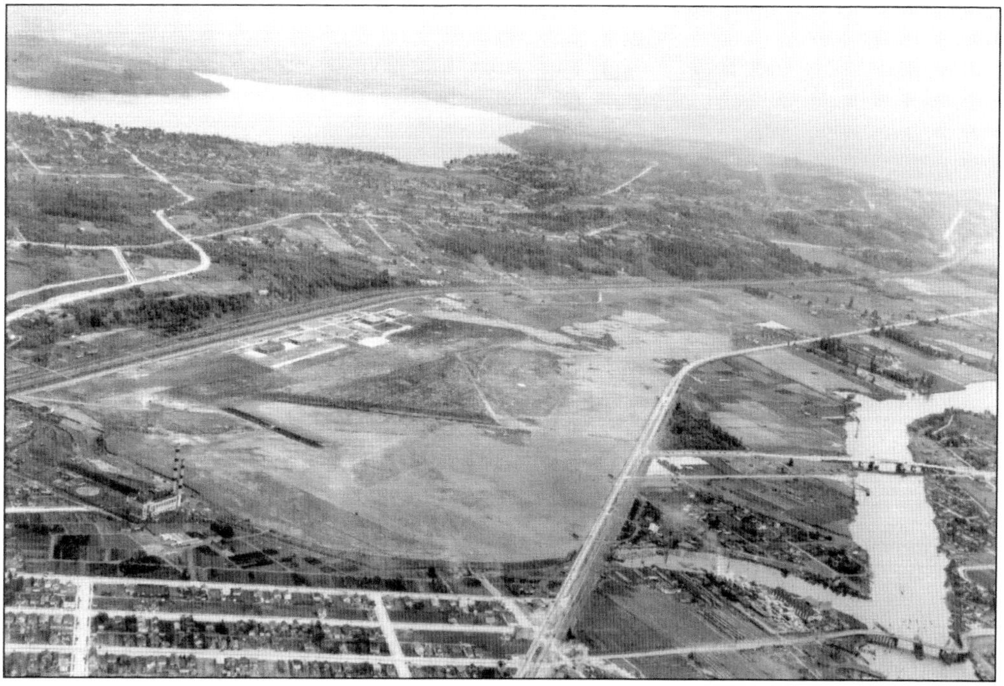

Here is an aerial photograph taken in 1933 of the Boeing Airplane Company. This image shows what Boeing's Plant Two looked like before the start of World War II. (Courtesy of Theresa Lytle.)

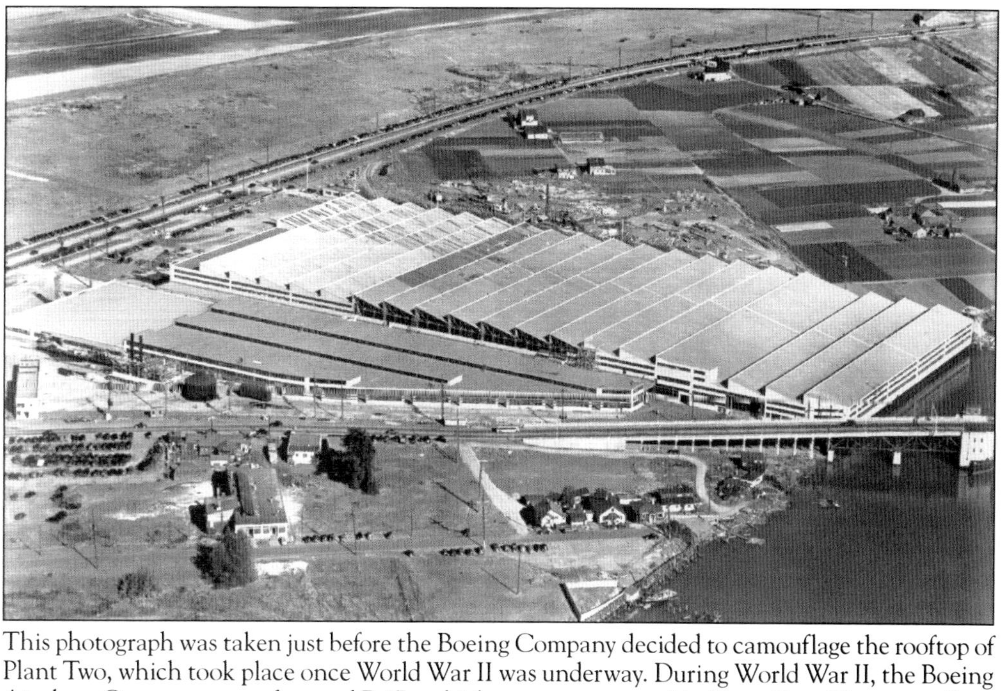

This photograph was taken just before the Boeing Company decided to camouflage the rooftop of Plant Two, which took place once World War II was underway. During World War II, the Boeing Airplane Company manufactured B-17s, which were constructed in Plant Two. The camouflage was put up to make Boeing look like a suburban community from the air, reducing its risk of becoming a target. (Courtesy of Theresa Lytle.)

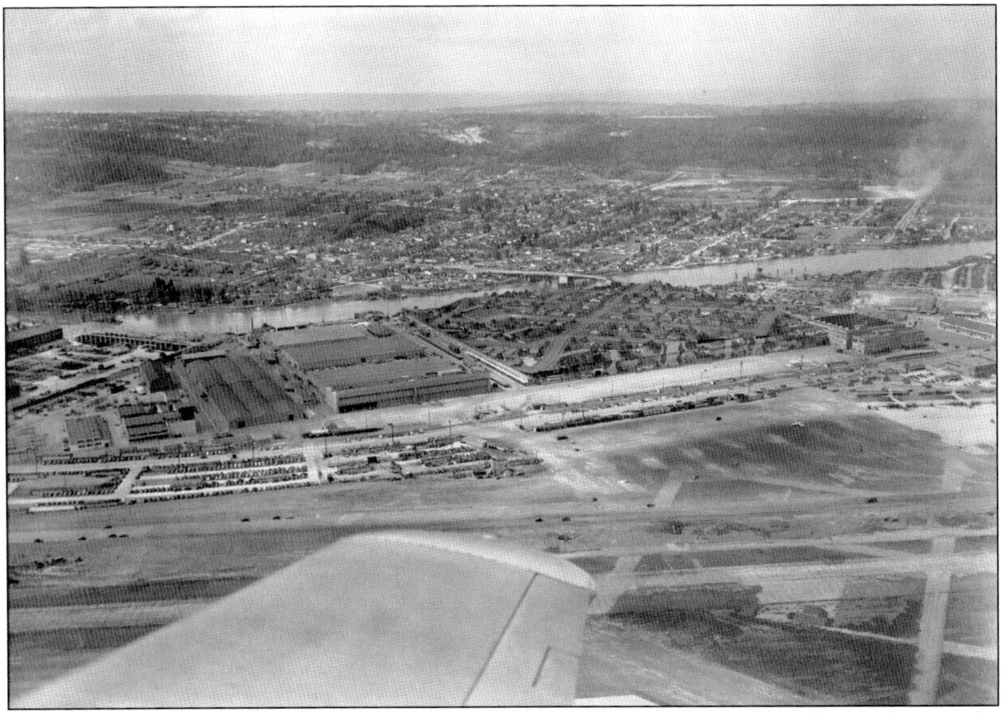

Taken from a Boeing B-17, this photograph overlooks the company in 1940. The airplane's right wing appears at the bottom of the photograph. (Courtesy of Theresa Lytle.)

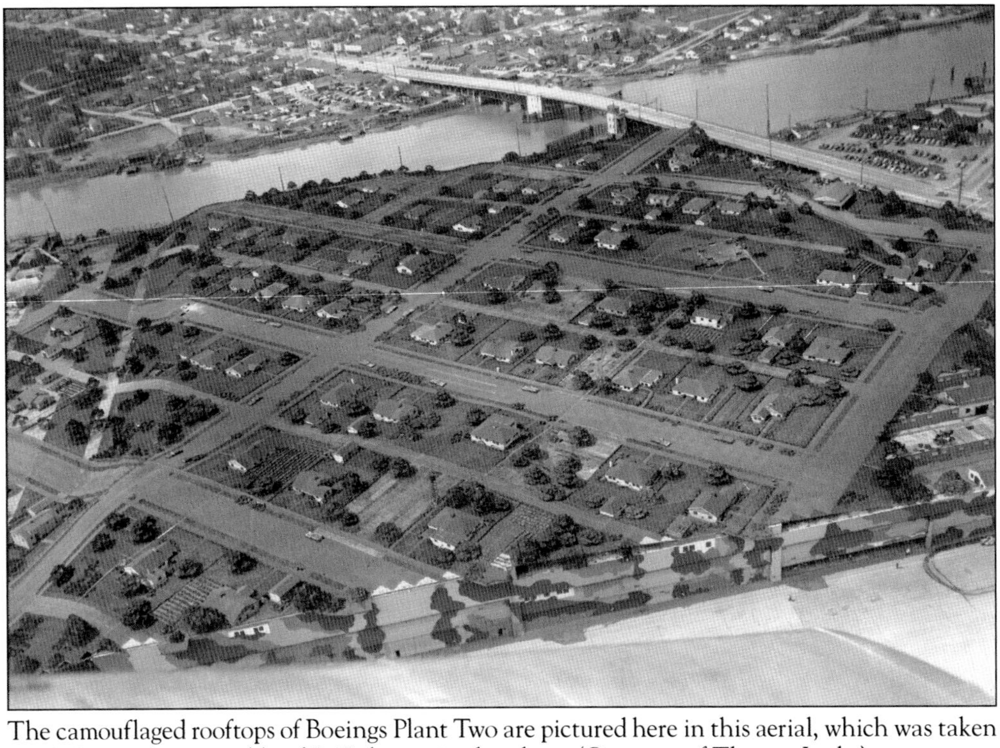

The camouflaged rooftops of Boeings Plant Two are pictured here in this aerial, which was taken in 1940 just after assembly of B-17s began in the plant. (Courtesy of Theresa Lytle.)

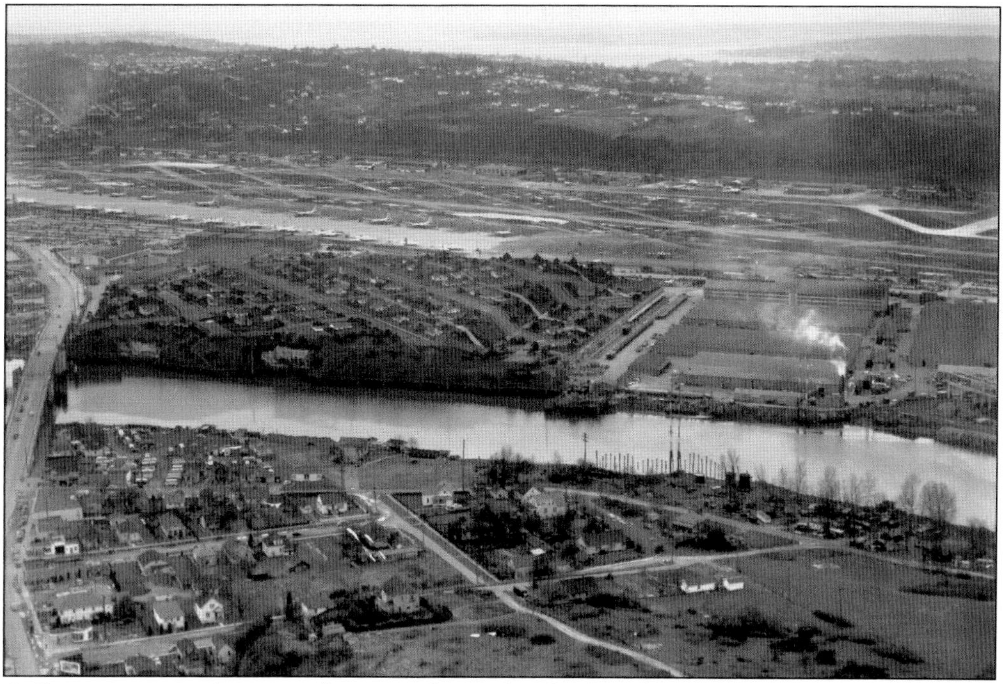

As Boeing continued to expand, more and more farmland was lost to development, as seen in this photograph that shows part of Boeing field and the Duwamish River. The date of this photograph is unknown. (Courtesy of Theresa Lytle.)

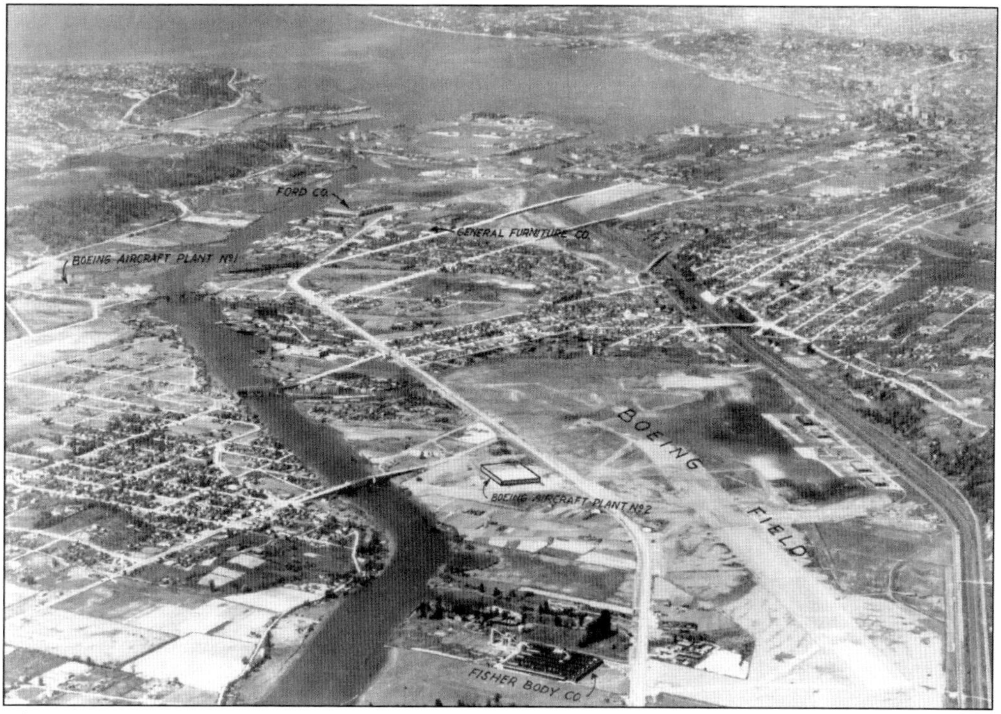

The Boeing Airplane complex sits among the South Park community, as seen in this high-altitude photograph taken by Boeing pilots. (Courtesy of Theresa Lytle.)

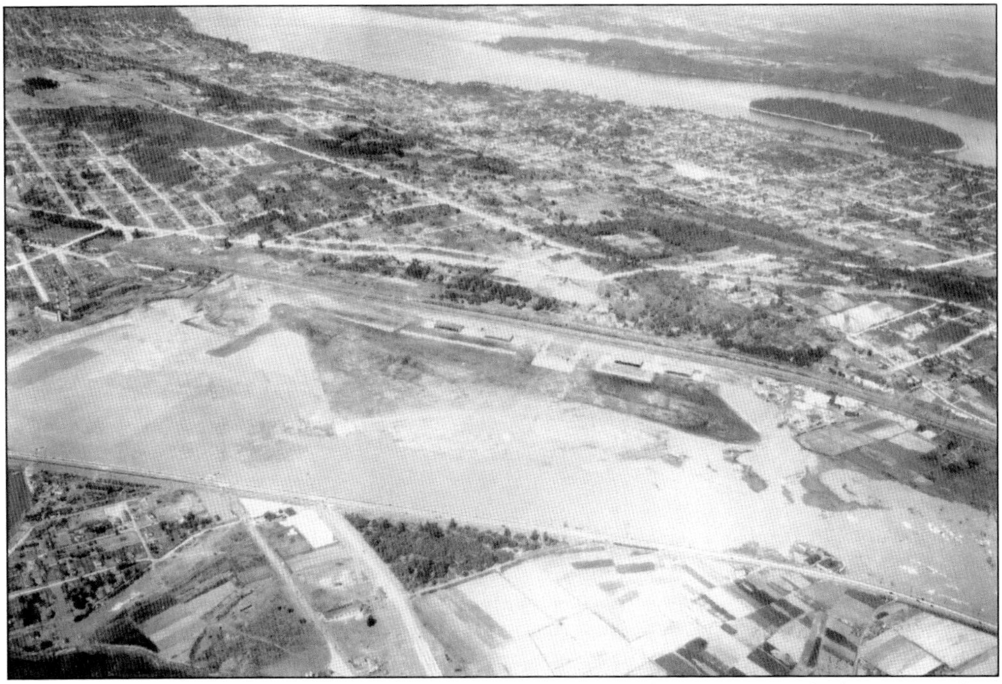

Taken in 1932, this aerial photograph shows the Boeing Airplane Company before its pending expansion. However, the company decided to remain in the Seattle area, assisted by a gift of several acres of land by Joe Desimone. (Courtesy of Theresa Lytle.)

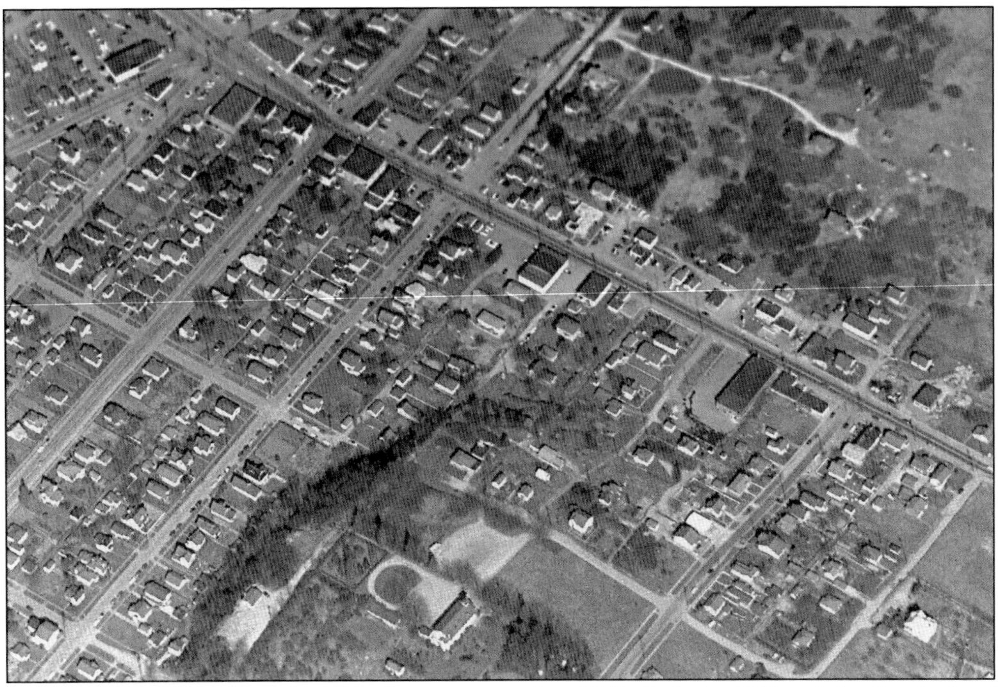

Here is the South Park neighborhood as it appeared in 1955. Catholic Hill and the Our Lady of Lourdes rectangular building are visible in the lower portion of this photograph. (Courtesy of Theresa Lytle.)

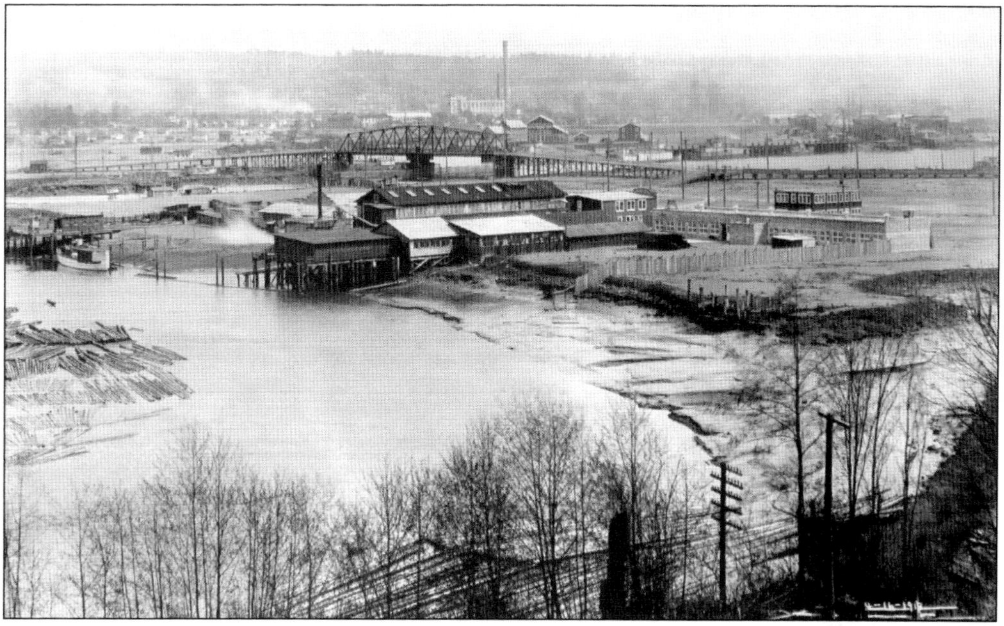

The Boeing plant is pictured here in 1918. The Boeing Airplane Company got its first big military order when its "C" model seaplane was accepted as a trainer by the U.S. Navy during World War I. The company opened a new plant on the west side of the Duwamish River to handle all this new business. The photograph shows the new factory, Plant One, of the Boeing Airplane Company. (Courtesy of MOHAI, No. SHS17645.)

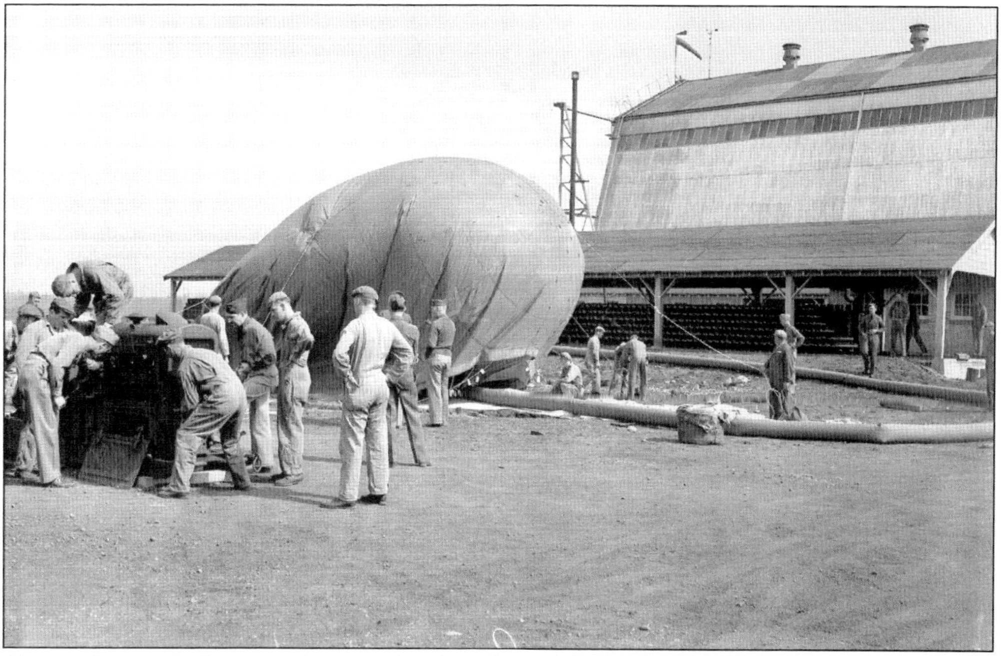

This is a barrage balloon on the ground in Seattle in 1942. During World War II, barrage balloons like this were flown on Catholic Hill and were used to guard against low-flying enemy air attacks. Each balloon was moored to a wagon by cables, which were strong enough to destroy any aircraft colliding with them. (Courtesy of MOHAI, No. 1986.5.643.3.)

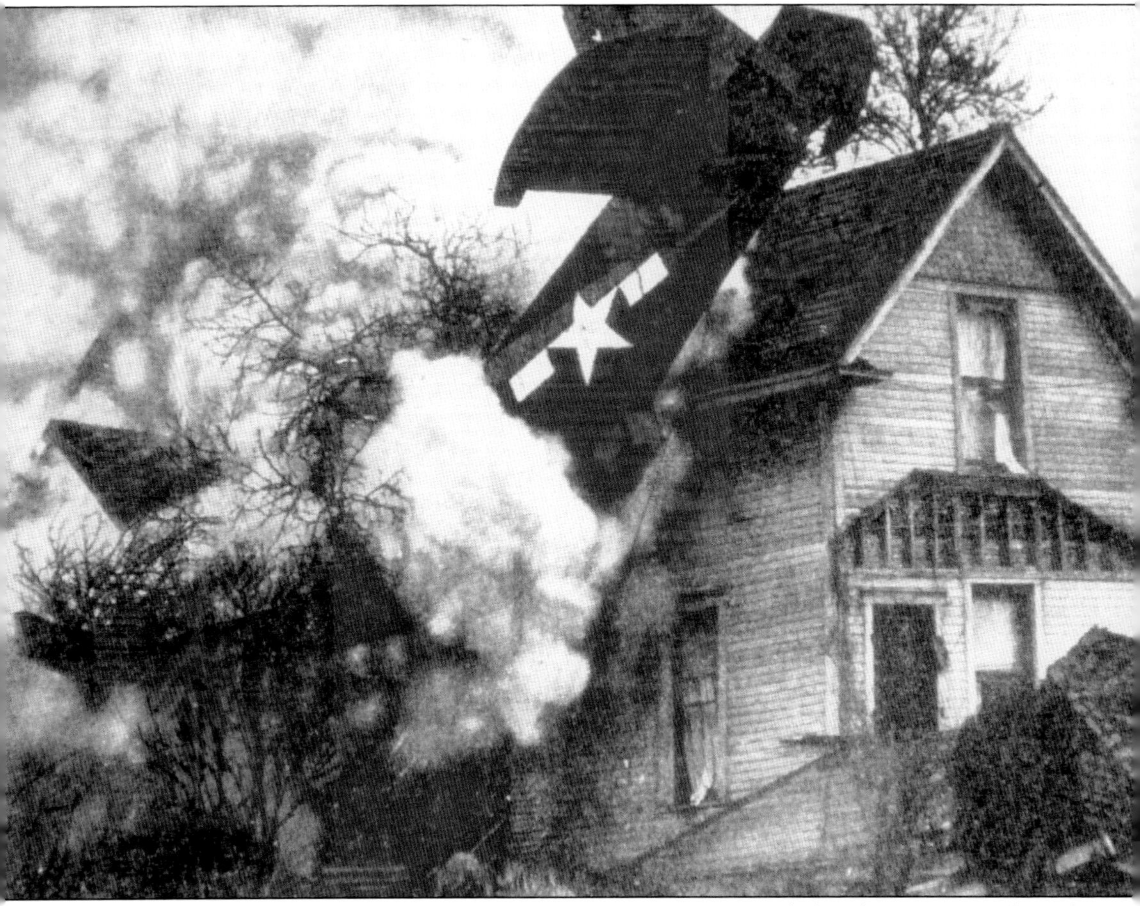

On February 9, 1946, at 10:15 a.m., this U.S. Navy Grumman torpedo bomber, on its way from the Sand Point Naval Station to Tillamook, Oregon, crashed into a house at 1206 Cloverdale Street in South Park. The pilot tried to land on Cloverdale Street but hit some power lines. Margaret Dillion (age 70), the owner was at home cooking beans when the crash occurred, as was Mary Daiver (age 79). The pilot, Paul Hull (age 27), escaped to a nearby vacant lot with a black eye and some scratches. The ladies in the house were both shaken but unhurt. The house was damaged to the point that it had to be demolished. The owner reportedly said, "Well, I guess I won't get to eat those beans." This photograph was in the personal collection of fire chief William Fitzgerald. (Courtesy of Richard Schneider.)

Six

COMMUNITY AND COMMUNITY ACTIVISM

Even though South Park's residents have traditionally been farmers and blue-collar workers, the neighborhood has a long history of community activism. In the early 1900s, as the South Park community continued its rapid growth, many citizens thought the district should be organized as a town. In December 1902, a petition for incorporation was circulated around the area, and after meeting with community approval, the district became the town of South Park on July 8, 1905.

An excerpt from the Duwamish Diaries, a book written by Cleveland High School students in 1949, states the following:

> In 1907 the citizens of South Park voted to become annexed to the City of Seattle because of the many advantages of being recognized as a part of the city. However, the election was declared illegal because the South Park area is not directly contiguous to the city. It was only after Southwest Seattle was annexed to the city that South Park was able to come in, which it did in March 1907. At the time that South Park joined the city of Seattle there were only 1,500 residents in the community of that number only 217 voted on the annexation issue. There were 181 votes in favor of the annexation and 36 votes against.

In 1913, at the prodding of the south end community at large, who could see the benefit of a navigable river, the Duwamish Waterway Commission and the Army Corps of Engineers completed the straightening of the Duwamish River.

In 1933, the South Park Ladies Improvement Club was established. Dues were 50¢ a year. The ladies met monthly in the clubroom of the South Park Field House and mobilized around community issues like installing a traffic signal at Eighth and Cloverdale Street, raising money for a movie projector, the kidney center, muscular dystrophy, and the Martha Washington School for Girls. This group evolved into the South Park Improvement Club.

In 1972, the South Park Seniors was established. At the same time, with city funds, the South Park Area Redevelopment Committee was started under the leadership of Tony Ferrucci and Bob Joiner. This committee was tasked with making neighborhood improvements in the wake of industrial rezoning.

In the 1980s, the South Park Crime Prevention Council was established to address the growing concern around public safety issues. In 2001, the name was changed to the South Park Neighborhood Association to incorporate the vision of both public safety and neighborhood improvement projects.

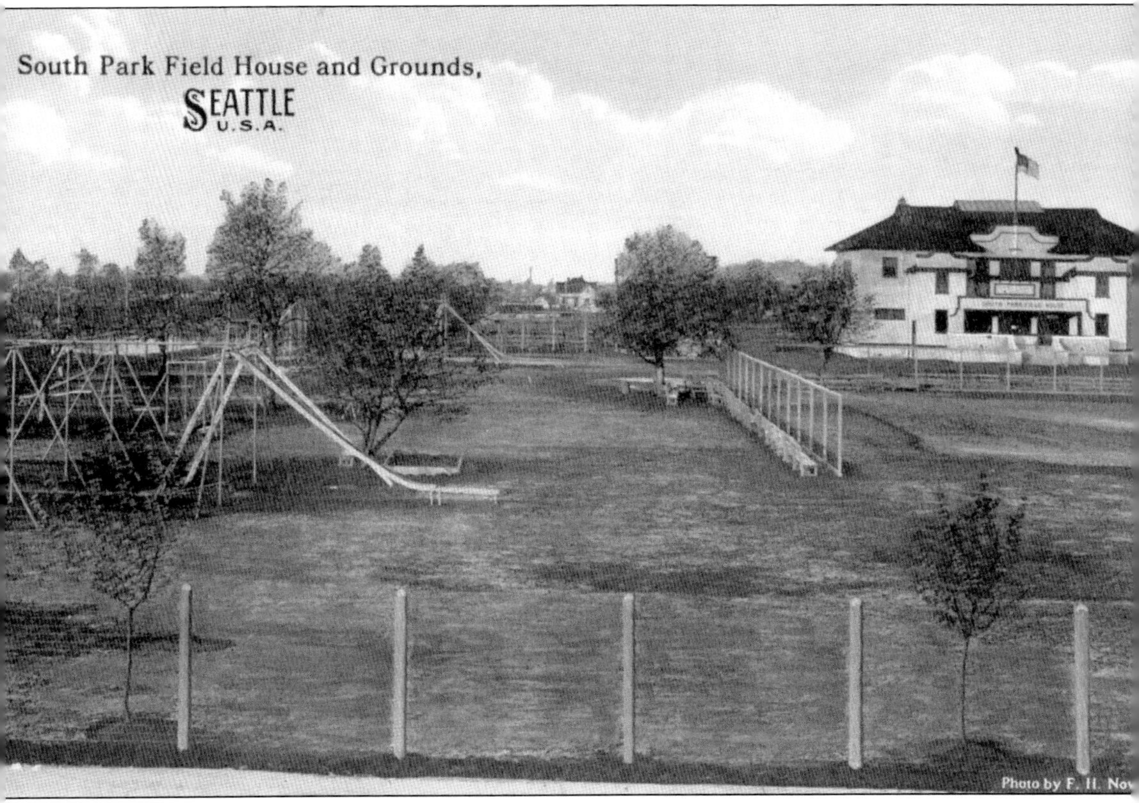

The South Park Field House was the largest of its kind west of the Mississippi. Here it is pictured on a postcard that South Park residents could mail to friends and family to make them envious of such a grand feature for such a small neighborhood. Before the construction of Highway 99, the South Park Playground and Field House had an expansive amount of property. The fruit trees left behind from the previous orchard that occupied this site provided an annual event in South Park called "Pie Days." Theresa Lytle recalls the big boys would shake the fruit trees while the young kids would gather the fruit in gunny sacks and take it home for their mothers to make pies. (Courtesy of MOHAI, No. 1982.156.6.)

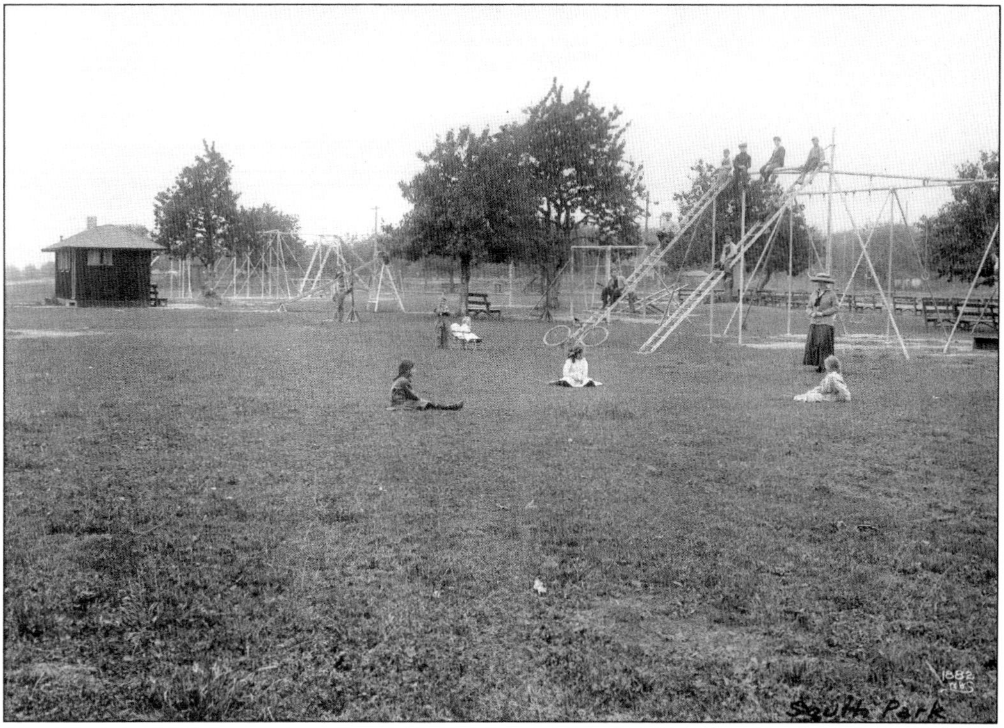

The South Park Playground is pictured here in 1910. The playground was known citywide for its nice amenities, which included large swing sets and many fruit trees left over from the Dunfield Orchards, which populated the site before its conversion to a recreation area. (Courtesy of the City of Seattle Municipal Archives.)

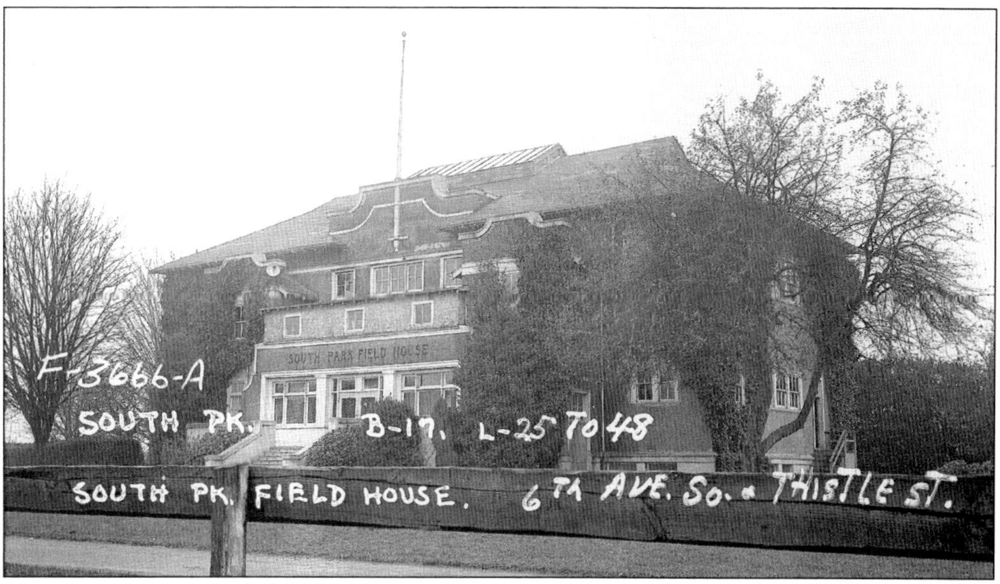

The original South Park Field House in 1937 was two stories and made of brick. The lines of the roof and the details of the old South Park Field House were mimicked in the new South Park Community Center when this one was torn down in 1989. (Courtesy of PSRA.)

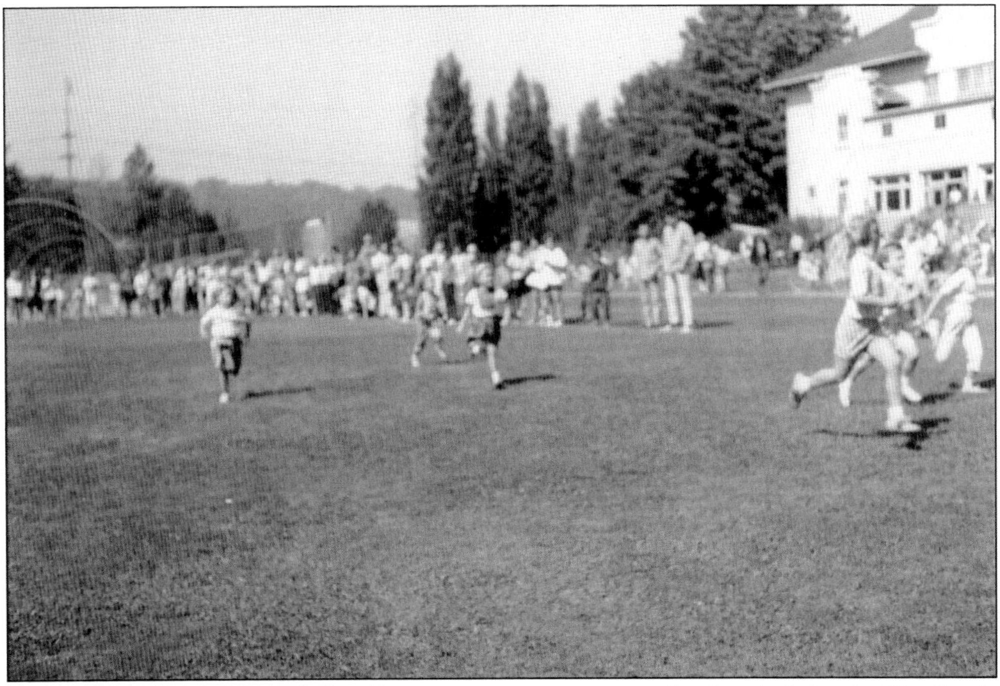

Always a popular event, the Labor Day races were entertaining for the whole family. The South Park Seniors would host the event at the South Park Field House. This image was taken in 1961. (Courtesy of the South Park Community Club.)

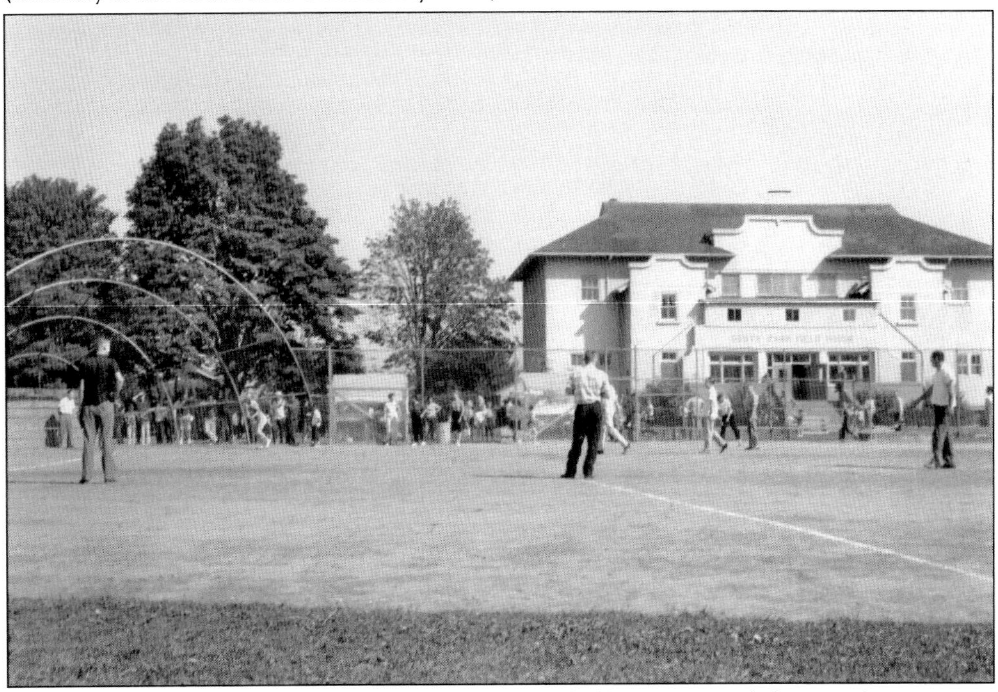

Long a tradition in South Park, Sunday afternoon baseball games provided respite from a seven-day workweek on the farms. Regular attendees included the Marras and their children. This photograph was taken in 1961. (Courtesy of the South Park Community Club.)

At a Labor Day dance in 1961, Georgina Collella demonstrated the latest dance moves. The Labor Day dance was widely regarded as one of the "don't miss events in South Park." (Courtesy of the South Park Community Club.)

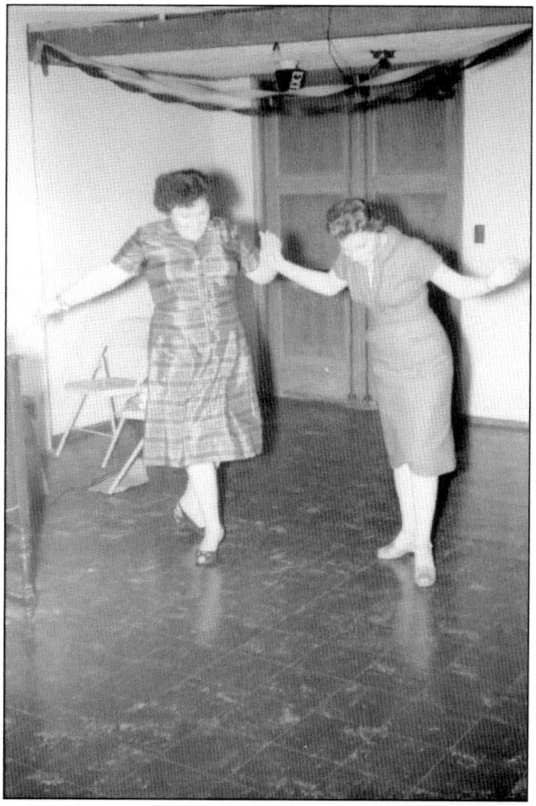

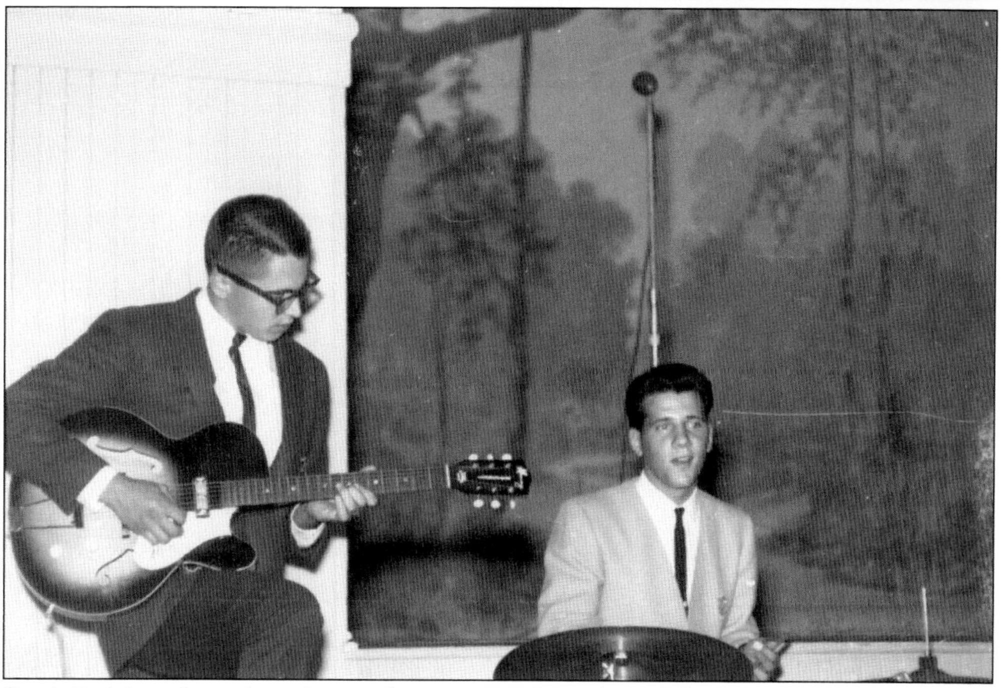

South Park has always been known for its events, festivals, and dances. Bo Collella is pictured above on the drums at a dance in 1961. (Courtesy of the South Park Community Club.)

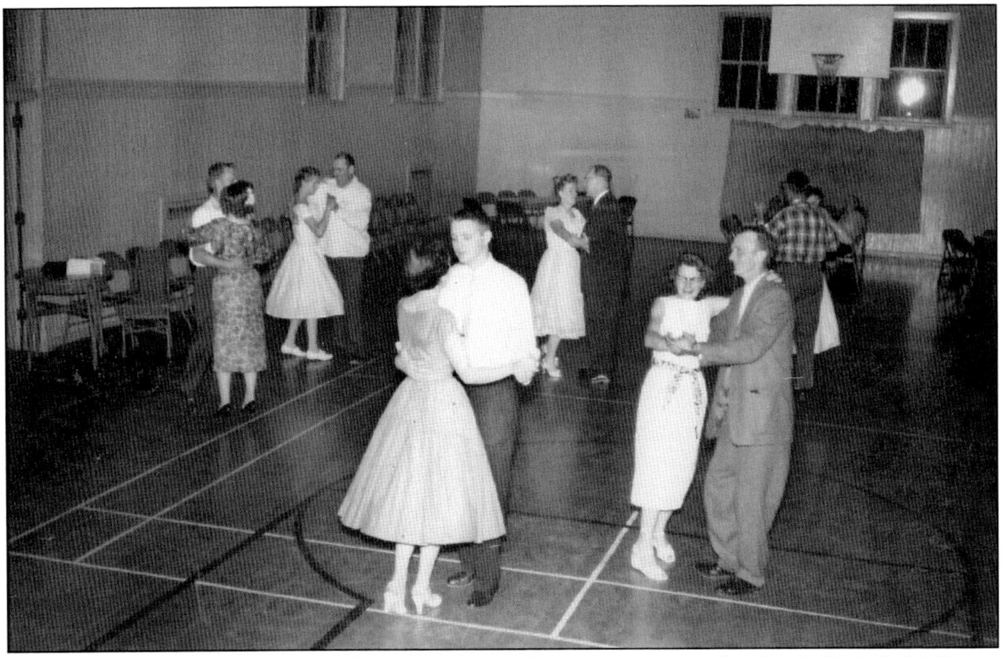

South Park residents are pictured here dancing in the gymnasium at the South Park Field House in 1961. The South Park Field House was oftentimes the gathering place for community events. The dances were always held in the gymnasium, which was located on the upper level of the building. (Courtesy of the South Park Community Club.)

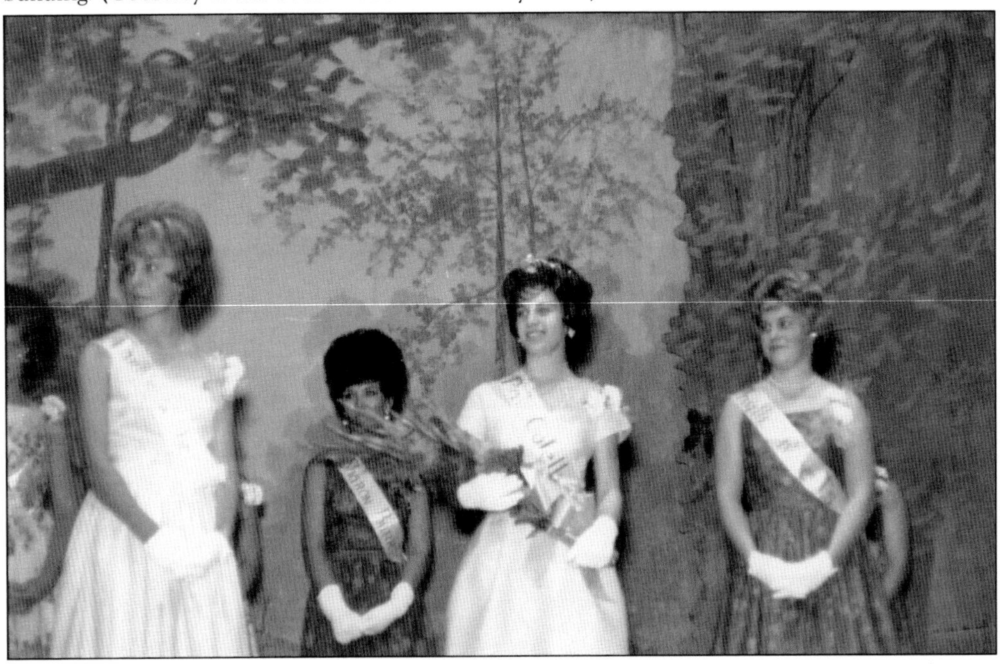

Pictured here are the queen and finalists of the 1961 Labor Day beauty pageant, an annual event in the South Park community that drew in people from surrounding Seattle neighborhoods. The Labor Day festival stopped being held when organizers got tired of the rain. By 1980, there were no longer Labor Day festivals in South Park. (Courtesy of the South Park Community Club.)

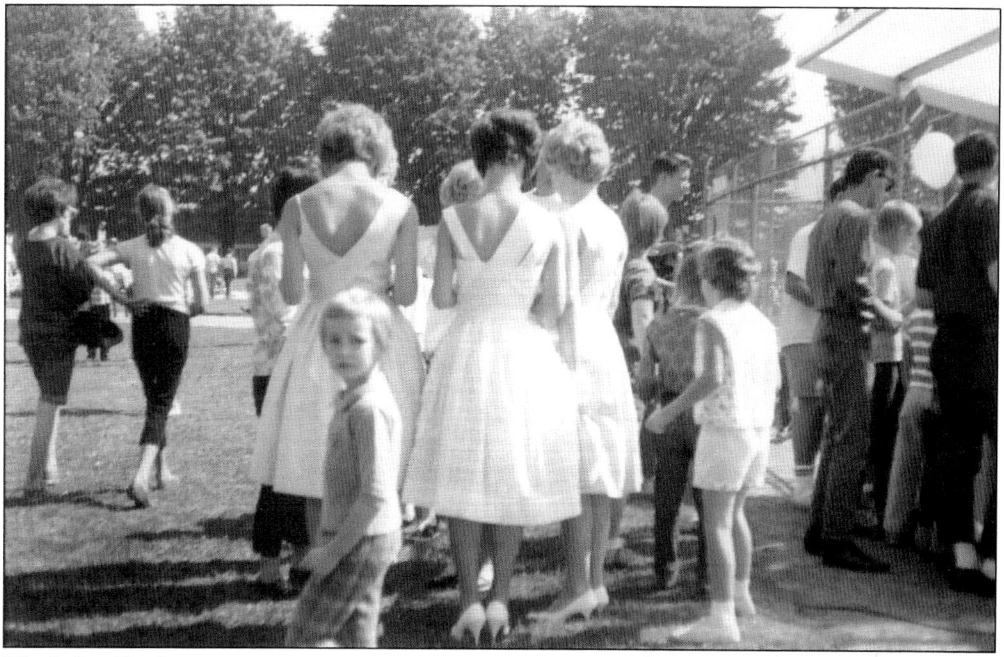

The Labor Day beauty pageant contestants are signing autographs in 1961. Those who participated in the pageant would compete in several categories for queen. The women were very popular with the residents and especially with the young girls from the neighborhood. (Courtesy of the South Park Community Club.)

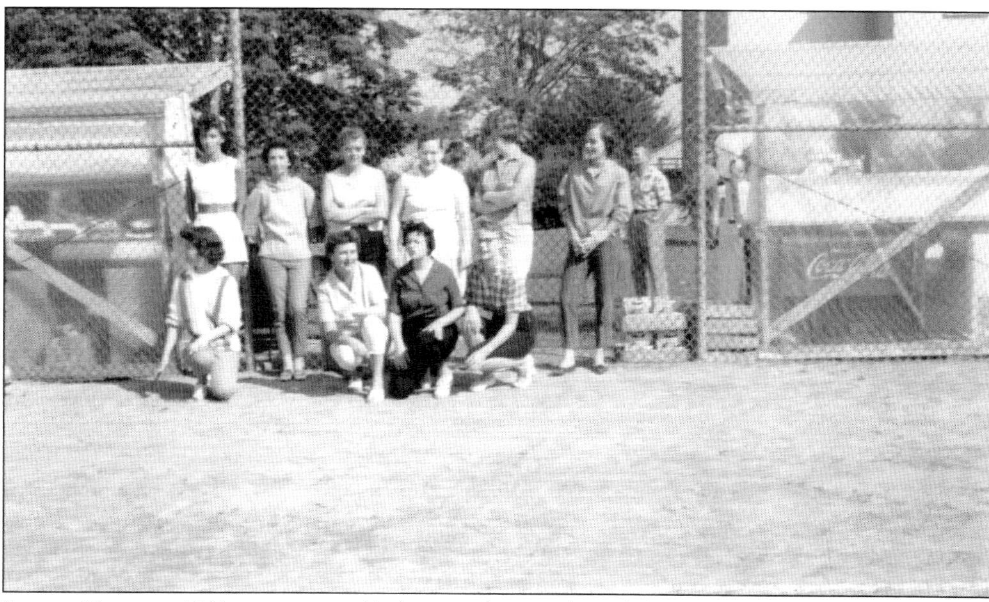

Pictured here in 1961 is a group of ladies on the South Park ball field. An informal team that occasionally played ball (but not against other neighborhood bar teams), they were the precursor to the present-day River Ratz, a baseball bar team that plays for the County Line and against other local bar teams. Theresa Lytle is pictured in the front row, second from the left. She recalled many impromptu neighborhood ball games being played at the South Park Field House on weekends. (Courtesy of the South Park Community Club.)

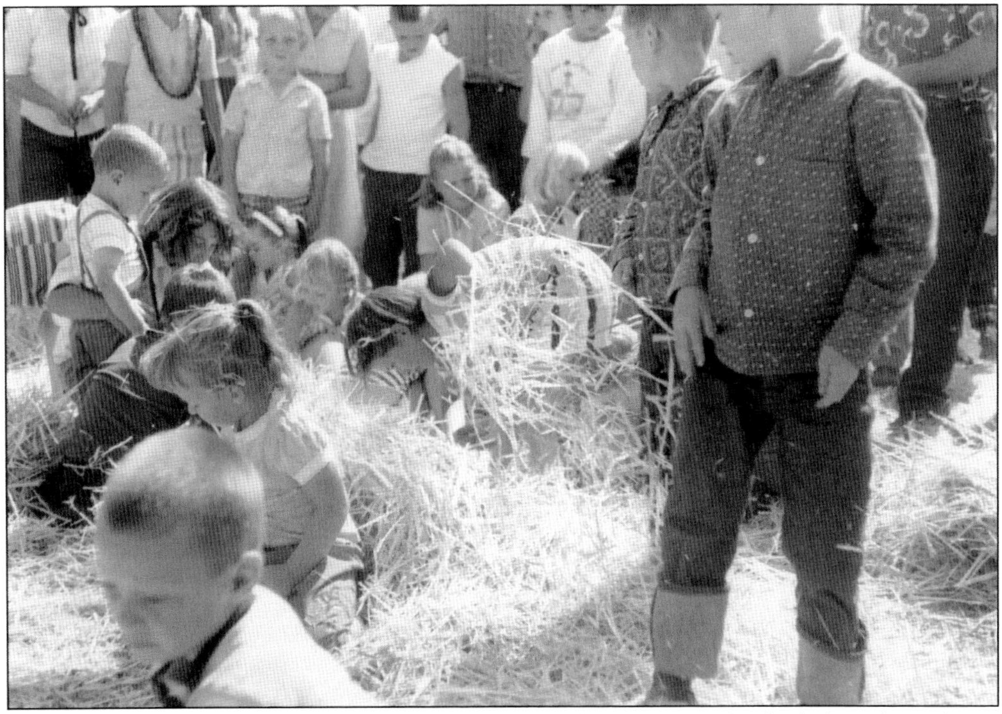

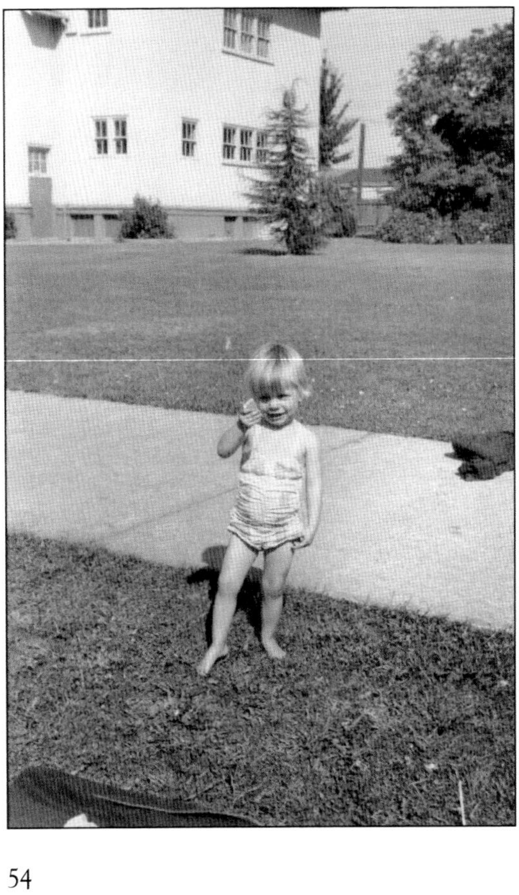

A favorite game for the kids at the Labor Day festival was "penny in a haystack." The event drew hundreds of local kids and their parents. The South Park Seniors purchased loads of hay and hid a single penny in one of the piles, and then local kids would rummage through them hoping to find the penny. These images are from 1963. The lucky winner of the penny in a haystack is pictured below after sorting through piles of hay to find a single penny. Hundreds of other kids competed in the race. (Both courtesy of the South Park Community Club.)

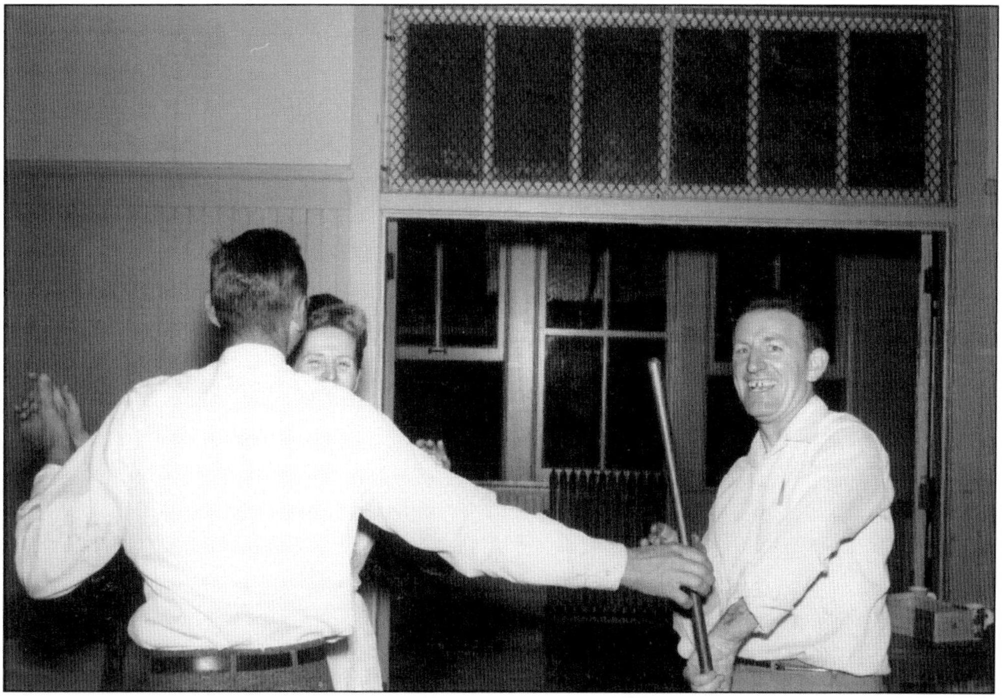

The Field House was a popular place for men to play shuffleboard and pool. (Courtesy of the South Park Community Club.)

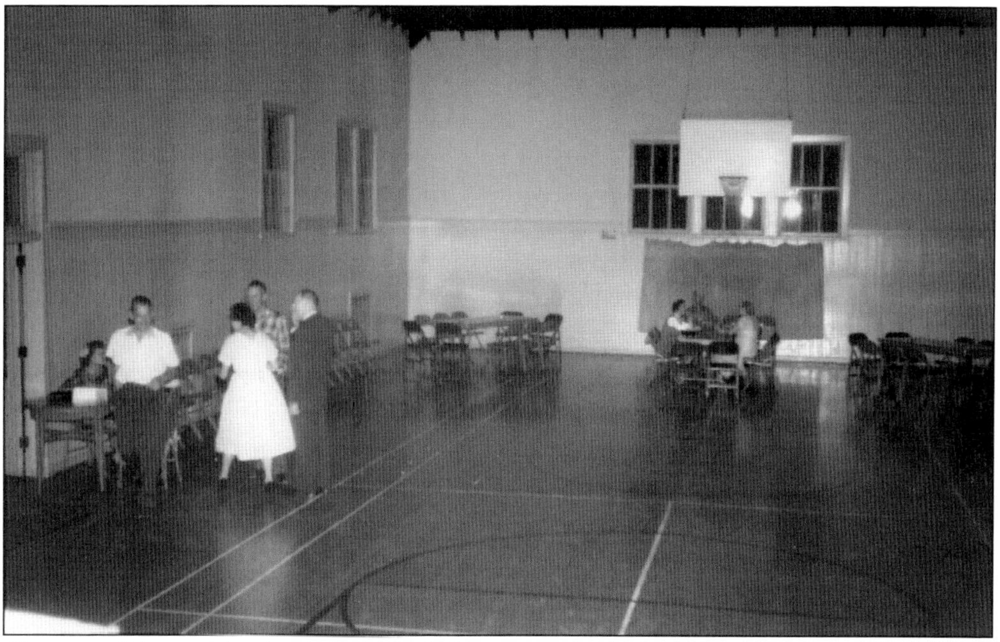

The second floor of the South Park Field House was a basketball court, but it was also used for dances sponsored by the South Park Community Club. The gym was open everyday of the week, and in later years, students from Concord School would often meet there after the school day ended. A stage was at one end of the basketball court and was used for community theater events. (Courtesy of the South Park Community Club.)

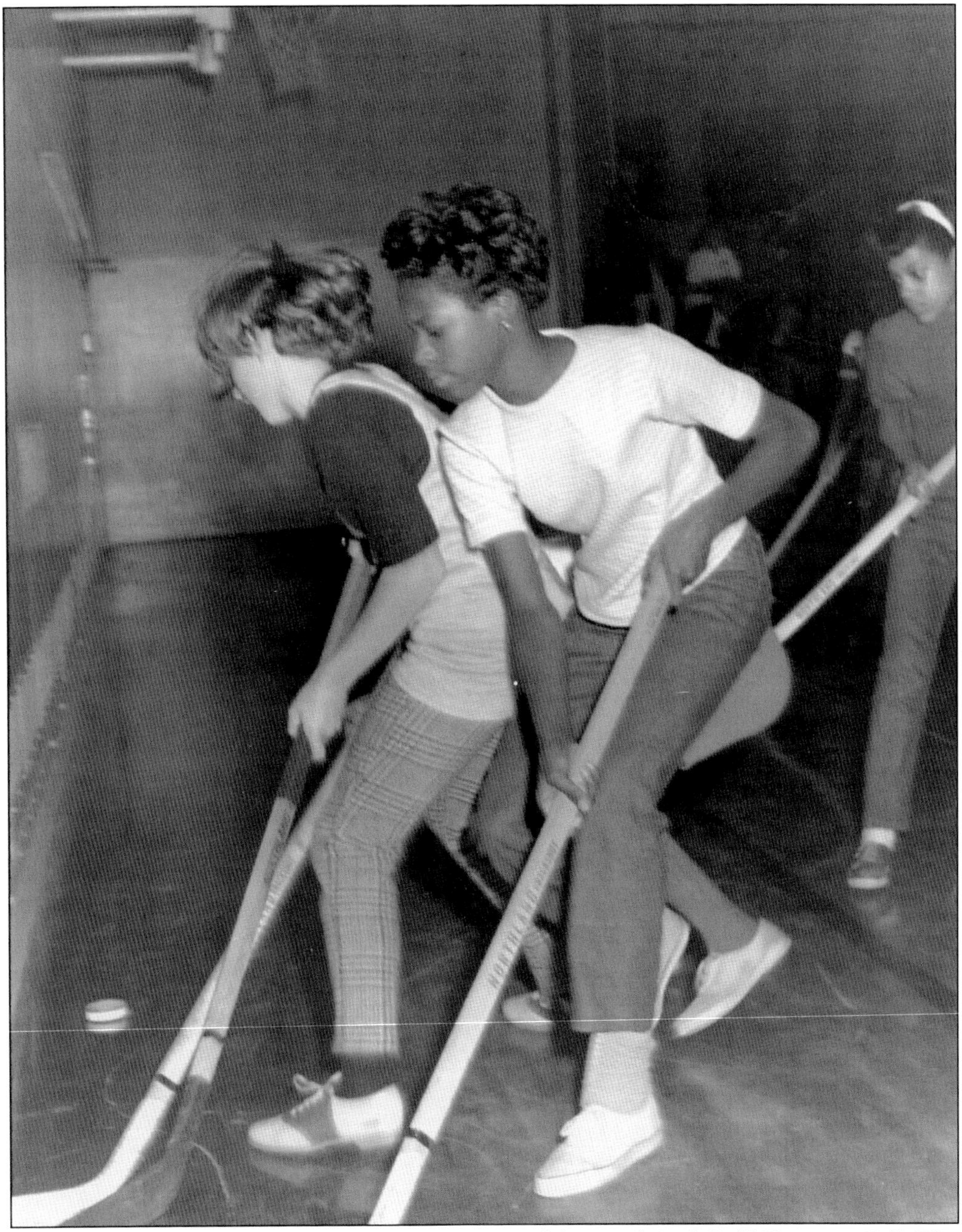

A group of students plays hockey in the gymnasium of the South Park Field House in 1963. The second story had a large basketball gymnasium that was used for many events beyond basketball, including hockey, dances, variety band shows, craft bazaars, and beauty pageants. (Courtesy of Theresa Lytle.)

South Park youth are pictured here squaring off under the watchful eye of community center staff in 1963. Historically, South Park has had many working-class families with children. The community center continues to provide positive activities for the diverse community of 3,800 residents, of which half are children. (Courtesy of Theresa Lytle.)

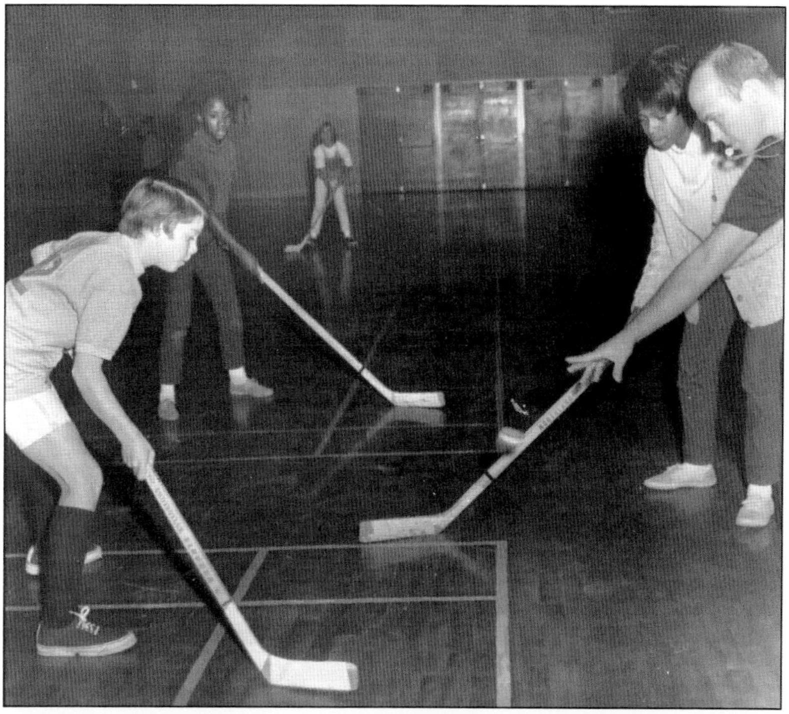

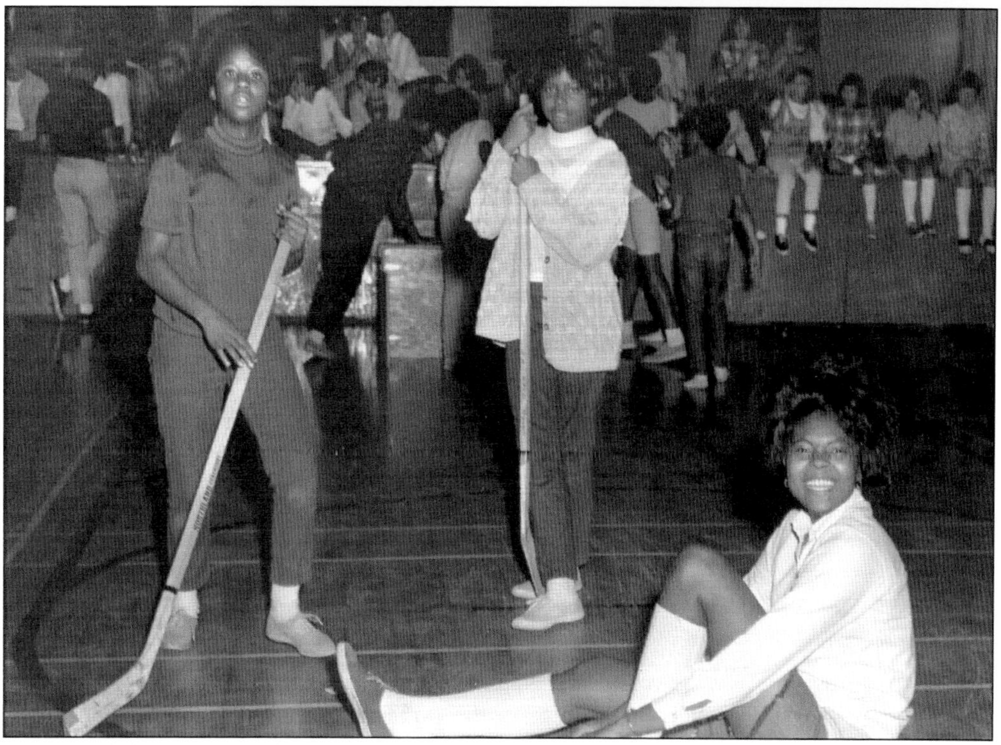

A group of elementary students is pictured here in 1963 enjoying a game of all-youth hockey. The event was held at the community center, which focused a majority of its programs and activities on young people, not unlike today. (Courtesy of Theresa Lytle.)

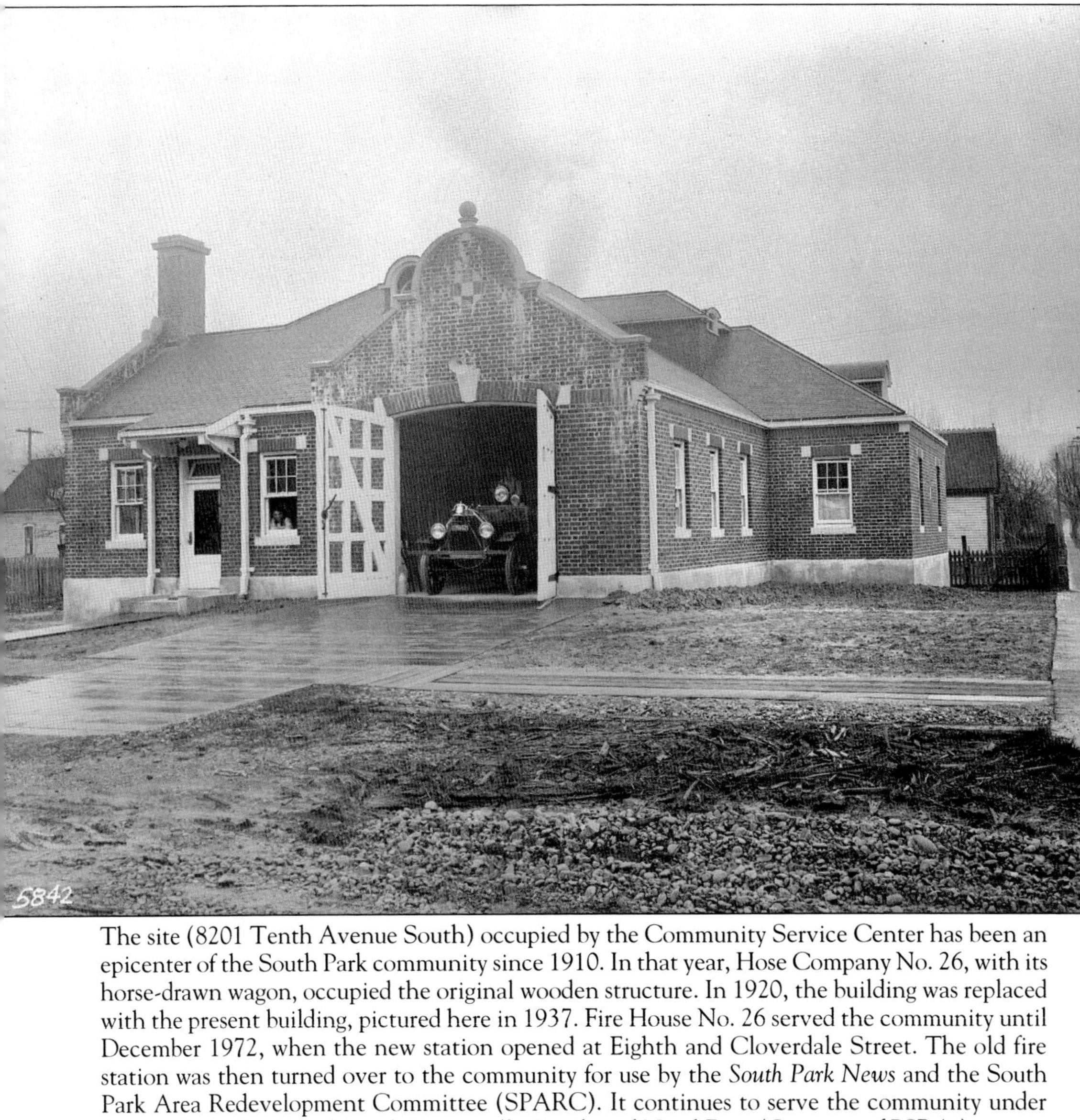

The site (8201 Tenth Avenue South) occupied by the Community Service Center has been an epicenter of the South Park community since 1910. In that year, Hose Company No. 26, with its horse-drawn wagon, occupied the original wooden structure. In 1920, the building was replaced with the present building, pictured here in 1937. Fire House No. 26 served the community until December 1972, when the new station opened at Eighth and Cloverdale Street. The old fire station was then turned over to the community for use by the *South Park News* and the South Park Area Redevelopment Committee (SPARC). It continues to serve the community under the gentle leadership of Joseph Pasquarella-Smith and Nigel Day. (Courtesy of PSRA.)

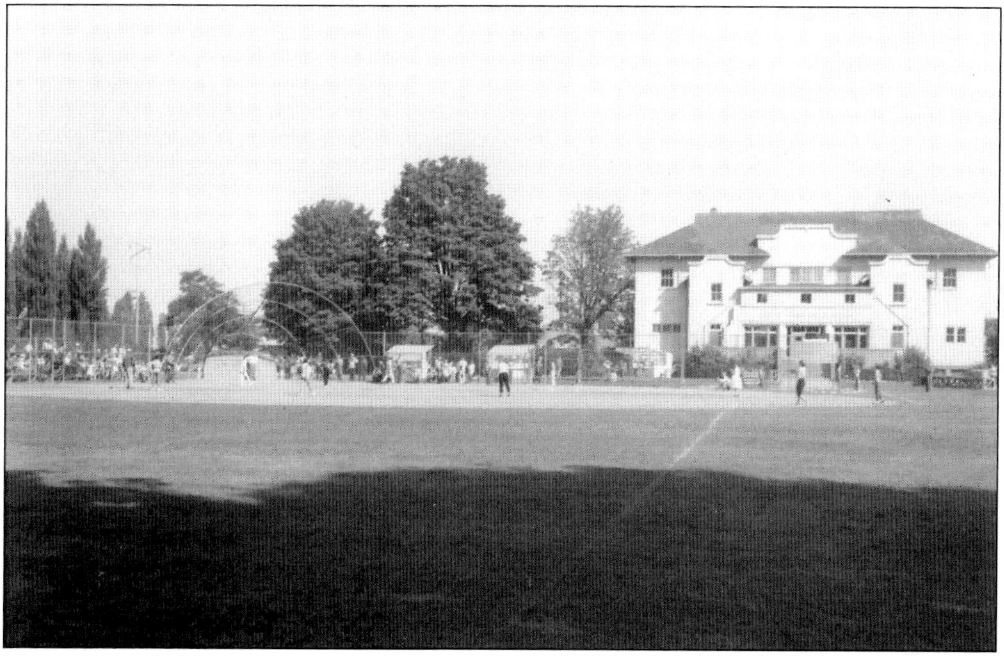

The 1961 Labor Day races were held at the South Park Field House. The lines of the roof and details of the old South Park Field House were mimicked in the new South Park Community Center in 1989. In this image, the once brick South Park Field House was painted white. (Courtesy of the South Park Community Club.)

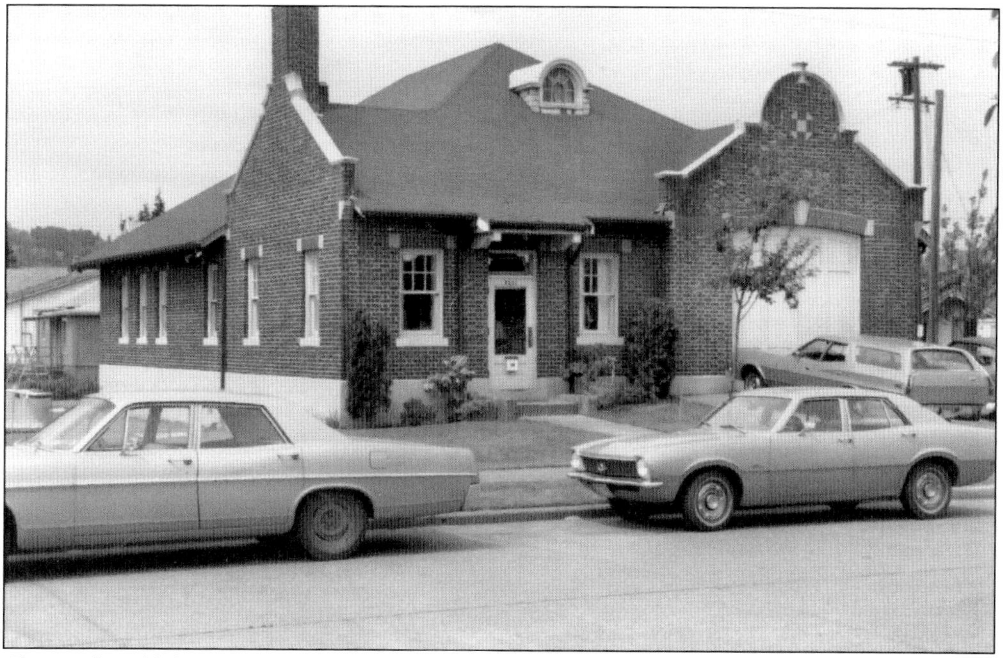

This is the old fire station in 1976, the year it was dedicated as the South Park Community Service Center. Today ECOSS and the Regina House Food Bank are located in the building. It is also used to host various neighborhood meetings and is known as the Neighborhood Center. The firemen's old lockers still adorn the entryway. (Courtesy of the South Park Seniors.)

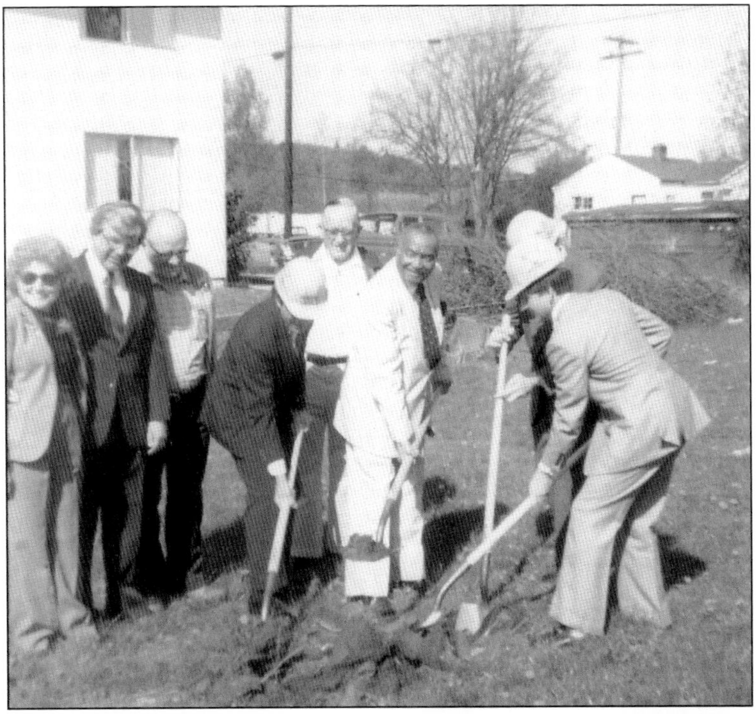

In 1983, the groundbreaking ceremony for the expansion of the South Park Community Service Center, or Neighborhood Center, was held. Mayor Charles Royer was present, along with city and local dignitaries. (Courtesy of the South Park Seniors.)

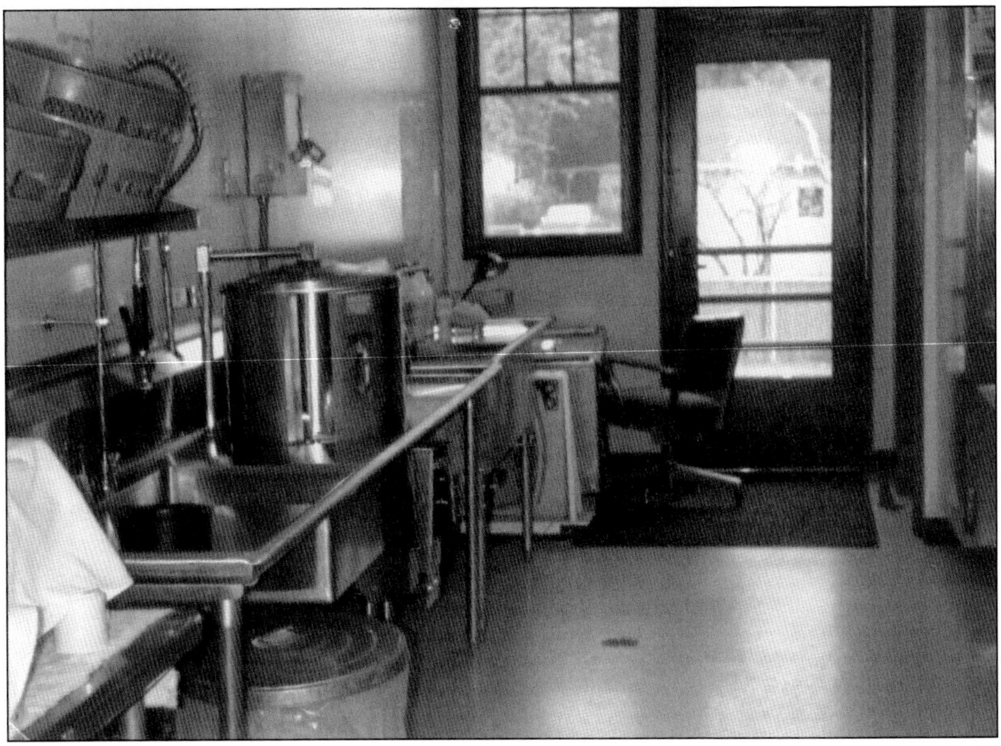

Here are the new kitchen facilities at the South Park Community Service Center in 1983. This kitchen continues to serve meals to South Park seniors and is used several times a year for community-wide potlucks and lunches. (Courtesy of the South Park Seniors.)

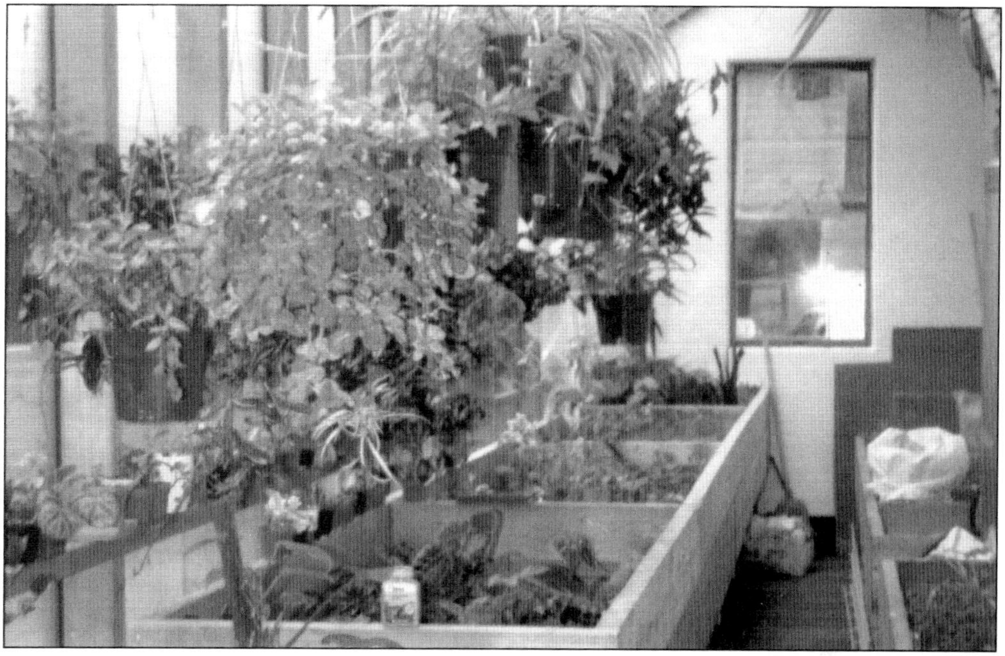

Pictured above in 1983 is the new greenhouse solarium at the South Park Community Service Center. This greenhouse provided a place for neighbors to garden, take classes on gardening, and raise money for the various community organizations. (Courtesy of the South Park Seniors.)

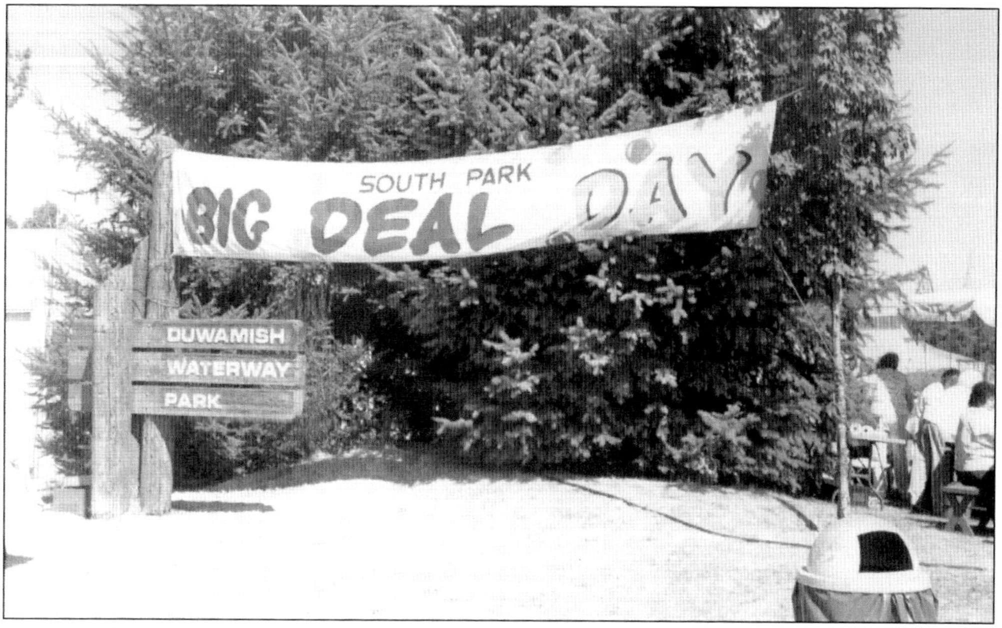

"Big Deal Day" started around 1987 and was typically cosponsored by the South Park Seniors, South Park Community Club, and South Park Crime Prevention Council. It quickly became known as one of South Park's community-wide celebrations and replaced the Labor Day festival as the annual community celebration. Big Deal Days stopped in the mid-1990s when Night Out Against Crime and La Fiestas Patrias became the annual community events. (Courtesy of the South Park Seniors.)

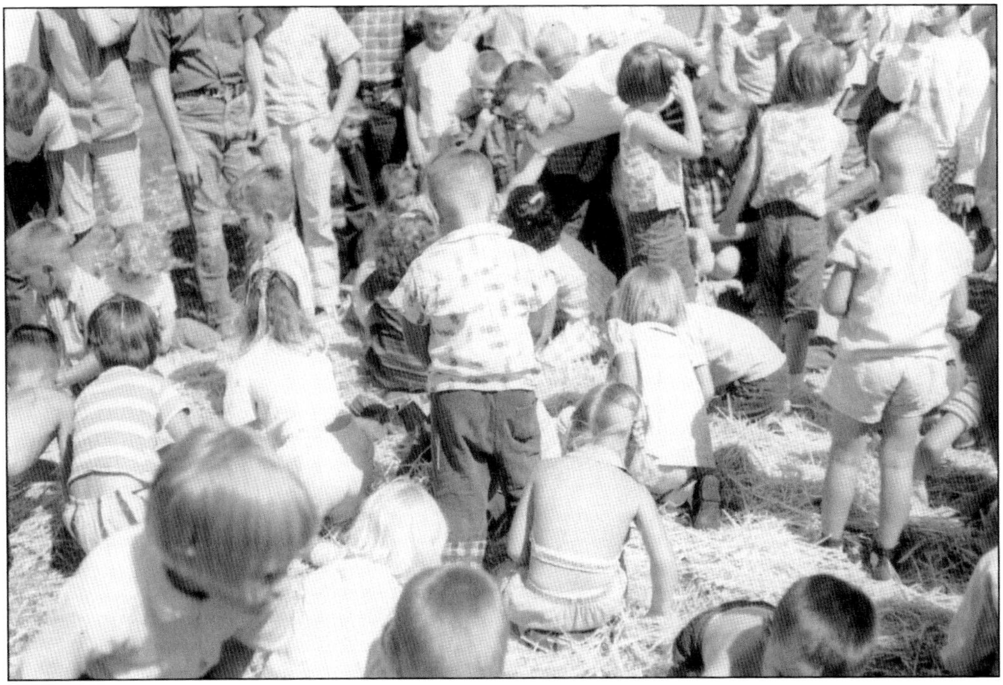

The kids are looking for the penny in the haystack, the extremely popular event for younger kids. This race took place at the South Park Field House in 1963. (Courtesy of the South Park Community Club.)

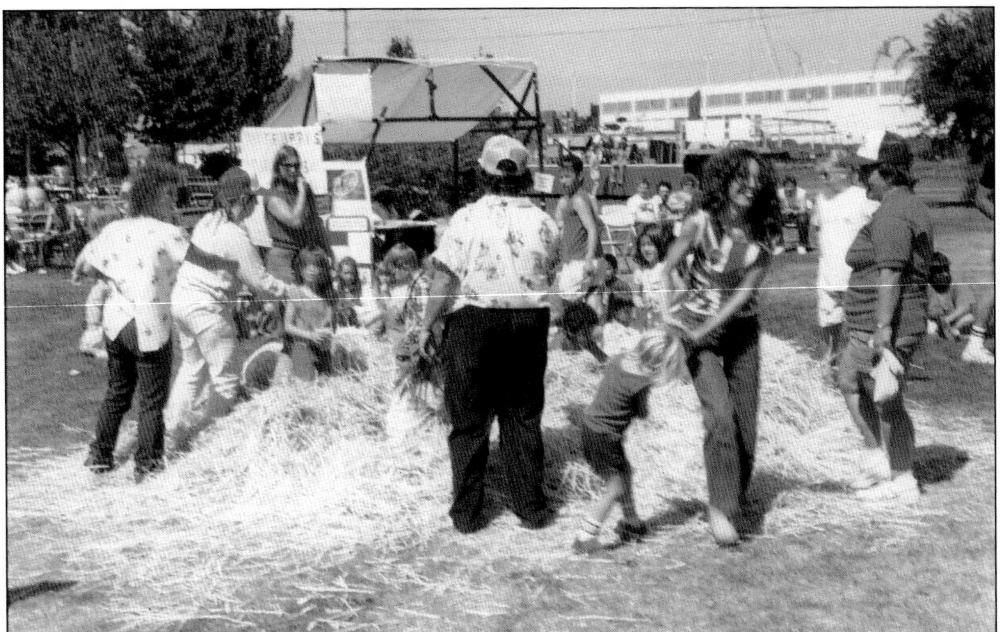

In 1987, children are looking for the penny in a haystack. Most did not care that a penny just did not go as far as it used to. This race took place at the Duwamish Waterway Park at the end of Tenth Avenue South. Boeing's plant is visible across the river. (Courtesy of the South Park Seniors.)

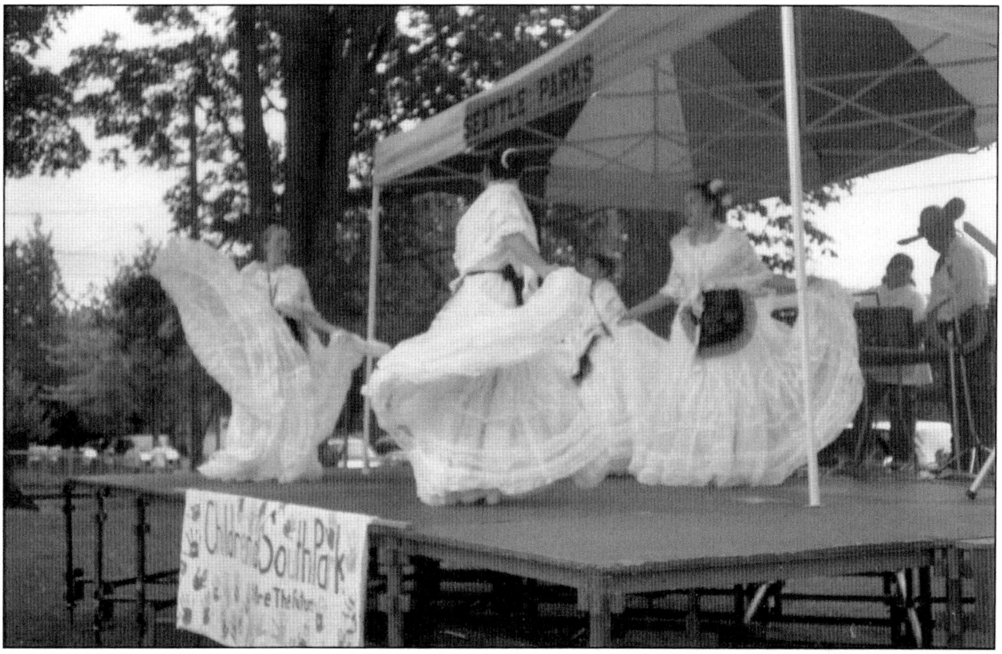

These South Park residents are Mexican folk dancing at Big Deal Days in 1987. This tradition continues with the La Fiestas Patrias festival held each year in South Park. La Fiestas Patrias is one of the few annual community-wide events still held in South Park. (Courtesy of the South Park Seniors.)

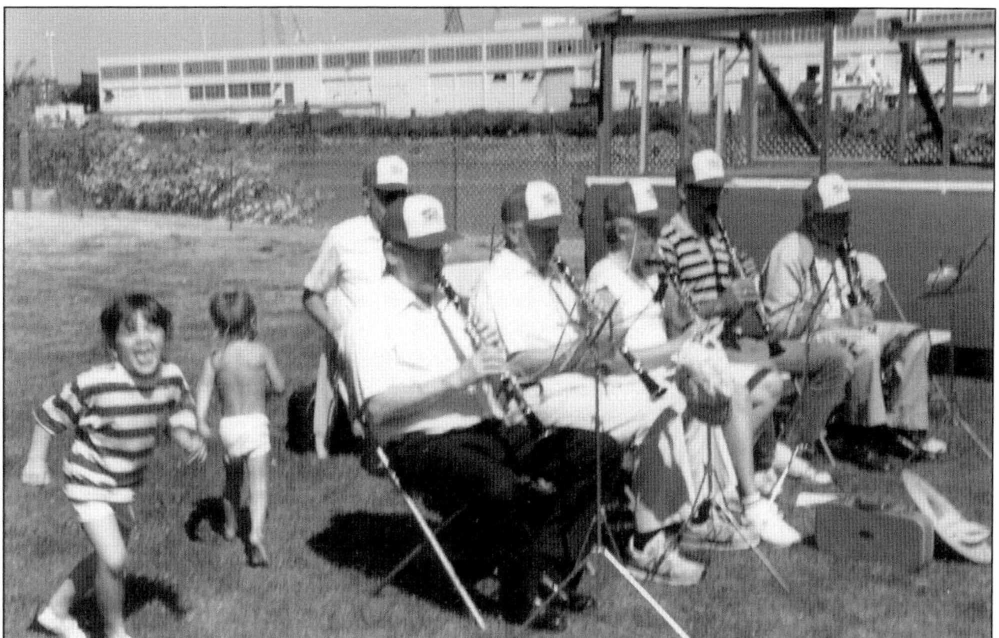

The South Park senior citizens' Variety Band entertains the young crowd at the 1987 Big Deal Days at Duwamish Waterway Park. The Variety Band played at events throughout the community and provided music for the dances held at the South Park Field House in the gymnasium. (Courtesy of the South Park Seniors.)

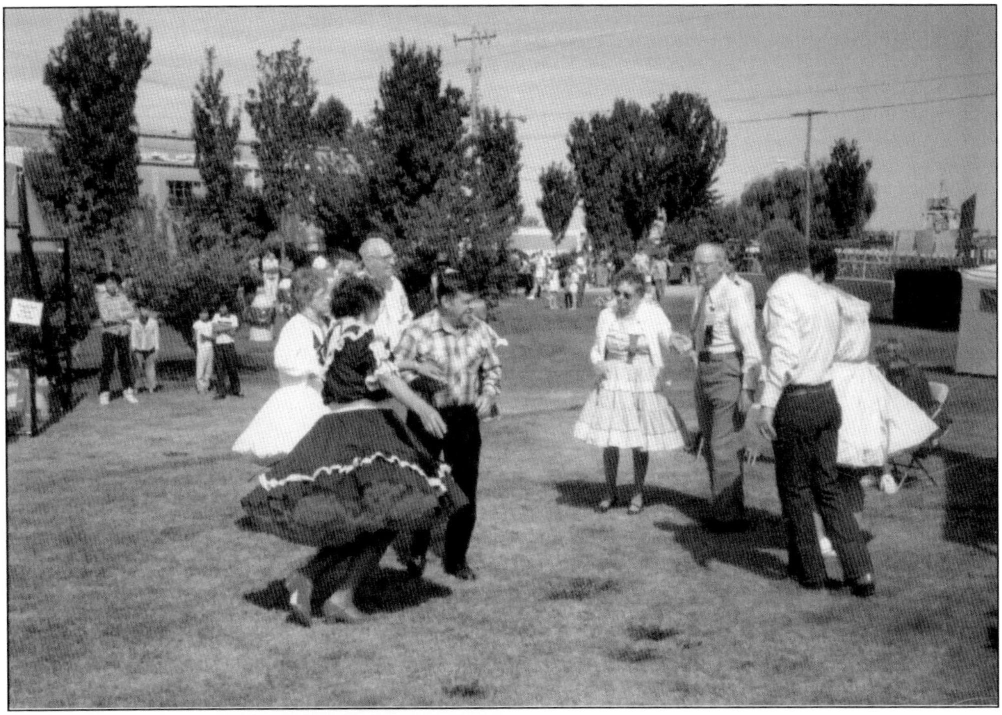

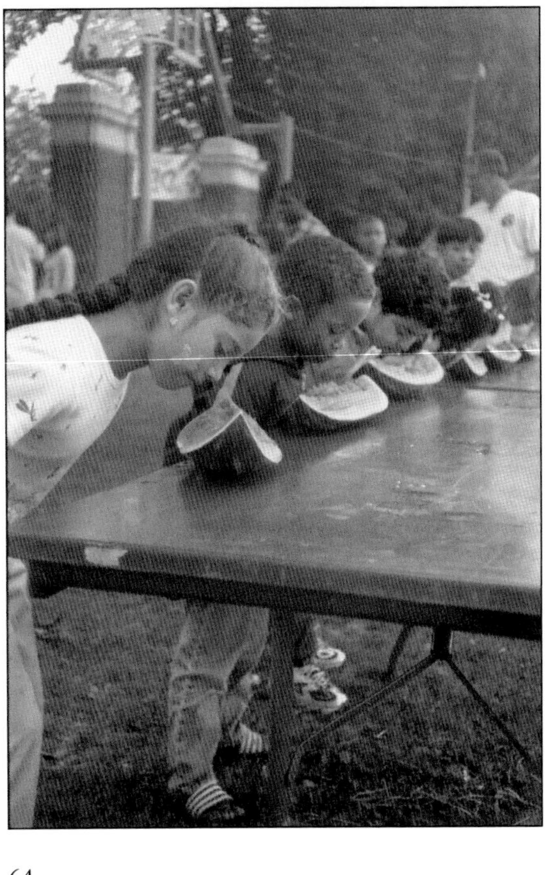

Square dancing was a mainstay of the Big Deal Days festivities and homage to the farming roots that were still present in South Park in the 1980s. Big Deal Days was a festival sponsored by the South Park Seniors, but it no longer takes place. (Courtesy of the South Park Seniors.)

The ever-popular watermelon-eating contest was always a big hit with young and old alike. This event was held at the South Park Field House in 1987. (Courtesy of the South Park Seniors.)

This is an actual copy of the petition signed by residents and given to the town council of South Park to begin the process of annexation into the city of Seattle. The town of South Park desired the city of Seattle's amenities, such as water and sewer. The names on this 1906 document, like McAllister, Middleton, McGee, Kelly, Mercer, Blanchard, Miller, Murdoch, Montan, Lingenfelter, Burdic, and Anderson, reflect how involved the farmers and business owners were in the community. (Courtesy of the City of Seattle Municipal Archives.)

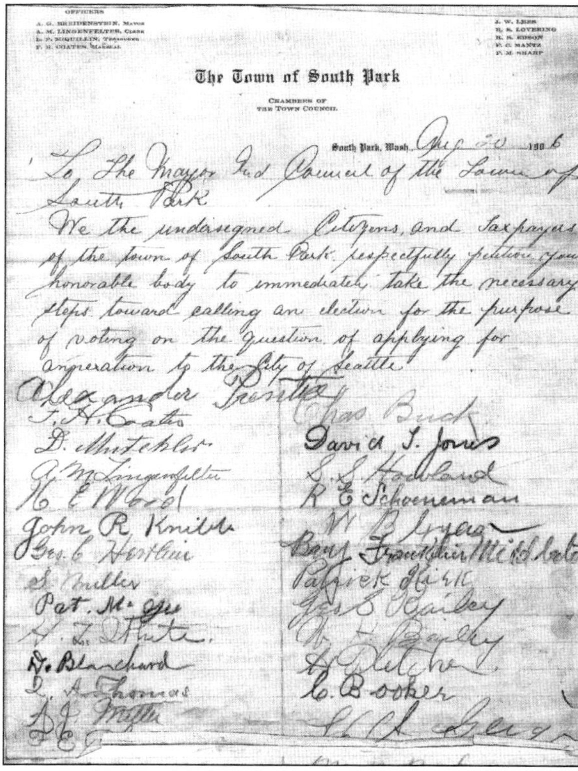

OFFICERS

A. M. LINGENFELTER, Clerk

J. W. LEES

F. M. SHARP

The Town of South Park

CHAMBERS OF THE TOWN COUNCIL

South Park, Wash., Aug 30 1906

To The Mayor and Council of the Town of South Park

We the undersigned Citizens and Taxpayers of the town of South Park respectfully petition your honorable body to immediately take the necessary steps toward calling an election for the purpose of voting on the question of applying for annexation to the City of Seattle

Alexander Prentice
Chas Buck
David J. Jones
A. M. Lingenfelter
R. E. Schoeneman
John R. Knible
Pat. McGee
D. Blanchard
C. Booker

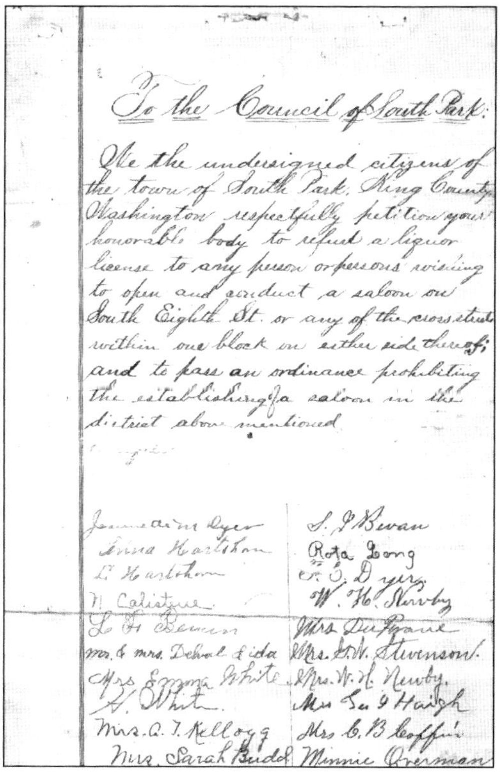

To the Council of South Park:

We the undersigned citizens of the town of South Park, King County Washington respectfully petition your honorable body to refuse a liquor license to any person or persons wishing to open and conduct a saloon on South Eighth St. or any of the cross streets within one block on either side thereof; and to pass an ordinance prohibiting the establishing of a saloon in the district above mentioned

S. J. Bevan
Rota Long
Mrs. J. W. Stevenson
Mrs Emma White
Mrs. W. H. Newby
Mrs. C. B. Coffin
Mrs. A. T. Kellogg
Mrs. Sarah Budd
Minnie Overman

Early records (1902–1907) of South Park revealed that the thickest folders are petitions and bonds for liquor licenses and street and water improvements. This is a letter from the residents of South Park requesting that an ordinance be written prohibiting the sale of alcohol on Eighth Avenue South, the main arterial and business core in South Park. The families of South Park did not want any saloons or taverns along the popular trolley line. (Courtesy of the City of Seattle Municipal Archives.)

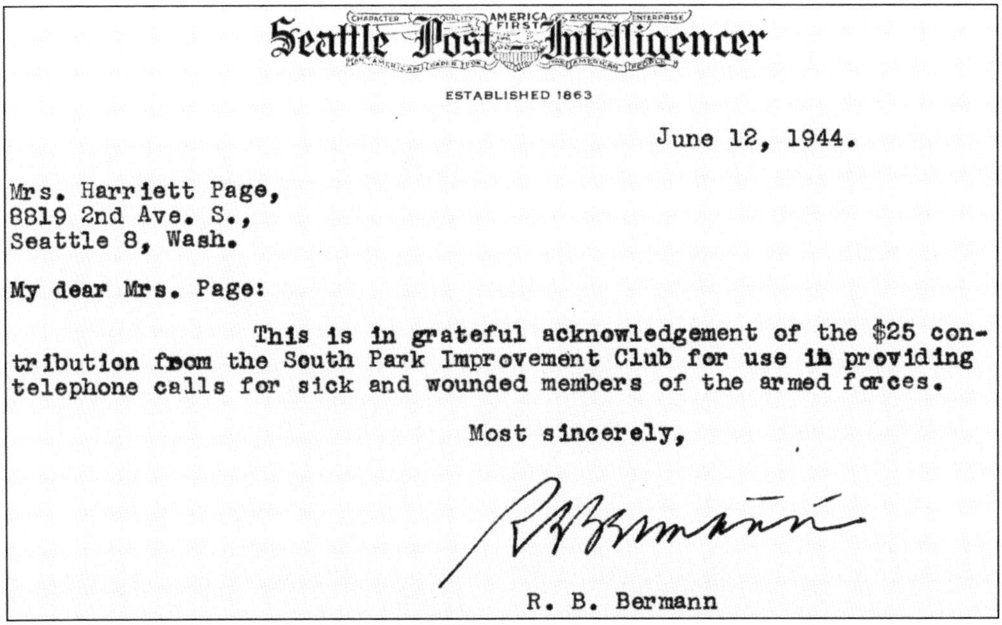

Seattle Post-Intelligencer

CHARACTER QUALITY AMERICA FIRST ACCURACY ENTERPRISE

ESTABLISHED 1863

June 12, 1944.

Mrs. Harriett Page,
8819 2nd Ave. S.,
Seattle 8, Wash.

My dear Mrs. Page:

This is in grateful acknowledgement of the $25 contribution from the South Park Improvement Club for use in providing telephone calls for sick and wounded members of the armed forces.

Most sincerely,

R. B. Bermann

When World War II began, many of South Park's young men were deployed throughout Europe and the Pacific. The South Park Ladies Improvement Club met in the clubroom at the South Park Field House and raised money for soldiers. Beacon Hill and South Park both had active chapters of ladies clubs. (Courtesy of the South Park Ladies Improvement Club.)

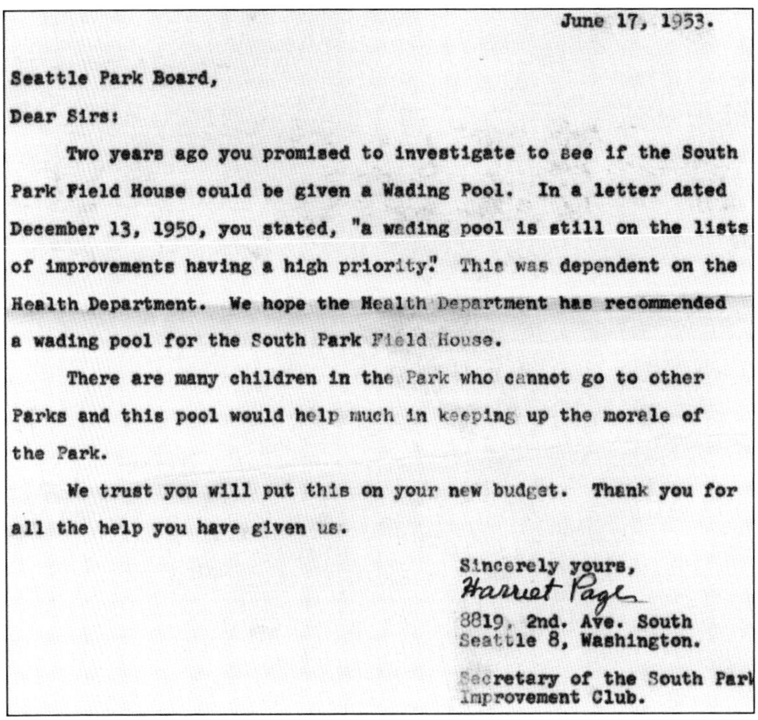

June 17, 1953.

Seattle Park Board,

Dear Sirs:

Two years ago you promised to investigate to see if the South Park Field House could be given a Wading Pool. In a letter dated December 13, 1950, you stated, "a wading pool is still on the lists of improvements having a high priority." This was dependent on the Health Department. We hope the Health Department has recommended a wading pool for the South Park Field House.

There are many children in the Park who cannot go to other Parks and this pool would help much in keeping up the morale of the Park.

We trust you will put this on your new budget. Thank you for all the help you have given us.

Sincerely yours,
Harriet Page
8819, 2nd. Ave. South
Seattle 8, Washington.

Secretary of the South Park
Improvement Club.

Pictured to the left is an urgent letter written by residents in the South Park community to the Parks Department, inquiring as to when exactly the wading pool was going to be implemented at the South Park Field House. The residents had been petitioning the Parks Department for three years. (Courtesy of the South Park Ladies Improvement Club.)

Seven

The River

At one point, on the west side of South Park, there were seven small creeks that came together as McAllister Creek, which boasted a 60-foot base where it entered the Duwamish River. McAllister Creek was one of the largest feeder creeks to the Duwamish.

By the late 19th century, the early residents had settled along the Duwamish River and learned to live with the ebb and flow of a river whose volume changed drastically based on the tide and rainfall. While the soil encouraged farming, annual winter flooding in the Duwamish flood plain commonly ruined houses and farmland. River ferry crossings still took the place of bridges, and flat-bottomed steamboats helped avoid the expense of deepening the river channel. By this time, the river had become more shallow, due in part to the construction of numerous wharves and piles that collected river debris and encouraged silt deposition. Early residents of South Park were frustrated with the difficulty they had navigating the then winding river. It is also clear that early city planners saw potential for the river being developed into a major industrial area served by a straightened and deep channel.

From 1910 to 1913, the Duwamish River was dredged and straightened and the once swampy, flat-like landscape of South Park dried up to some degree. Industry boomed on the lower Duwamish waterway. As a result, the lower Duwamish River is one of the most industrialized waterways in Washington State. Chemicals in airport runoff and from World War II bomber construction at Boeing, the heavy metals in ship paint, the arsenic in cement material, the oil in storm water from city streets, and sewage from overflowing city and county sewage pipes contributed to the U.S. Environmental Protection Agency listing the river as a Superfund site on September 13, 2001.

Because South Park residents were, and are, mostly non-English speaking with a lower income, the cleanup of the Duwamish River became an environmental justice issue. South Park community members along with environmental organizations like the Environmental Coalition of South Seattle (ECOSS), the Duwamish River Cleanup Coalition, People for Puget Sound, and the Duwamish tribe are advocating for a cleanup that protects the river and its wildlife and stops recontamination. There are also efforts underway to restore the habitat along the river's edge to make the environment more hospitable for juvenile salmon on their way from spawning grounds to the saltwater of Elliot Bay.

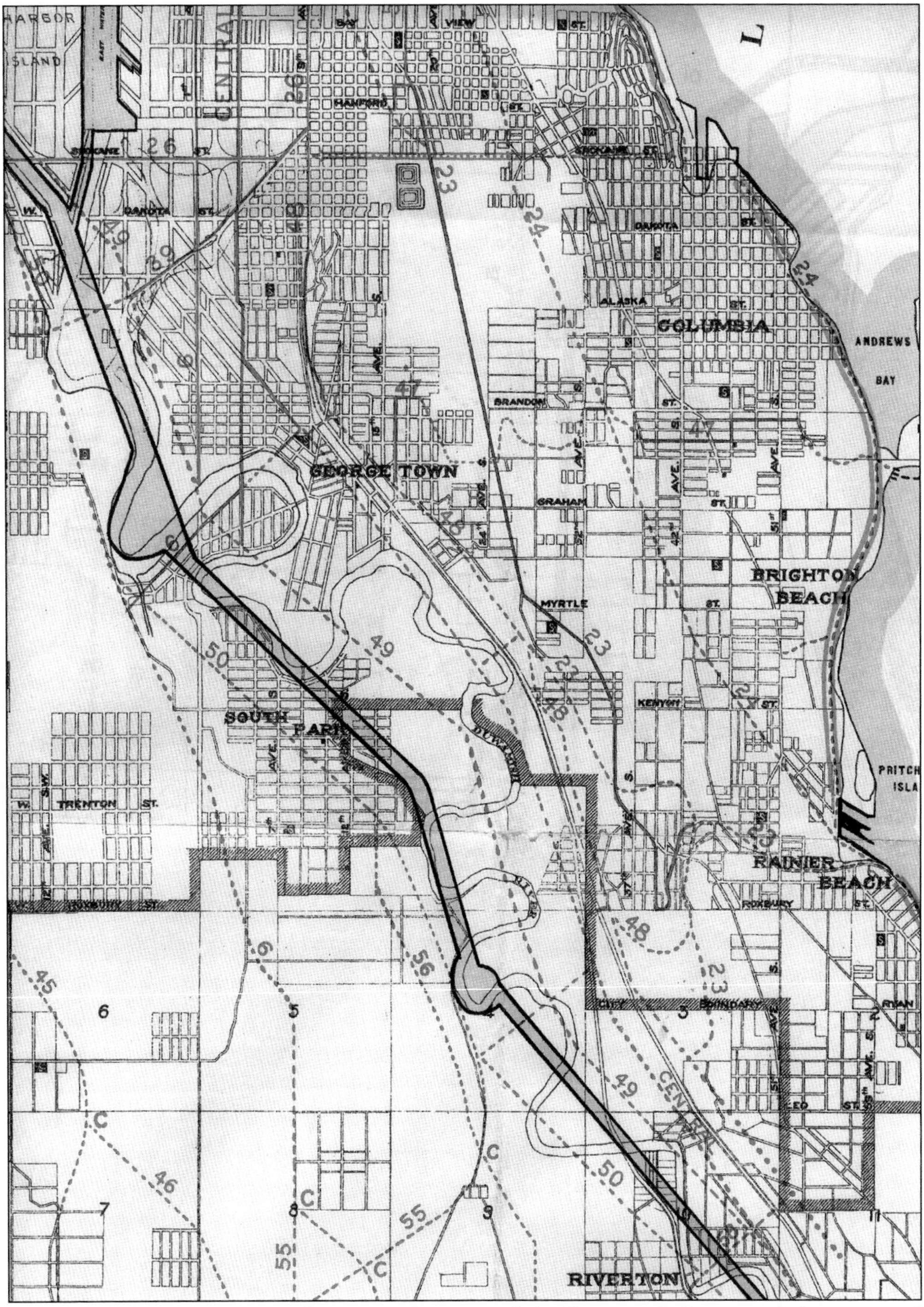

This 1910 map depicts both the original curves of the Duwamish River and the proposed straightening. Since the South Park neighborhood was such a marshy area, the residents supported the river straightening proposed by the City of Seattle. (Courtesy of Richard Strong.)

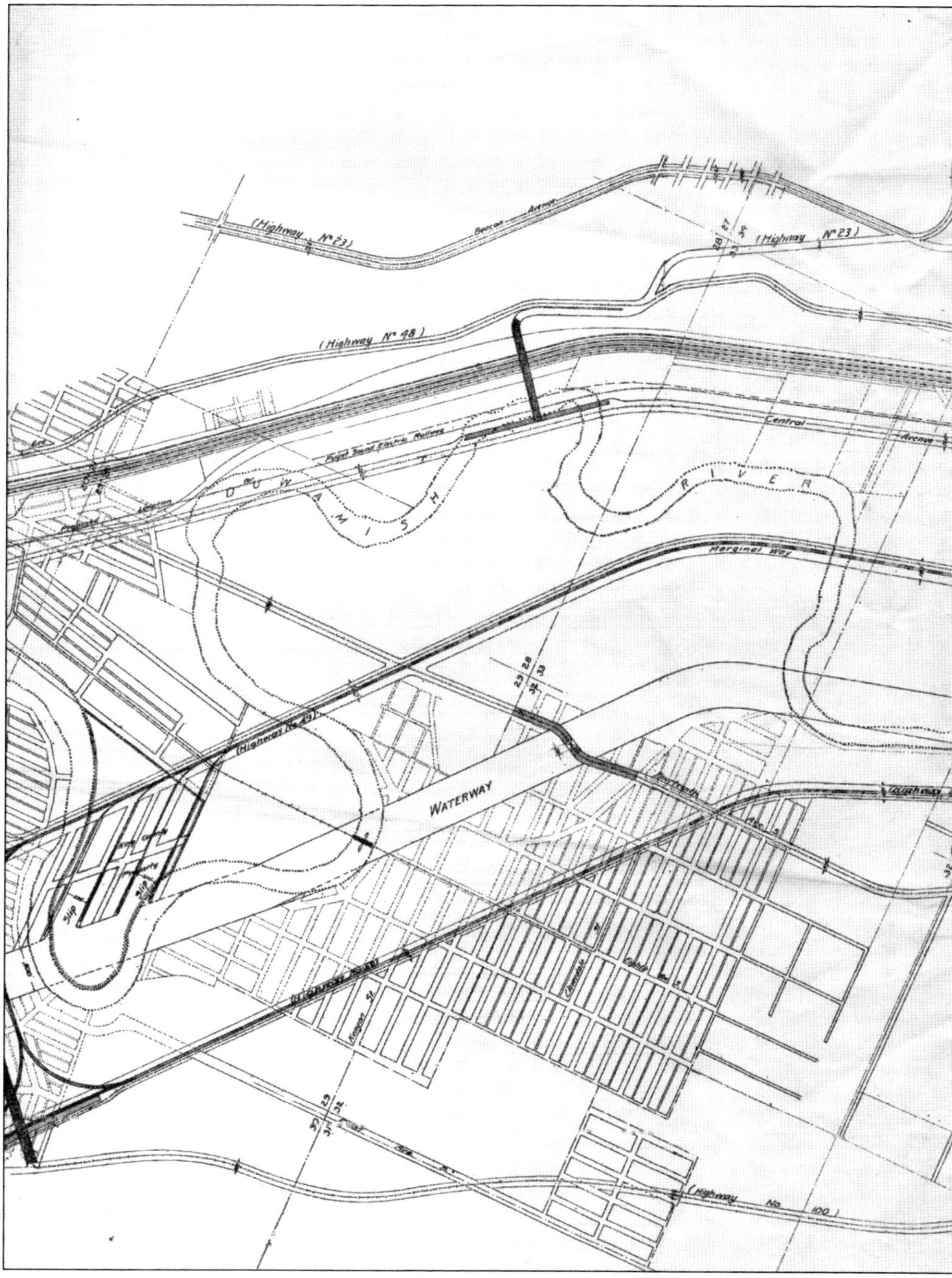

Above are a city planner's 1911 drawings for the proposed straightening of the Duwamish River. The proposal was accepted, and the river straightening was completed by 1913. There were plans to dredge and straighten the Duwamish all the way to Tukwila, a few miles south of South Park. That dredging was not completed, however, as Seattle's other waterways in Elliot Bay, Lake Union, and Ballard provided abundant access for commerce. (Courtesy of Richard Strong.)

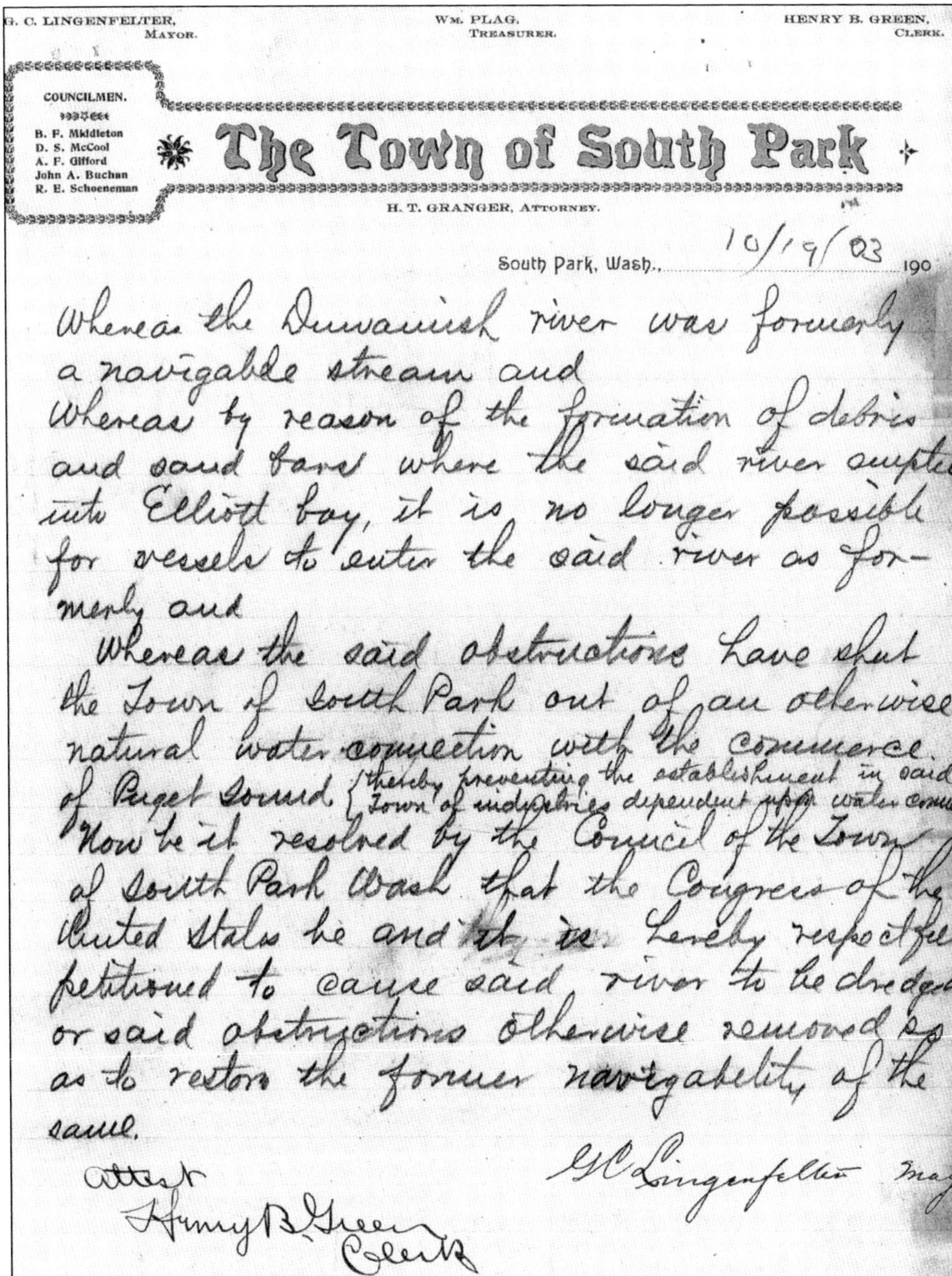

G. C. LINGENFELTER, MAYOR. WM. PLAG, TREASURER. HENRY B. GREEN, CLERK.

COUNCILMEN.
B. F. Middleton
D. S. McCool
A. F. Gifford
John A. Buchan
R. E. Schoeneman

The Town of South Park

H. T. GRANGER, ATTORNEY.

South Park, Wash., 10/19/03 190

Whereas the Duwamish river was formerly a navigable stream and
Whereas by reason of the formation of debris and sand bars where the said river empties into Elliott bay, it is no longer possible for vessels to enter the said river as formerly and
Whereas the said obstructions have shut the Town of South Park out of an otherwise natural water connection with the commerce of Puget Sound {thereby preventing the establishment in said Town of industries dependent upon water connect[ion]
Now be it resolved by the Council of the Town of South Park Wash that the Congress of the United States be and it is hereby respectfully petitioned to cause said river to be dredged or said obstructions otherwise removed so as to restore the former navigability of the same.

Attest
Henry B. Green
Clerk

G C Lingenfelter Mayor

A 1903 letter, written by Mayor G. C. Lingenfelter and clerk Henry B. Green of the Town of South Park, asked the U.S. Congress to dredge the river and make it navigable; apparently debris was regularly blocking passage to Elliot Bay. As homes and businesses were built on the river's edge and as the river swelled and receded, it was not unusual for logs and debris to collect in the river. South Park residents recognized early on that the river's navigability was tied to their need for commerce and flood control. (Courtesy of the City of Seattle Municipal Archives.)

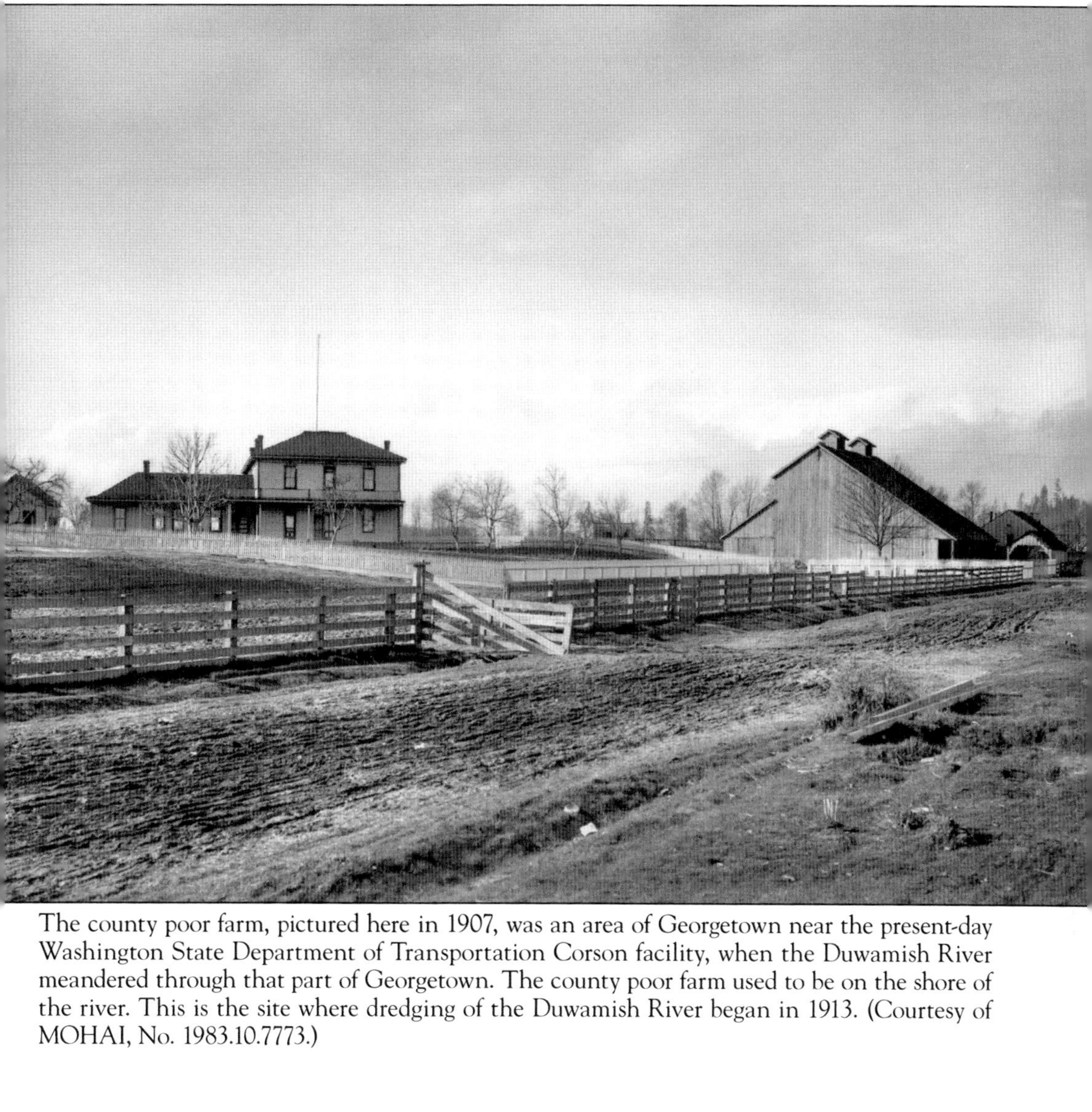

The county poor farm, pictured here in 1907, was an area of Georgetown near the present-day Washington State Department of Transportation Corson facility, when the Duwamish River meandered through that part of Georgetown. The county poor farm used to be on the shore of the river. This is the site where dredging of the Duwamish River began in 1913. (Courtesy of MOHAI, No. 1983.10.7773.)

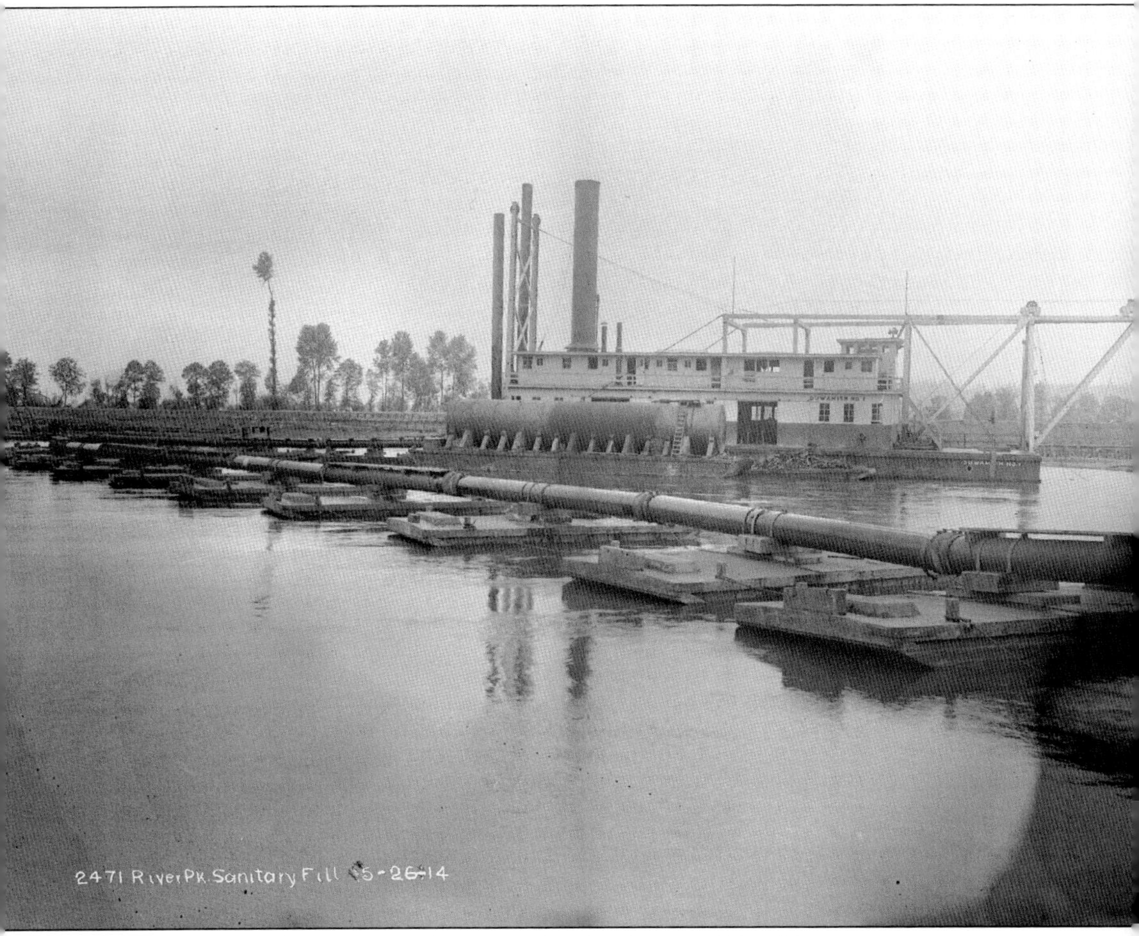

The dredging of the Duwamish began on October 14, 1913. The Waterway Commission's intent was to sell excavated dirt as fill to other parts of the city. Approximately one-third of the cost to dredge the river was covered by the sale of this fill. The *Duwamish I*, seen here in 1914, was a dredging device used to create deep channels to accommodate large vessels. (Courtesy of the City of Seattle Municipal Archives.)

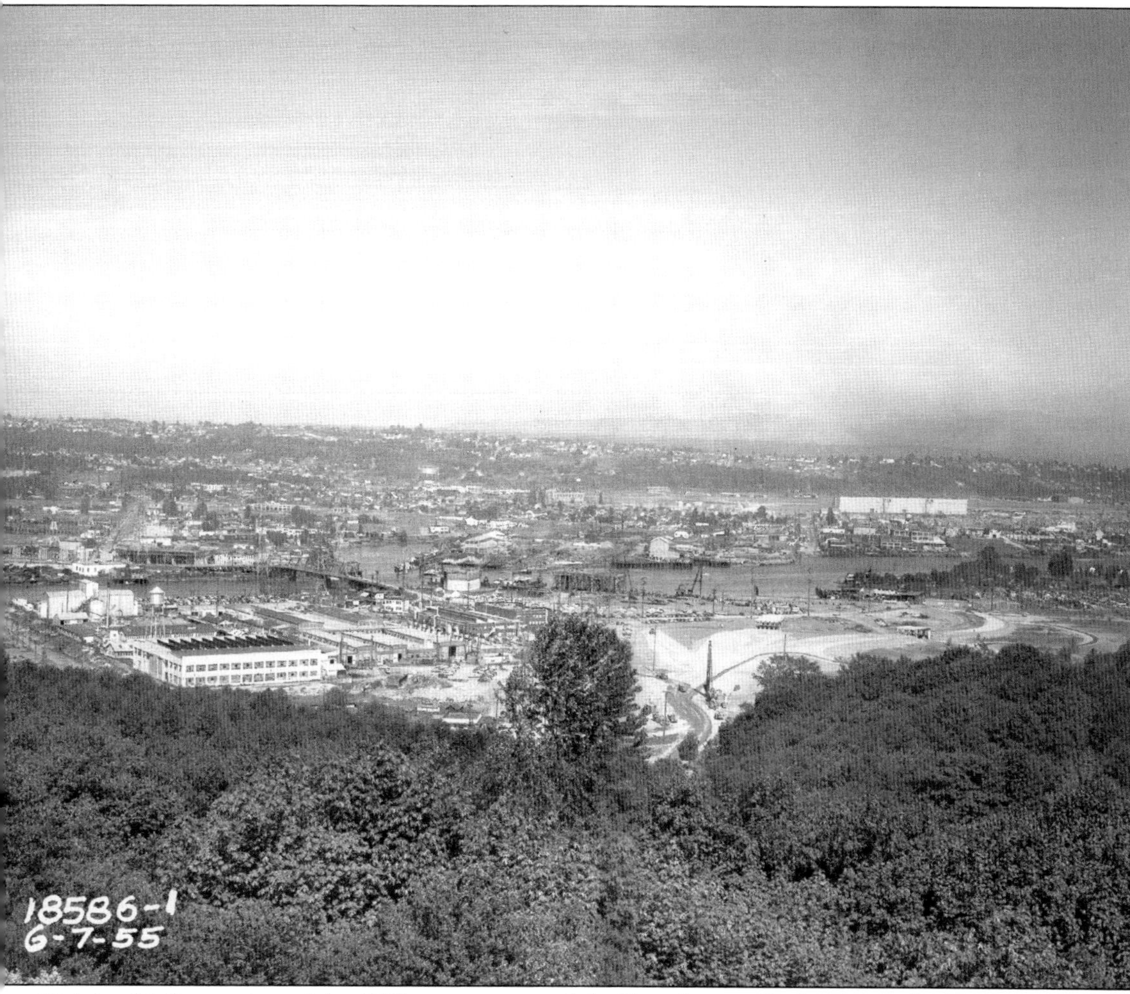

This is a bird's-eye view of the 1955 construction of the First Avenue Bridge. In the background are Beacon Hill, Georgetown, and South Park. The First Avenue Bridge, completed in 1956, was the second bridge built across the Duwamish at that site. (Courtesy of the City of Seattle Municipal Archives.)

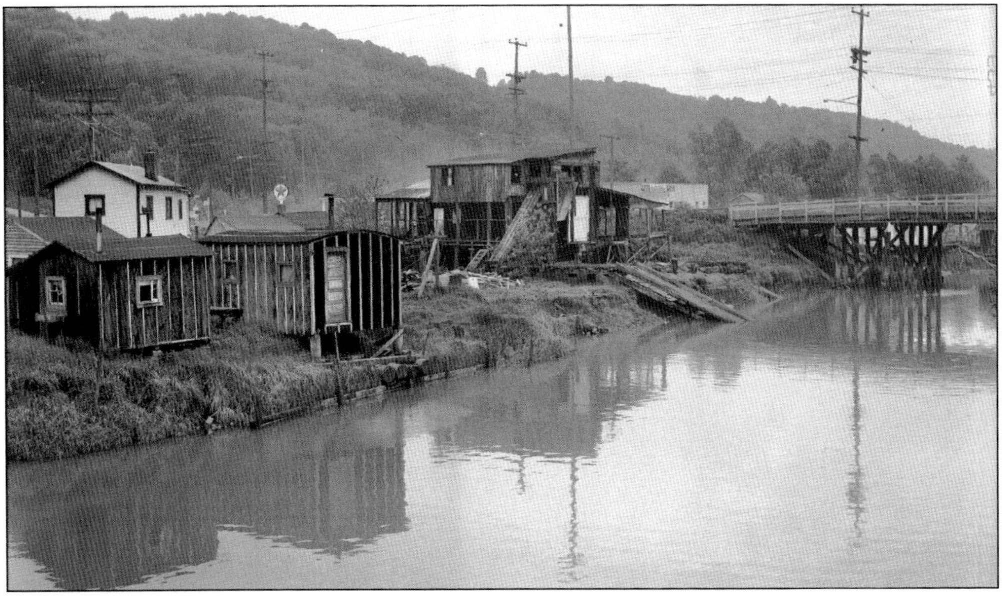

In 1953, McAllister Slough—named after one of the early owners, John McAllister, who also owned a large brickyard in South Park in the late 1800s—was the area just south of the current First Avenue Bridge. The McAllister clan had many acres along old First Avenue South from Kenyon Street north to the current site of the First Avenue Bridge. These shanties were removed for the First Avenue South Bridge construction in 1955. (Courtesy of the City of Seattle Municipal Archives.)

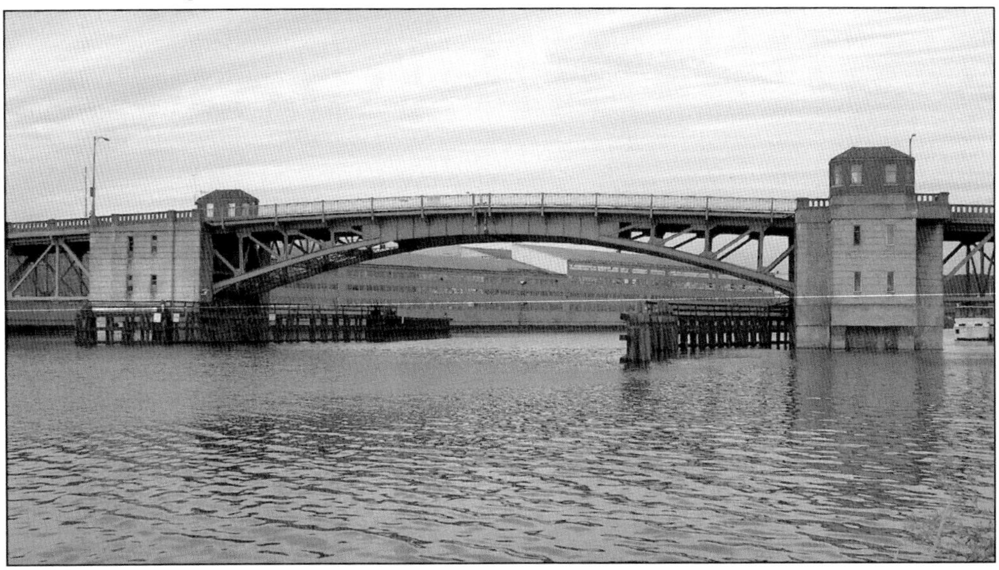

The South Park Bridge was built between 1929 and 1931. Because it is the only operational example of a Scherzer rolling lift bascule bridge in Washington, the bridge is listed on the National Register of Historic Places. The 1894–1895 Tower Bridge in London and the Scherzer rolling lift Van Buren Street Bridge in Chicago are considered prototypes of modern bascule bridges. The bascule bridge, with its advantages of a wide center channel free of piers and fast-operating speed, is well suited for South Park's heavy bridge traffic, which is frequently interrupted by marine traffic. (Courtesy of the South Park Neighborhood Association.)

Eight

Business, Bridges, and Transportation

The center of South Park's retail core has shifted over the years as the locations of the bridges across the river shifted from Eighth Avenue South to Fourteenth Avenue South. In South Park's formative years, Eighth Avenue South and Dallas Avenue contained the hub of services frequented by residents. The trolley took passengers south on Eighth Avenue and headed east on Cloverdale Street, where the tracks ended at the intersection of Fourteenth and Cloverdale Street. Genovese Cash and Grocery on Eighth Avenue South, Barnes Grocery on Eighth and Thistle, Yocum's Mercantile at Eighth and Cloverdale Street, and B. F. Middleton's Grocery store on Dallas Avenue were examples of successful businesses dependent upon transportation arterials from the Eighth Avenue Bridge. Valley Road (which intersected with South Eighth, Washington Boulevard, South Tenth, South Eleventh, Lookout Street, and McNatt Street) housed the bulk of the saloons (according to administrative records from town of South Park).

With the demise of the Eighth Avenue Bridge and the construction of the new South Park Bridge at Fourteenth Avenue South in 1931, the business district of Fourteenth Avenue was born. The Fourteenth Avenue retail core had something for everyone, including a Safeway grocery store, a bakery, a clothing store, eight taverns, and even a dance and pool hall on the second floor of South Park Hall.

The 256-unit housing project, South Park Courts, strongly supported this new, thriving business district. Unfortunately the housing created for war workers in 1945 was torn down in 1978 to make way for industry. The demolition of the vibrant housing project, coupled with the decline of Boeing, was disastrous for Fourteenth Avenue South, which seems deserted compared to days of old.

In 1974, reporter Michael Sweeney accurately details the then booming retail core on Fourteenth Avenue South:

> There, as if stamped out of some hundred-year-old mold are the café, the second-hand shop, realty agency, gas station, drug store, furniture store, dime store, cleaners, grocery store—all silently facing one another across a string straight stretch of street and sidewalk. At the Cheerie Daze Café, a fixture on Main Street since World War II, head waitress Fumi Sakuma scurries from the lunch counter in front to the bar in back through the dining room and kitchen between. The lunch crowd, she reports, as the jukebox clicks in a fresh country sadness, is mostly Boeing workers and local merchants.

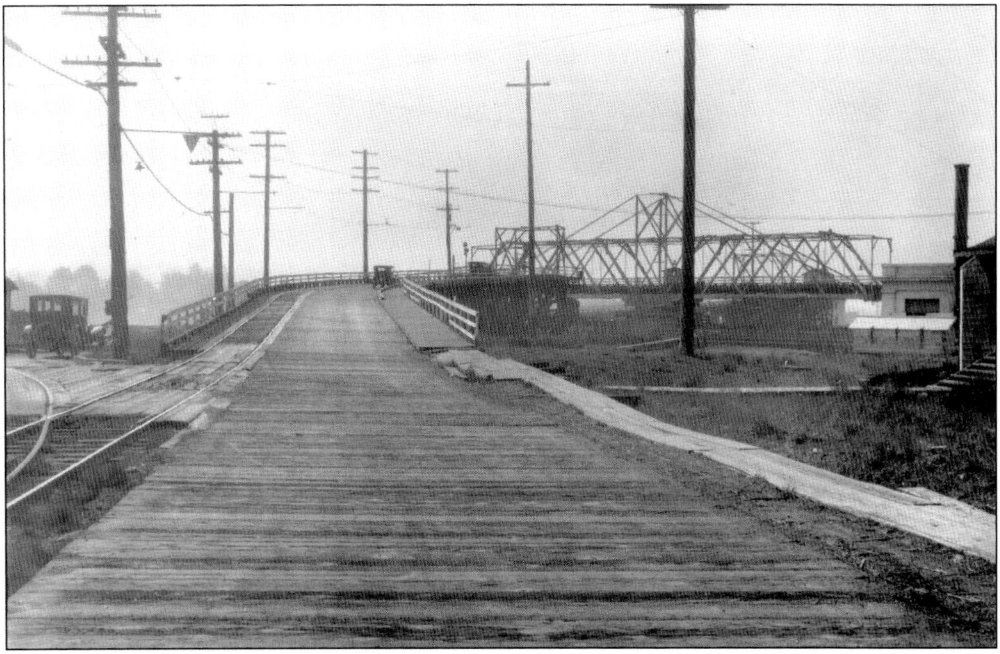

The Eighth Avenue drawbridge is pictured here looking east in 1920. In later years, passengers were let off to walk across the bridge rather than risk a collapse from the full weight of the trolley car. Currently, this street end is the Eighth Avenue South Park. (Courtesy of the University of Washington Libraries, Special Collections, SMR 202.)

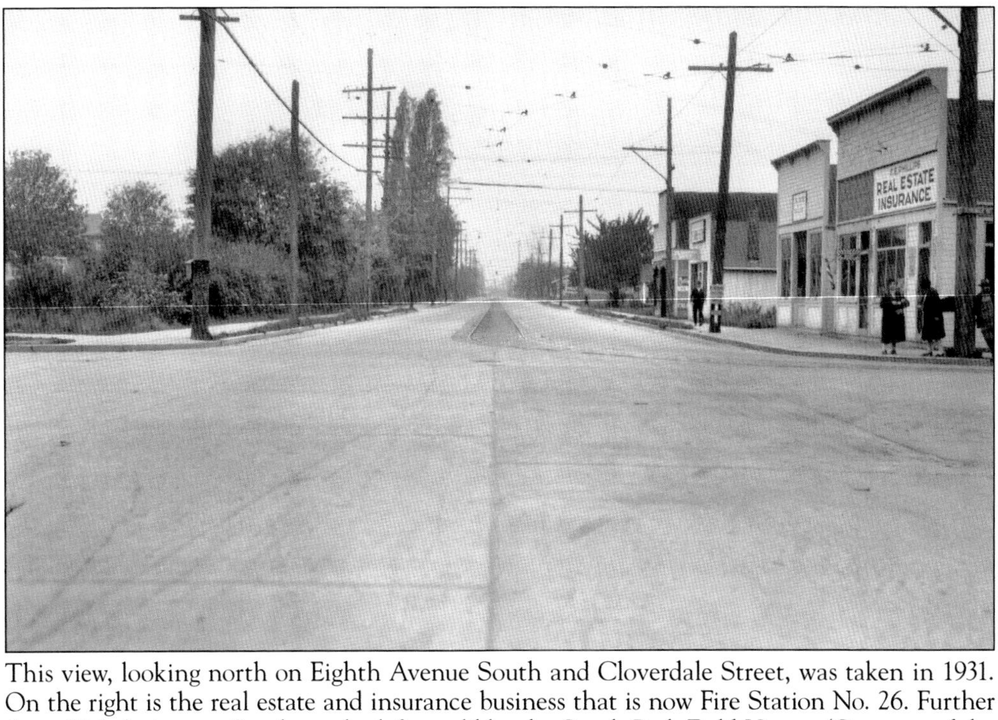

This view, looking north on Eighth Avenue South and Cloverdale Street, was taken in 1931. On the right is the real estate and insurance business that is now Fire Station No. 26. Further down Eighth Avenue South on the left would be the South Park Field House. (Courtesy of the University of Washington Libraries, Special Collections, SMR 273.)

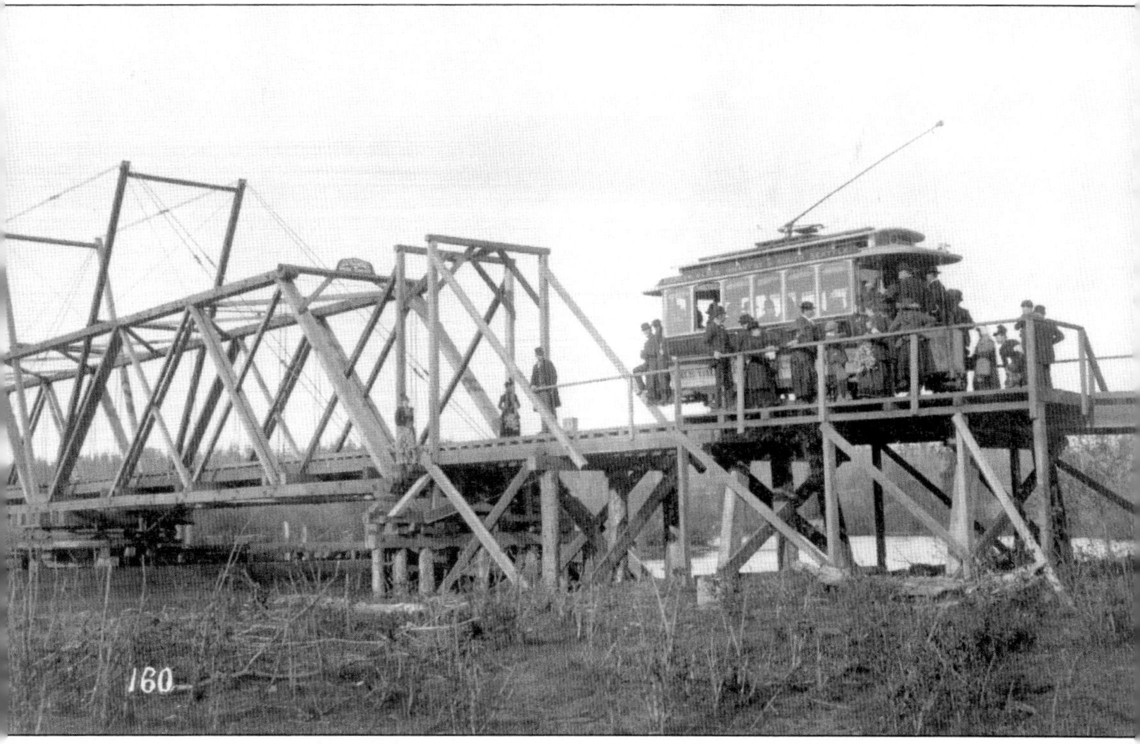

With an excursion party onboard, this Grant Street Electric Railway streetcar crosses the Duwamish River at Eighth Avenue South in 1891, before the Duwamish River was straightened. The streetcar rail line determined early development in South Park along Eighth Avenue, connected South Park to Georgetown, then resumed its route on the other side of the river down Carleton Avenue, the main transportation arterial through Georgetown, unlike Corson and Ellis Avenues, which serve as today's arterials. Today Fourteenth Avenue South is the main arterial connecting South Park and Georgetown. (Courtesy of Frank La Roche, University of Washington Libraries, Special Collections, La Roche 160.)

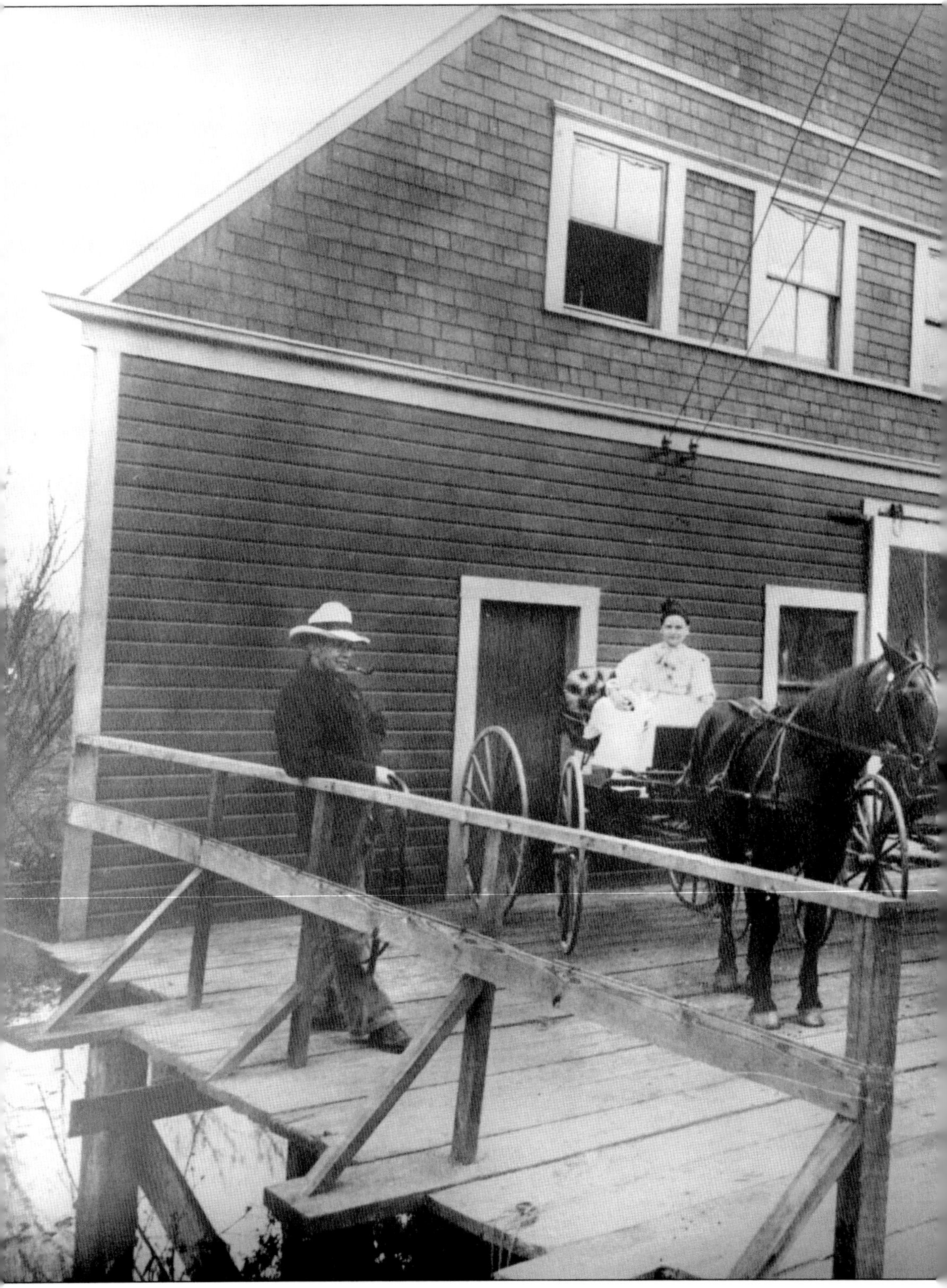

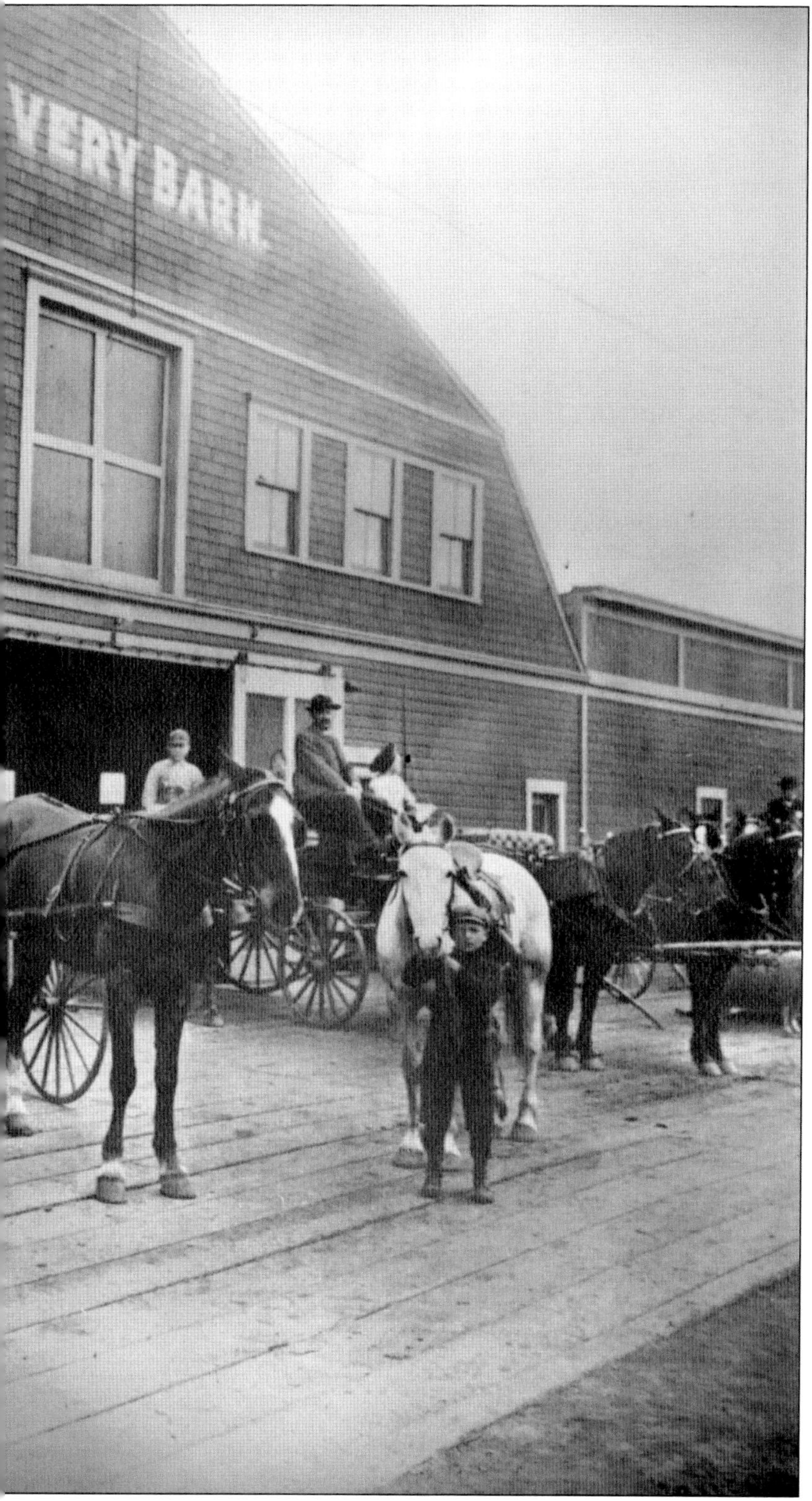

The South Park Livery Stables were located where Twelfth Avenue South and Dallas Avenue meet. This photograph was taken around 1900. Horses and wagons continued to be the common method of transportation (in addition to the trolley car) in Seattle from 1850 until 1920 when the automobile was introduced. Resident Theresa Lytle recalls playing with her brother under the remains of the pier-like foundation. Currently, part of this triangle lot is undeveloped. The other part of the lot is covered with housing built in the 1940s during the war-housing boom in South Park. (Courtesy of Theresa Lytle.)

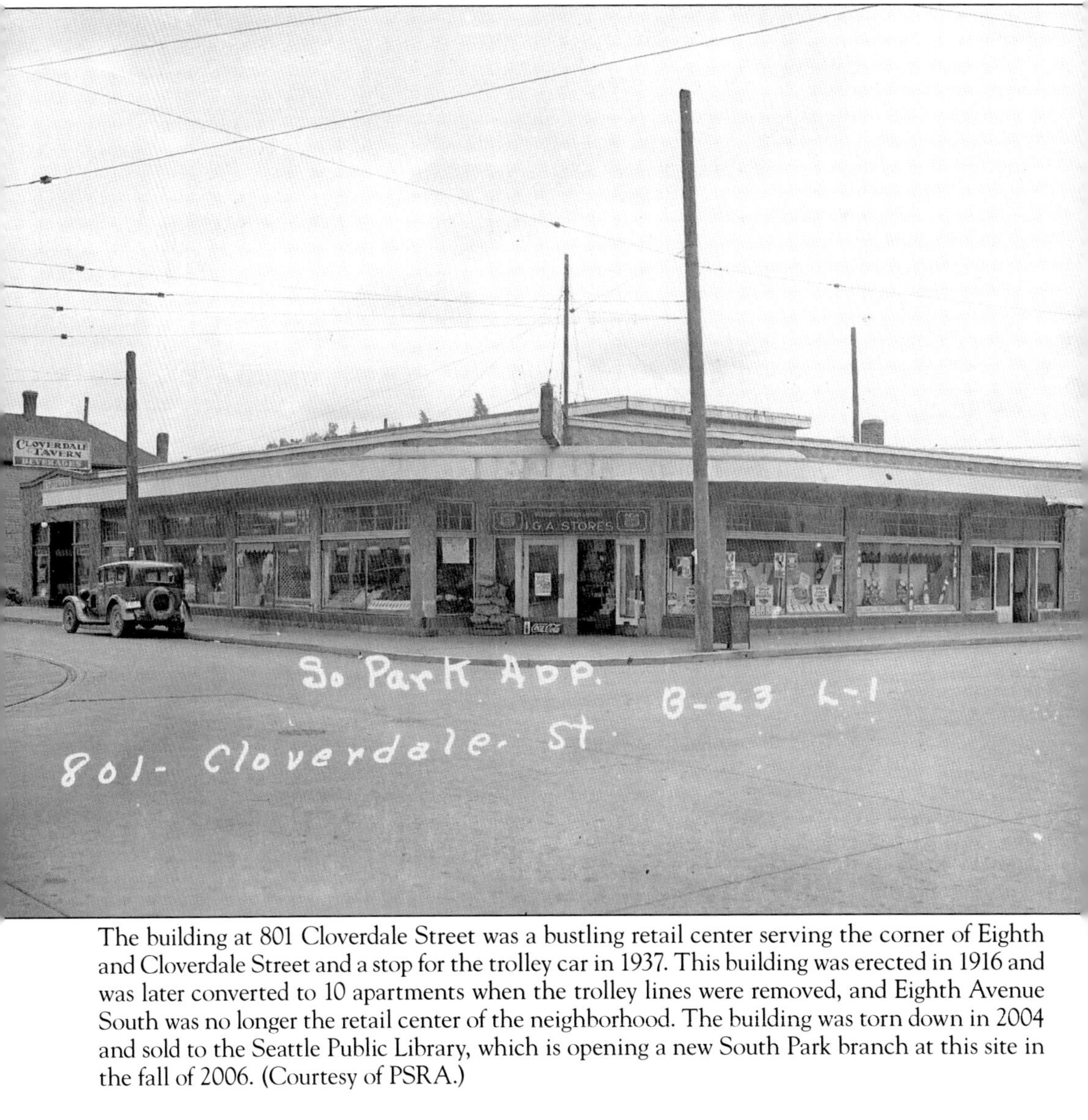

The building at 801 Cloverdale Street was a bustling retail center serving the corner of Eighth and Cloverdale Street and a stop for the trolley car in 1937. This building was erected in 1916 and was later converted to 10 apartments when the trolley lines were removed, and Eighth Avenue South was no longer the retail center of the neighborhood. The building was torn down in 2004 and sold to the Seattle Public Library, which is opening a new South Park branch at this site in the fall of 2006. (Courtesy of PSRA.)

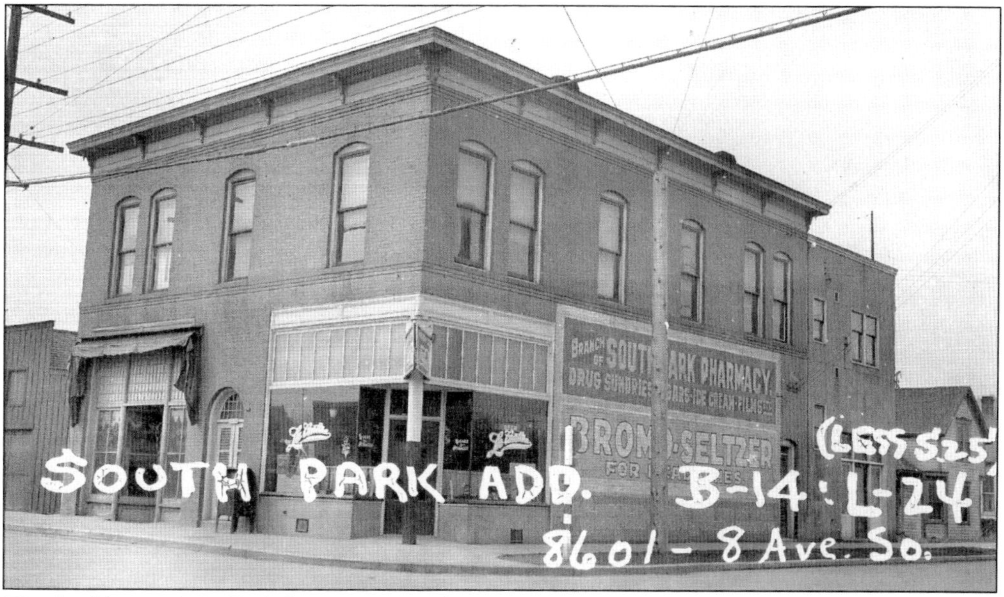

This building at 8601 Eighth Avenue South, pictured here in 1937, is also known as La Cantina, which was the name of the bar that operated on the first floor before it was closed in the mid-1990s. In 1907, William Woolsey applied for a liquor license for the Cloverdale Bar, which preceded La Cantina. Historically, this building was always used as a neighborhood commercial building because it was located on the trolley line. (Courtesy of PSRA.)

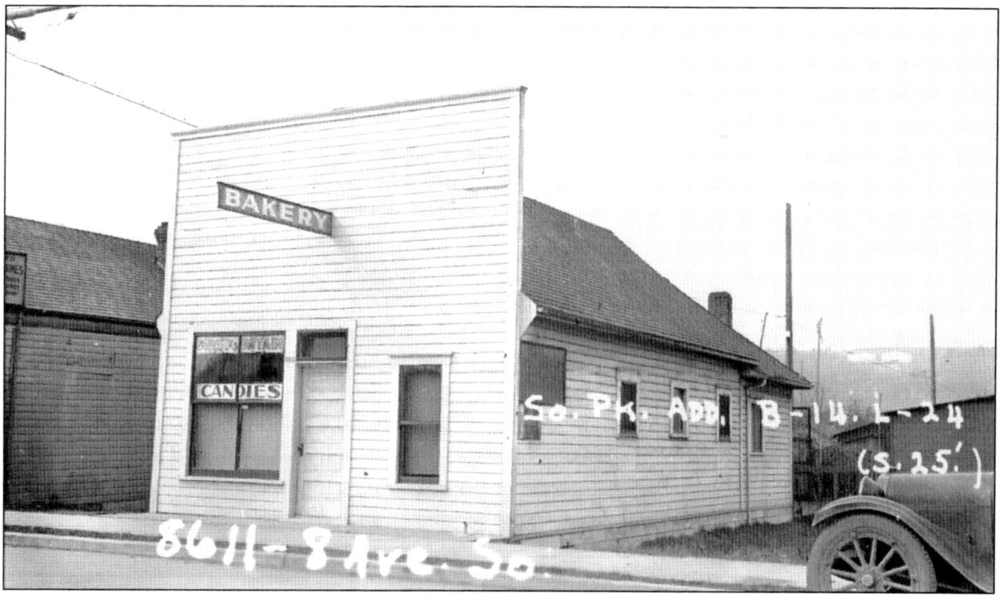

This bakery, located at 8611 Eighth Avenue South, was owned by Charles O. Boggs. The building is pictured here in 1937 before it was remodeled into a residential dwelling. The original structure was built in 1908, when Eighth Avenue South was the major transportation arterial in South Park. Today Eighth Avenue South dead ends a short distance from this building, where Highway 99 dissects the neighborhood. (Courtesy of PSRA.)

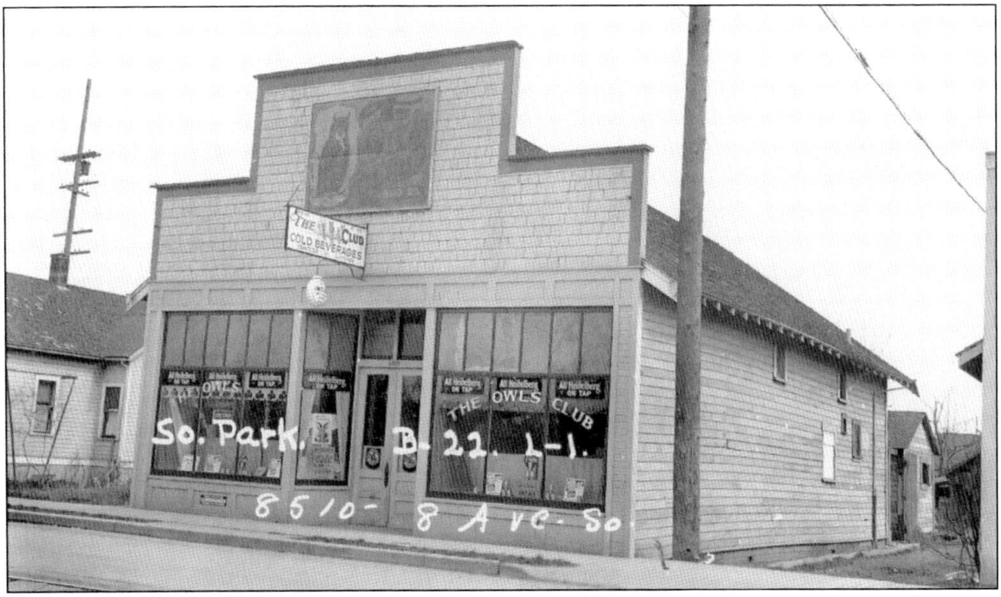

This building at 8510 Eighth Avenue South, pictured here in 1937 as neighborhood tavern The Owl's Club, was constructed around 1910 and owned by Albert Tillotson in 1939. In 1943, Lord Our Righteous Church purchased the property and remodeled it into a church. Today this church is called the South Park Baptist Missionary Church. (Courtesy of PSRA.)

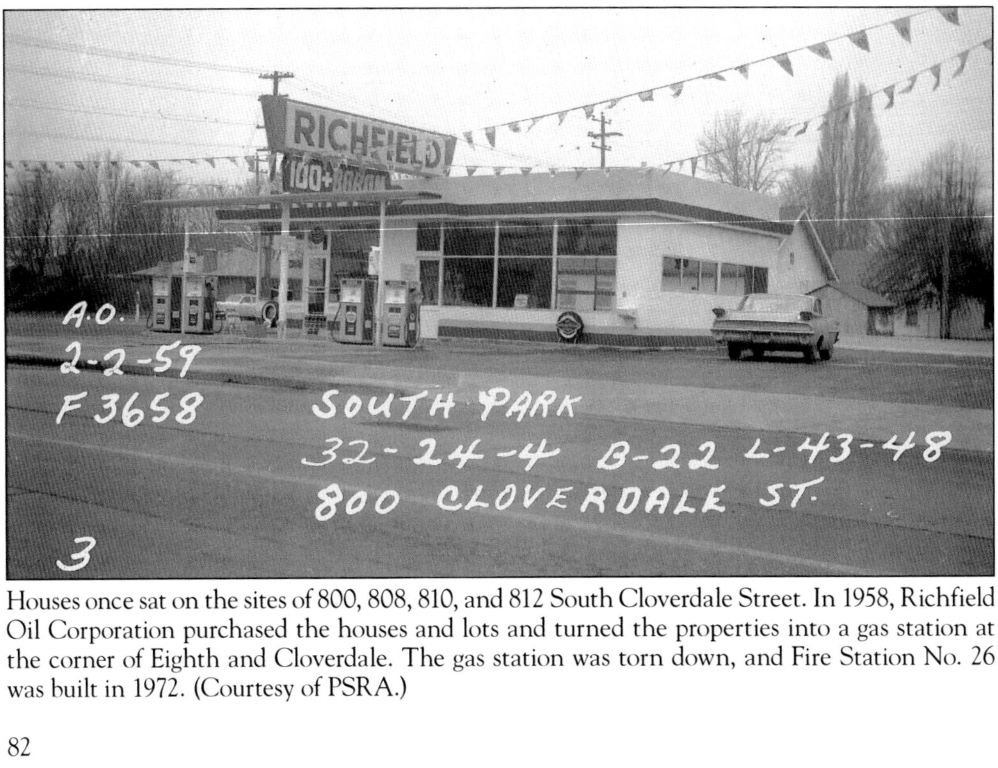

Houses once sat on the sites of 800, 808, 810, and 812 South Cloverdale Street. In 1958, Richfield Oil Corporation purchased the houses and lots and turned the properties into a gas station at the corner of Eighth and Cloverdale. The gas station was torn down, and Fire Station No. 26 was built in 1972. (Courtesy of PSRA.)

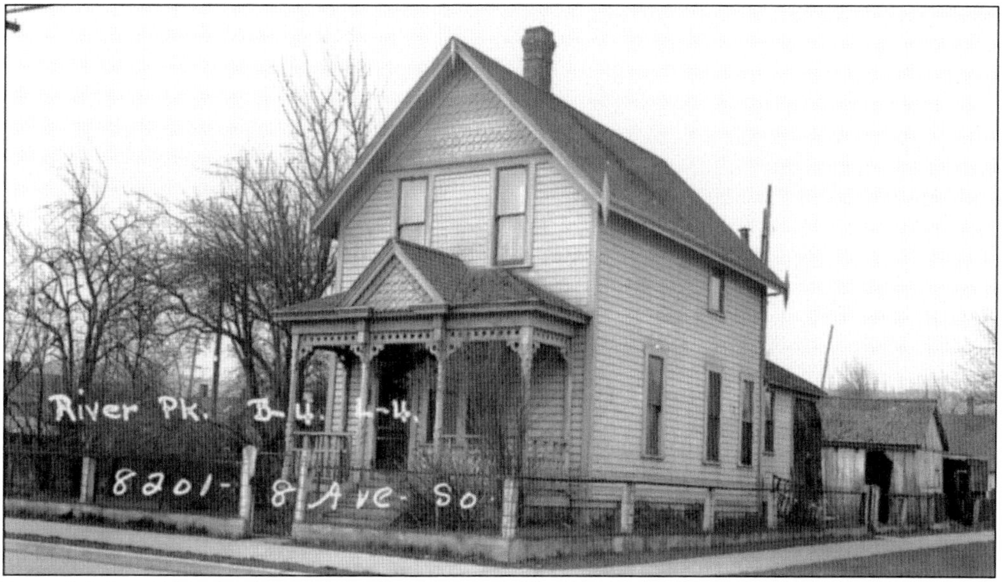

Remodeled in 1920, this is 8201 Eighth Avenue South in 1937. The home was built in 1892. A 1937 assessor noted it was "on the car and bus line," because the electric trolley car ran down Eighth Avenue South. It no longer retains the ornate details on the porch. (Courtesy of PSRA.)

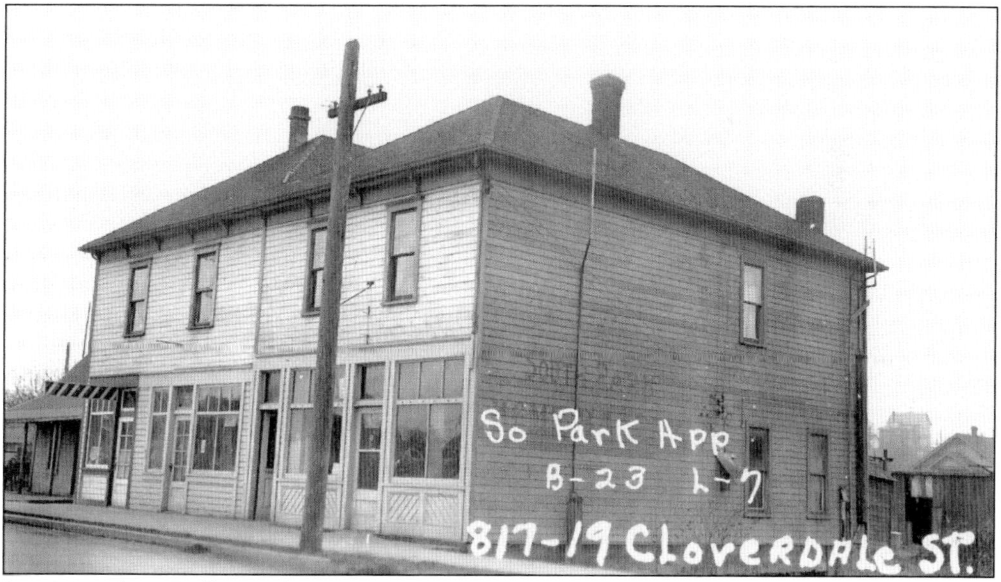

In 1918, when Dallas and Rosie Hanes owned the building at 817–819 South Cloverdale Street, it was both stores and apartments. Originally constructed in 1900, it housed soldiers and provided meals during World War II. In 1957, the ground floor was remodeled from stores and storefronts to apartments. It continues to be a nine-unit apartment building. (Courtesy of PSRA.)

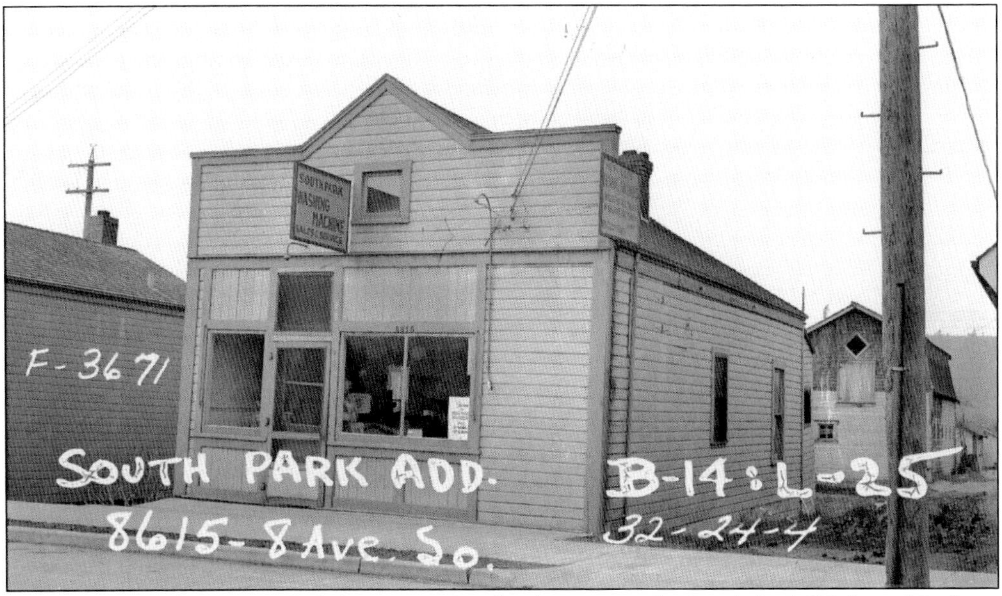

This 1937 view shows 8615 Eighth Avenue South when it was the South Park Washing Machine Sales and Service. This building is still standing and is part of the South Park Tongan Assembly of God buildings. (Courtesy of PSRA.)

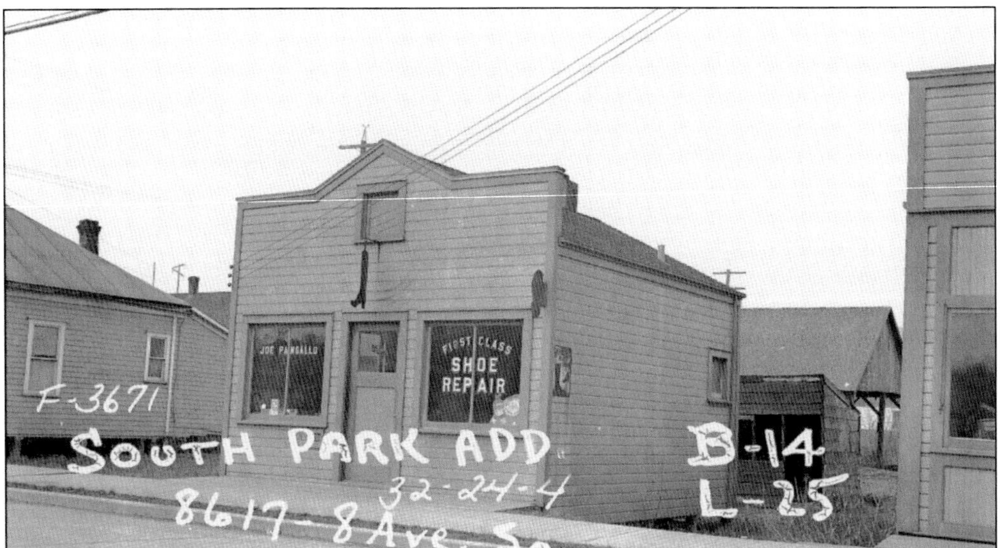

Once a shoe repair store, the building at 8617 Eighth Avenue South is still standing and still looks like an old storefront. This lot is zoned commercial but is used for the South Park Tongan Assembly of God. (Courtesy of PSRA.)

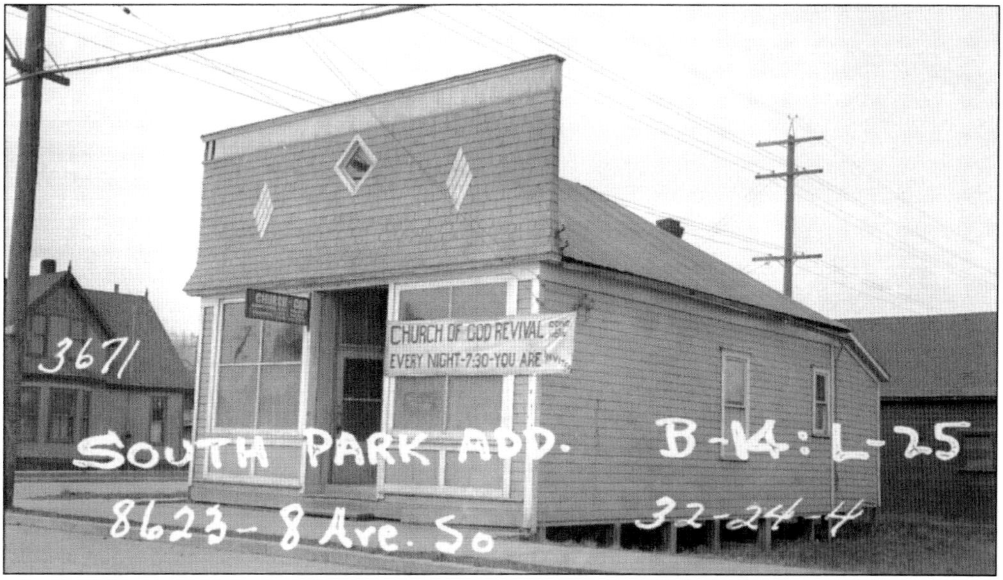

This building housed the Church of God located at 8623 Eighth Avenue South. This structure remains unaltered and is the main building used for hosting religious services at the South Park Tongan Assembly of God. It is zoned commercial, which is perhaps a remnant zoning assignment when Eighth Avenue South was the major retail core of South Park. (Courtesy of PSRA.)

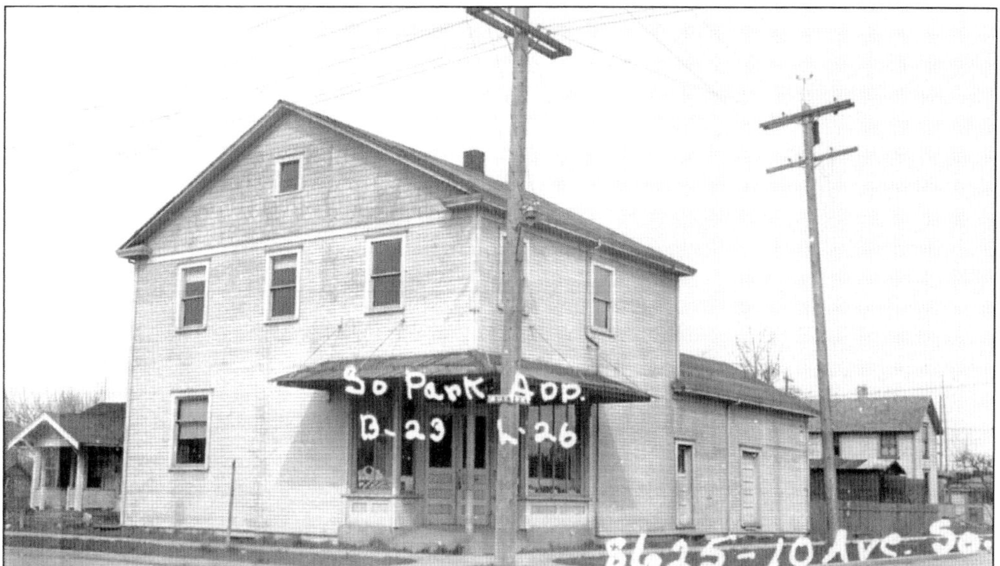

Pictured here in 1937 is 8625 Tenth Avenue South; an apartment building originally constructed in 1918 as a store. It is now a triplex surrounded by single-family housing. As the commercial areas of South Park changed with the relocation of transportation arterials, many of the commercially zoned properties were turned into multifamily housing despite the single-family zoning for that particular block. (Courtesy of PSRA.)

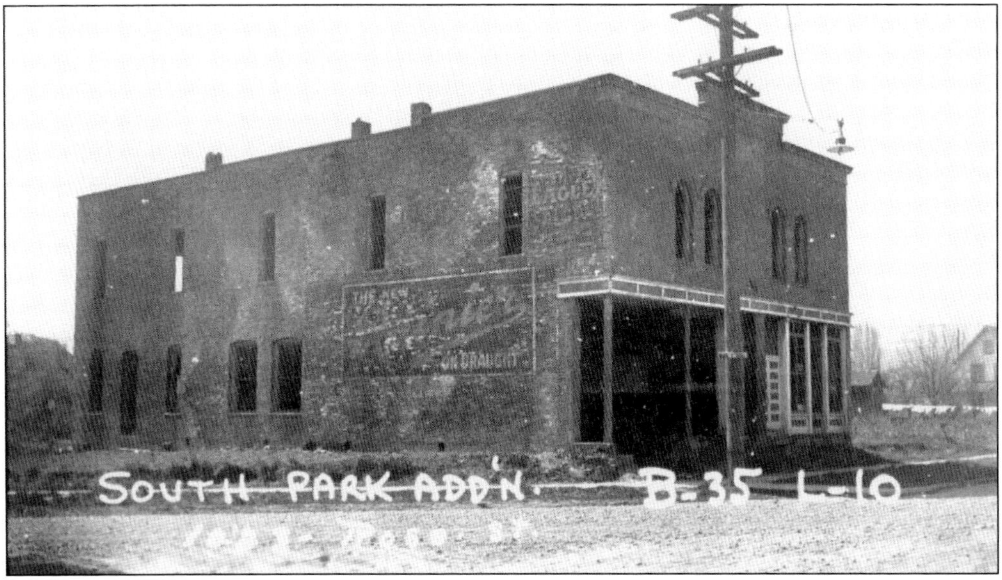

Prior to being Glacier Frozen Food Locker storage, 1023 Rose Street's original structure was built in 1906 and owned by Glacier Cold Storage. There used to be a bar in part of this building that served pitchers of beer out the back door to neighborhood kids, who had strict instructions "not to spill." All but part of one wall was torn down around 1944 and replaced with the building that is now known as 8305 Dallas Avenue South and houses a candle factory. (Courtesy of PSRA.)

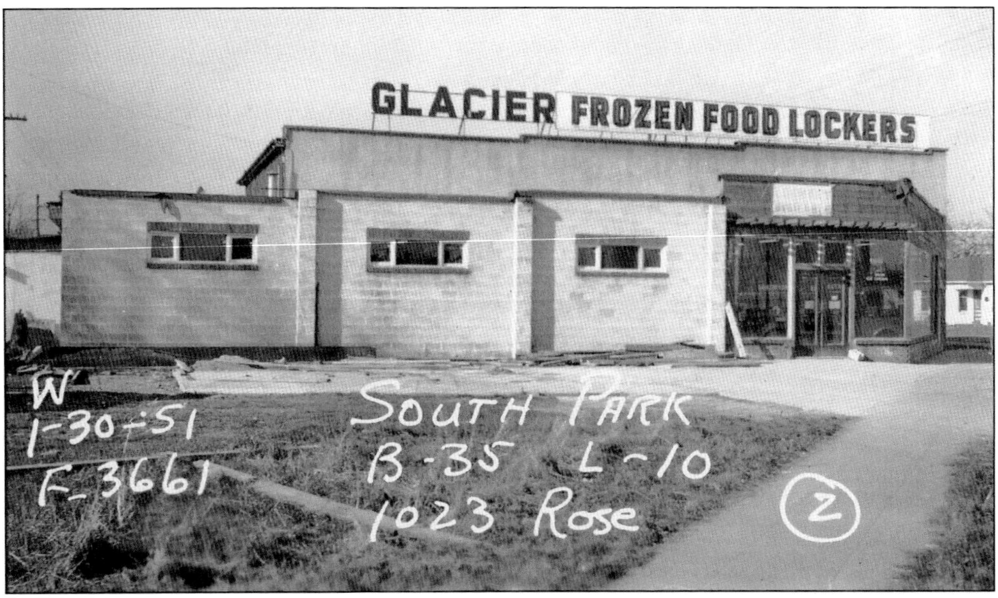

Glacier Frozen Food Lockers at 1023 Rose Street is pictured here in 1951. The address of this same building changed from 1023 Rose to 8305 Dallas Avenue when the owners moved which street the front entrance faced. It is currently being used as a candle factory and is surrounded by single- and multifamily housing.

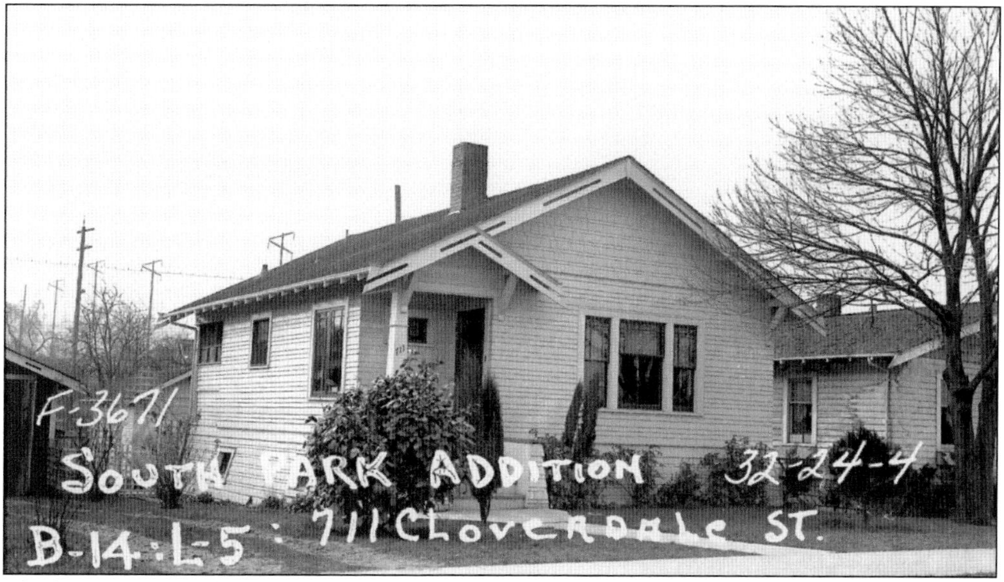

The house at 711 Cloverdale Street was owned by Fred Yocum, who purchased the property in 1925 and built this house in 1928. He rented the house for $22.50 per month in 1937. Fred Yocum, an enterprising South Park resident, owned a few homes and commercial businesses from 1920 to 1960. Although the house was torn down to make way for Highway 99, a new Habitat for Humanity house was built at the address. (Courtesy of PSRA.)

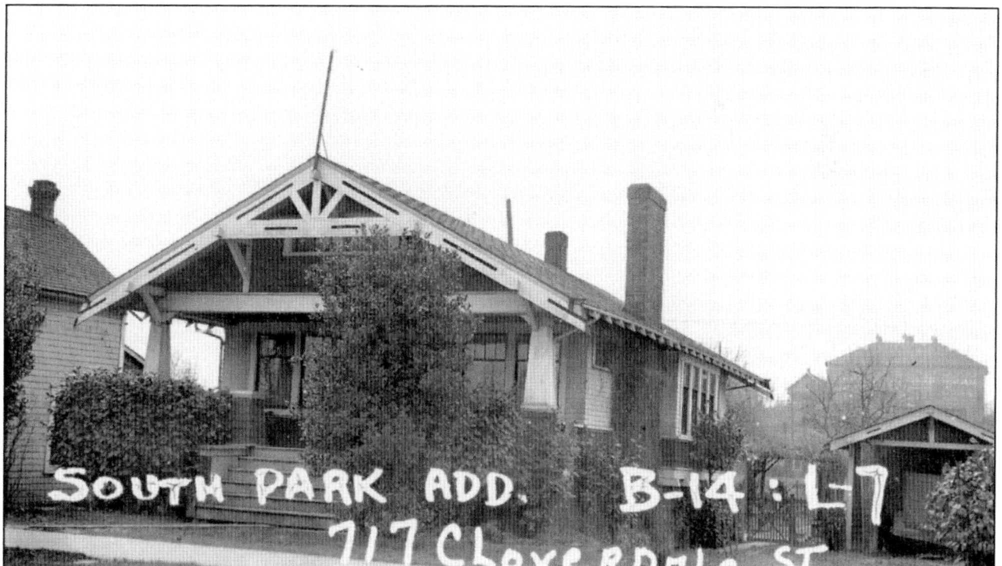

The house at 717 Cloverdale Street was another home owned by Fred Yocum. It was moved to 838 Director Street in the 1950s. There were many houses near this address that were either torn down or moved to Director and Trenton Streets to make way for Highway 99. Concord Elementary can be seen in the background. (Courtesy of PSRA.)

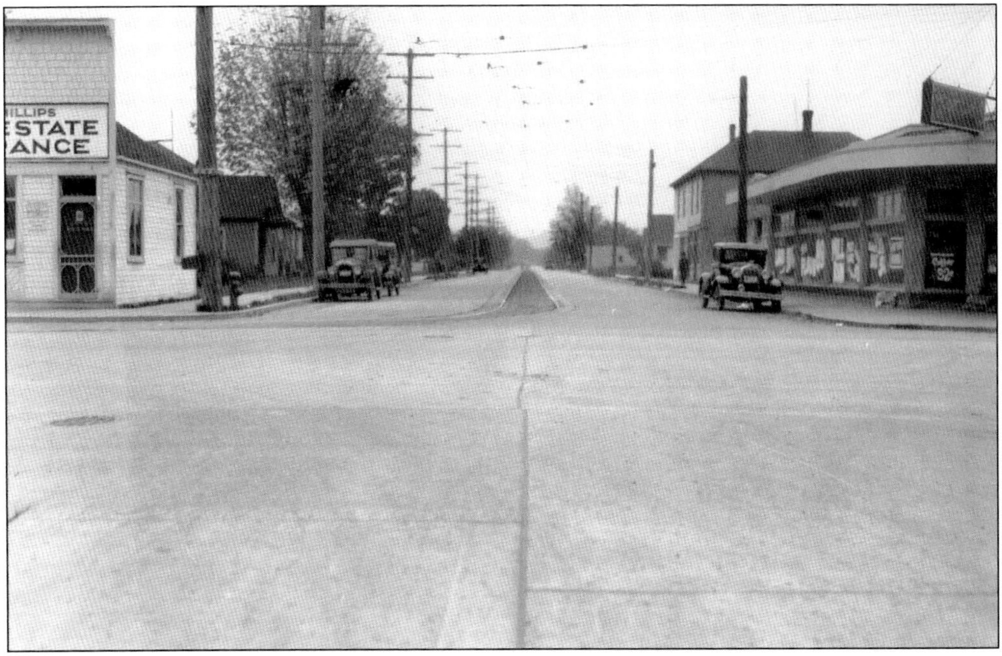

Looking east on Cloverdale Street in 1931, Yocum's Mercantile is on the right and further down (also on the right) is an apartment building that remains in 2006. Today Fire Station No. 26 is on the left, and the new South Park library is on the right. (Courtesy of University of Washington Libraries, Special Collections, SMR 274.)

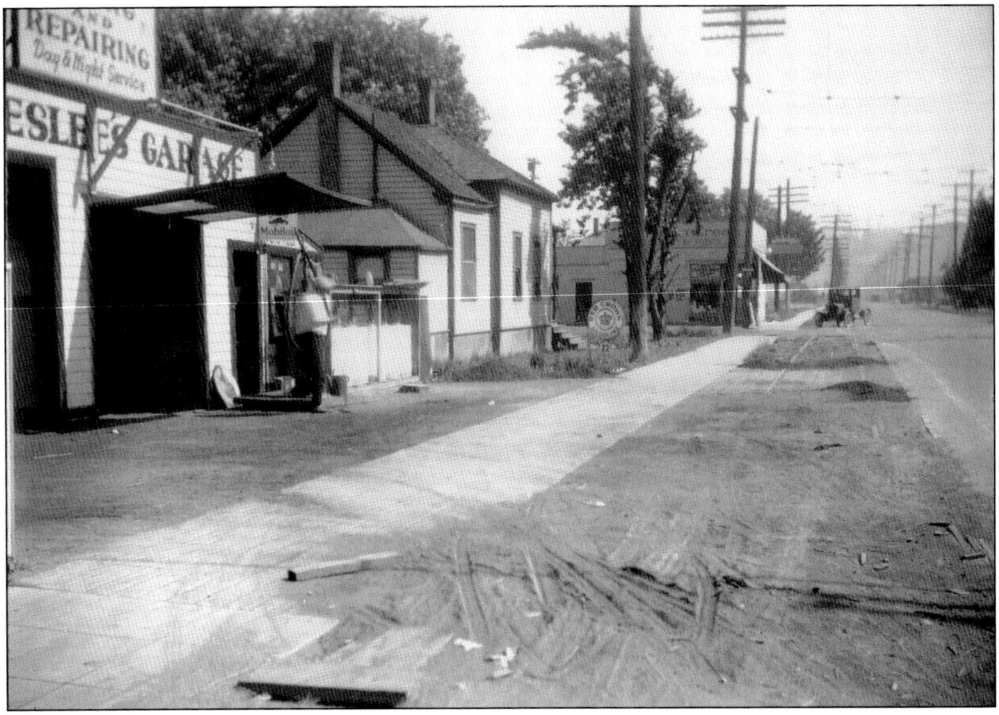

This view of Fourteenth Avenue South in 1925 looks south down Fourteenth Avenue and Cloverdale Street. (Courtesy of University of Washington Libraries, Special Collections, SMR 230.)

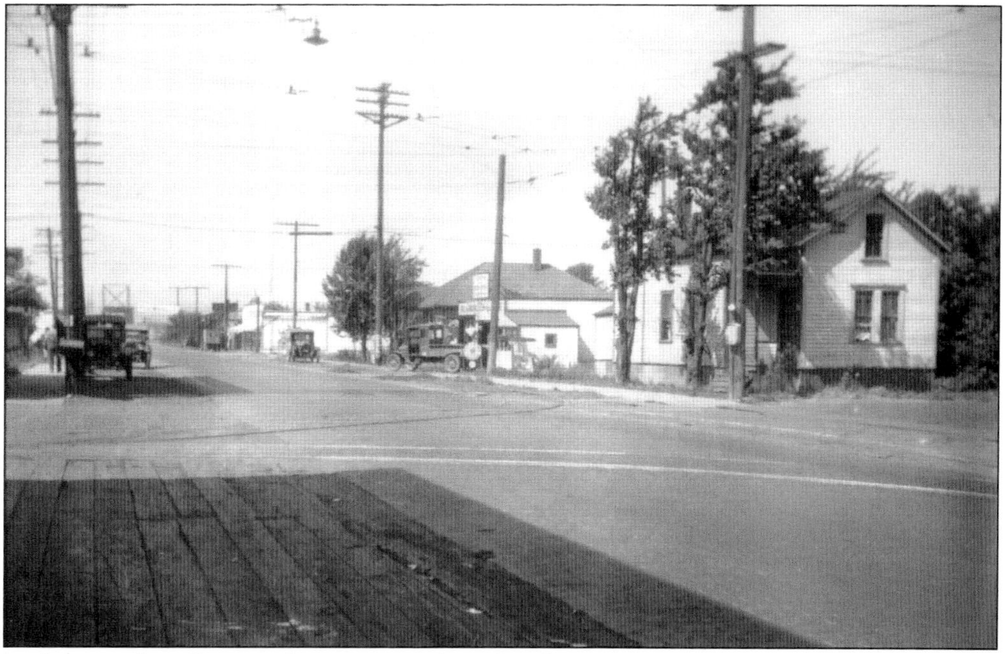

Looking north on Fourteenth Avenue South on October 9, 1925, note the brick road, and in the far distance, a glimpse of the first wooden Fourteenth Avenue Bridge, which was constantly plugged with debris that kept it from opening for marine traffic. (Courtesy of University of Washington Libraries, Special Collections, SMR 229.)

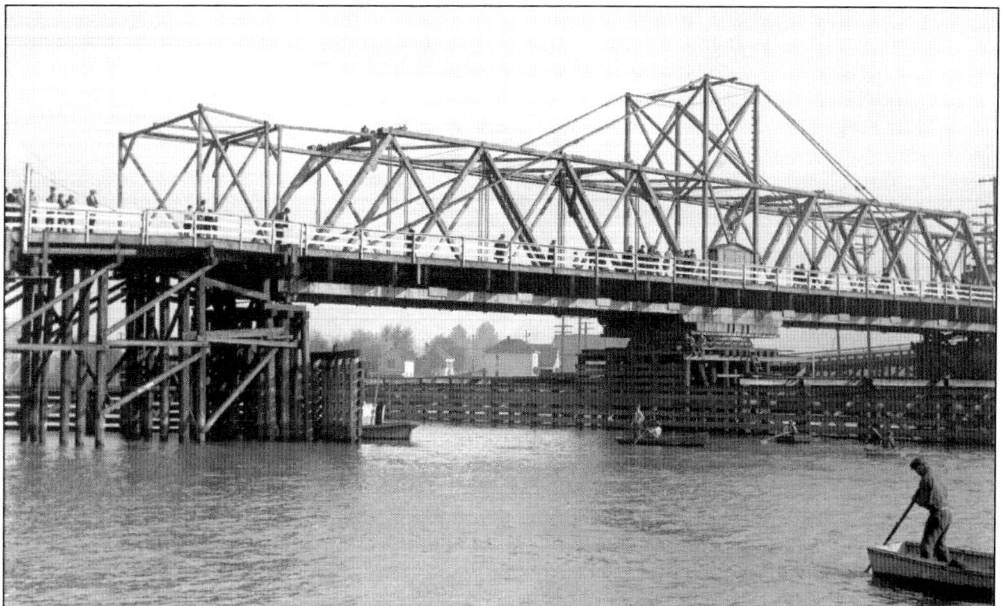

The Eighth Avenue South Bridge is visible here as it looked in 1925. This bridge, although in the same location, was different from the original Eighth Avenue streetcar bridge erected in 1891. The Eighth Avenue South Bridge was built in 1914–1915 to accommodate both trolley cars and automobiles. This bridge closed in July 1937, a result of age and the new South Park Bridge that crossed the river at Fourteenth Avenue South. (Courtesy of MOHAI, No. PI20659.)

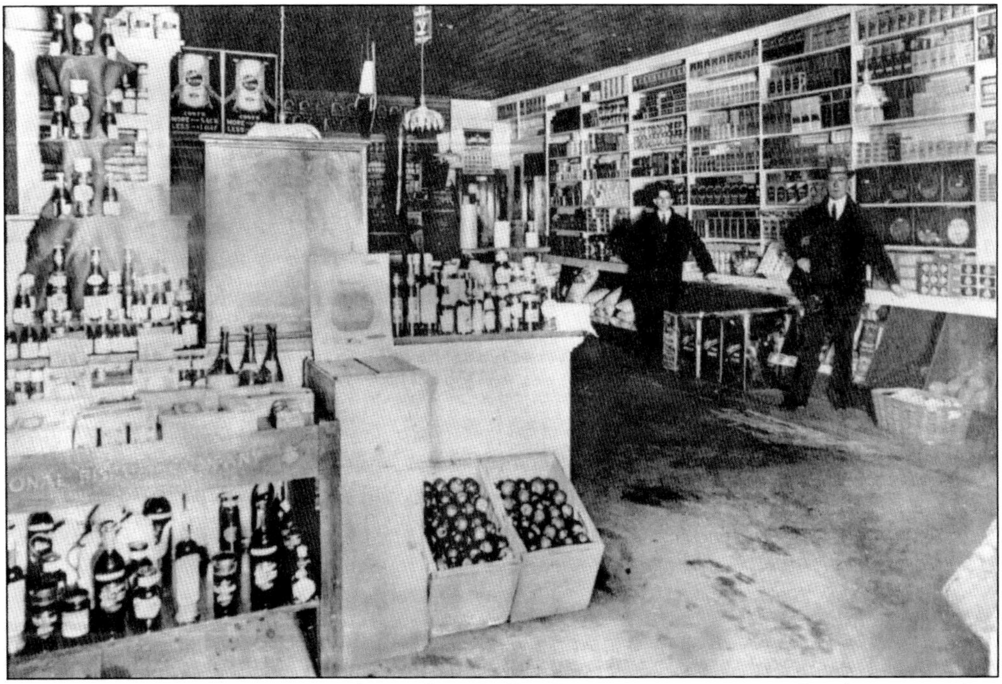

The B. F. Middleton grocery was located on Dallas Avenue among many other businesses that supported the families that lived in South Park. Middleton also built the home located at 1005 Southern Street. (Courtesy of the South Park Seniors.)

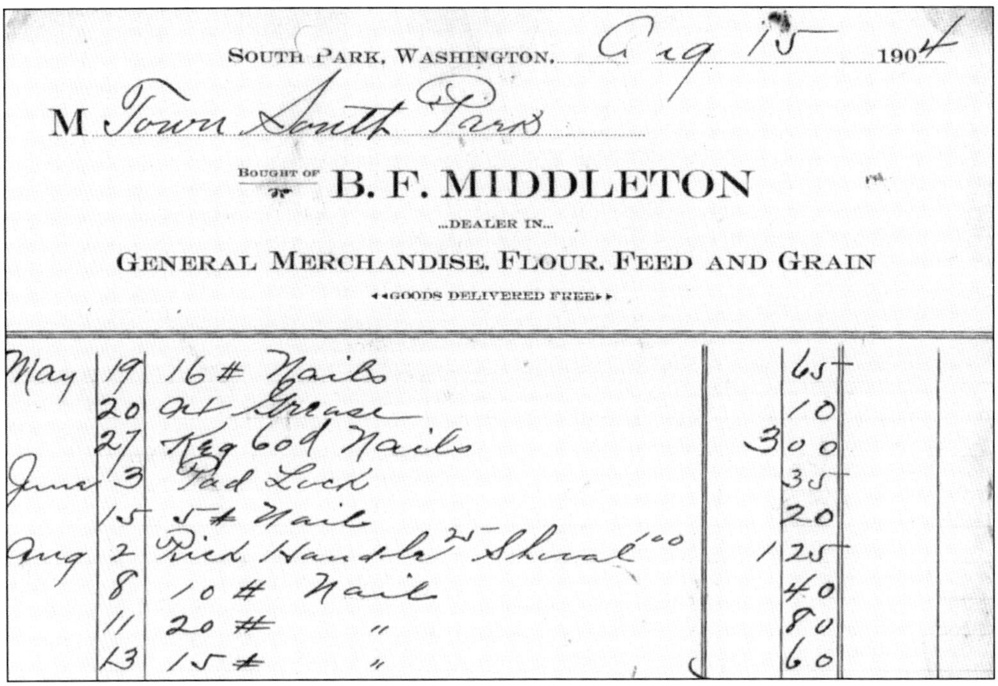

SOUTH PARK, WASHINGTON, Aug 15 1904

M Town South Park

BOUGHT OF B. F. MIDDLETON

...DEALER IN...

GENERAL MERCHANDISE, FLOUR, FEED AND GRAIN

◂◂GOODS DELIVERED FREE▸▸

May	19	16# Nails		65
	20	Qt Grease		10
	27	Keg 60d Nails	3	00
June	3	Pad Lock		35
	15	5# Nail		20
Aug	2	Pick Handle 25 Shovel 100	1	25
	8	10# Nail		40
	11	20# "		80
	13	15# "		60

Pictured above in 1904 is a receipt from B. F. Middleton's grocery store. The town of South Park regularly ran a tab at the store, according to Old Town of South Park treasury records in the City of Seattle Municipal Archives. (Courtesy of the City of Seattle Municipal Archives.)

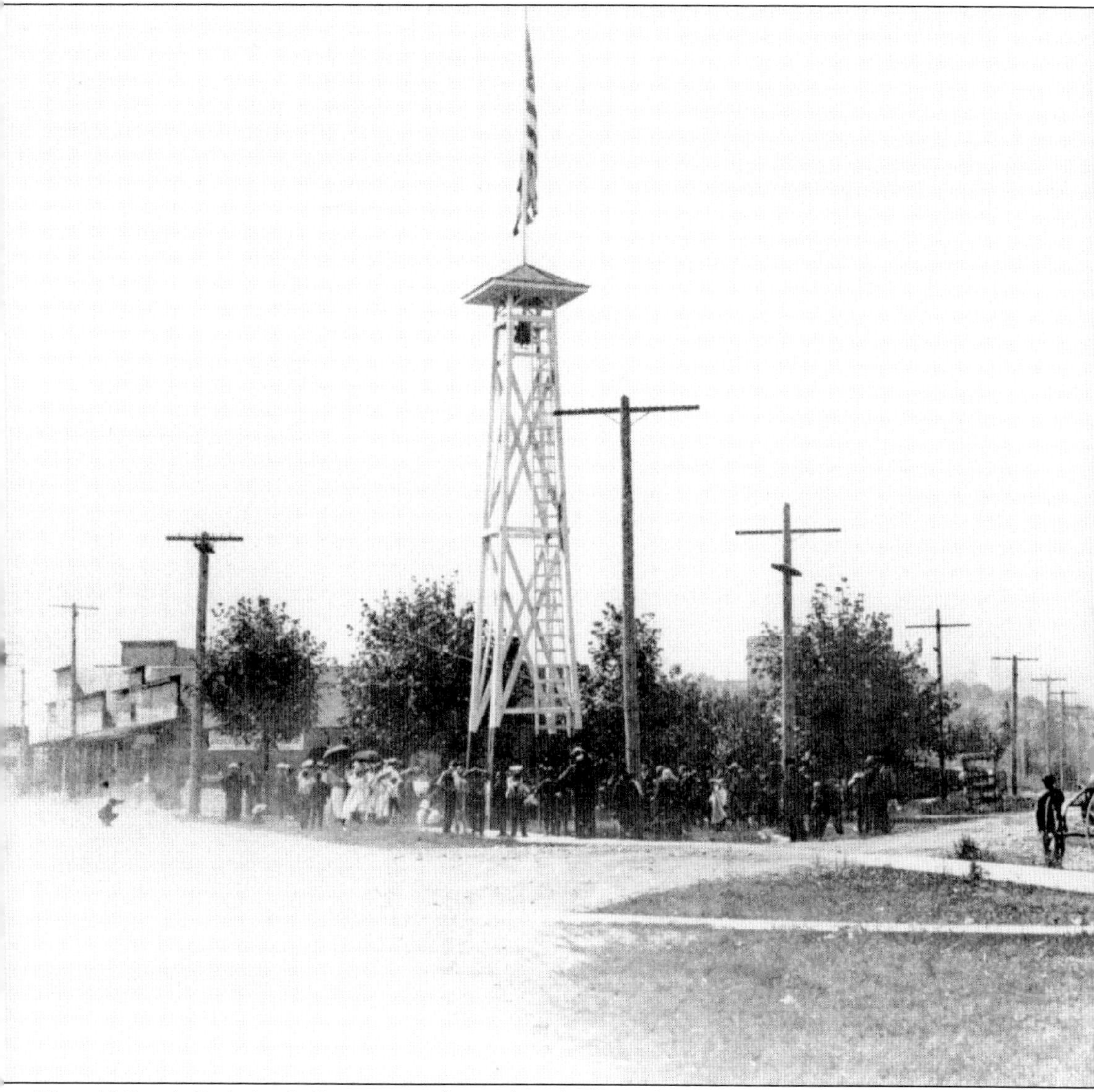

The old South Park fire bell tower was located at the triangle of Dallas Avenue and Sullivan, close to where the Triangle Park and bench are currently located. B. F. Middleton's grocery store was across the street (it can be seen in the left side of the photograph) from the bell tower. The old wooden fire station was just beyond the left edge of this late-1890s or early-1900s photograph. Horses then drew the fire wagon, and Dallas Avenue was a major retail core for South Park. (Courtesy of Theresa Lytle.)

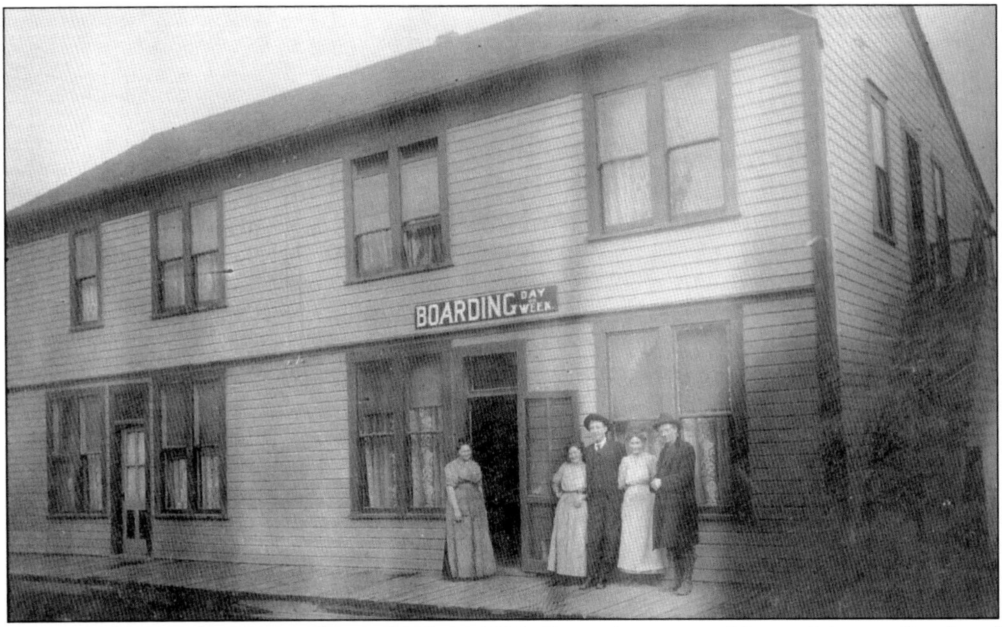

Pictured above is the Montan house, built in 1894. Owner/proprietor Minnie Montan lived and ran a boardinghouse there until 1950. A finished basement room, with its own fireplace and a hidden separate entrance, suggest that the boardinghouse was used as a speakeasy in the 1920s. Minnie's husband operated a barbershop in the building that now sits on the corner of Dallas Avenue and South Southern Street. (Courtesy of the Anderson family.)

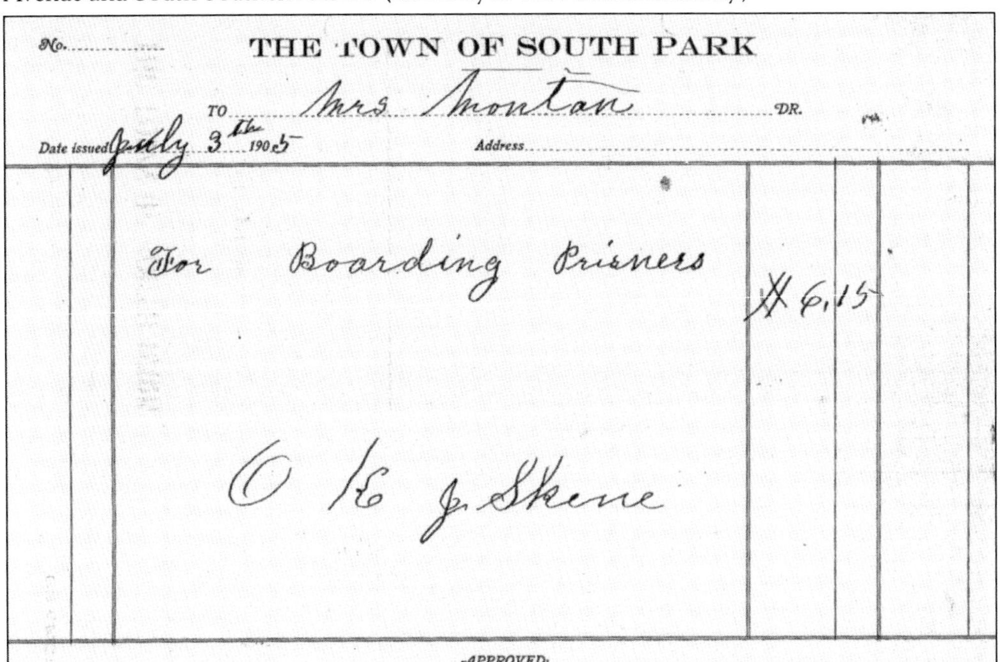

No. ....

THE TOWN OF SOUTH PARK

TO Mrs Montan DR.

Date issued July 3th 1905 Address

For Boarding Prisners $6.15

O K J. Skene

APPROVED:

At one point, Minnie Montan was paid by the town of South Park to board prisoners. The location of the town jail is unclear, but it could not have been too far from Montan's house on Dallas Avenue. (Courtesy of the City of Seattle Municipal Archives.)

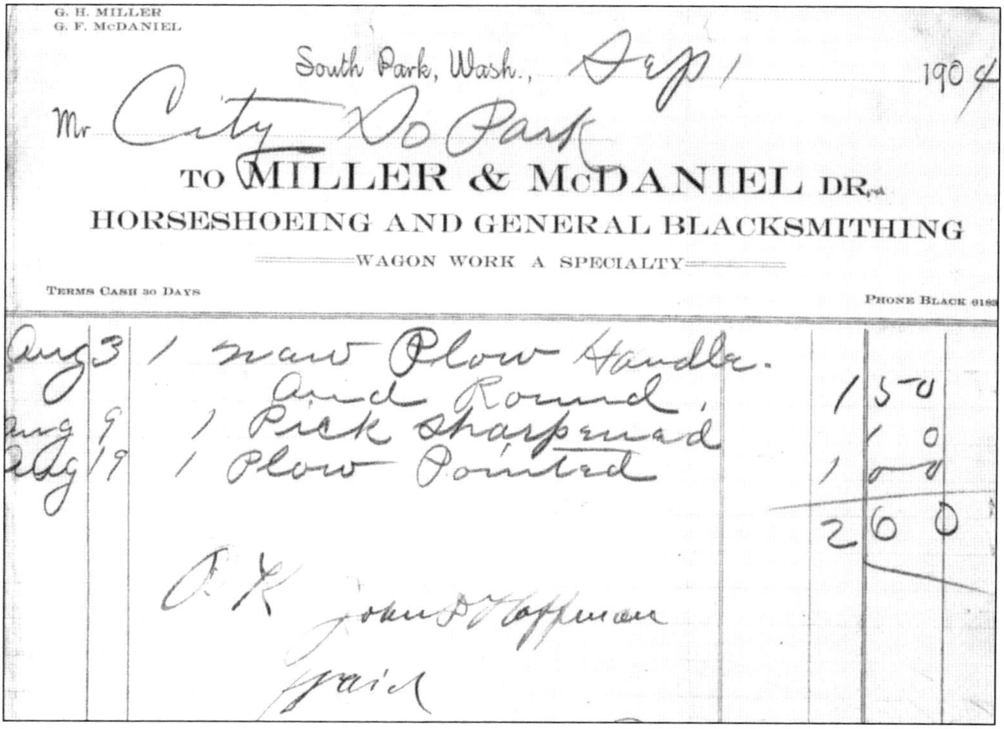

G. H. MILLER
G. F. McDANIEL

South Park, Wash., Sep 1 1904

Mr City Do Park

TO MILLER & McDANIEL DR.

HORSESHOEING AND GENERAL BLACKSMITHING

WAGON WORK A SPECIALTY

TERMS CASH 30 DAYS — PHONE BLACK 6183

Aug	3	1 new Plow Handle and Round	1 50
Aug	9	1 Pick sharpened	1 0
Aug	19	1 Plow Pointed	1 00
			2 60

O.K. John D. Hoffman

paid

The Millers ran a blacksmith shop not far from the livery stables on Dallas Avenue South. The South Park businesses easily supported all the needs of the farmers and families who lived in the area. Because horses were used on farms and for transportation, there were several blacksmiths in South Park. (Courtesy of the City of Seattle Municipal Archives.)

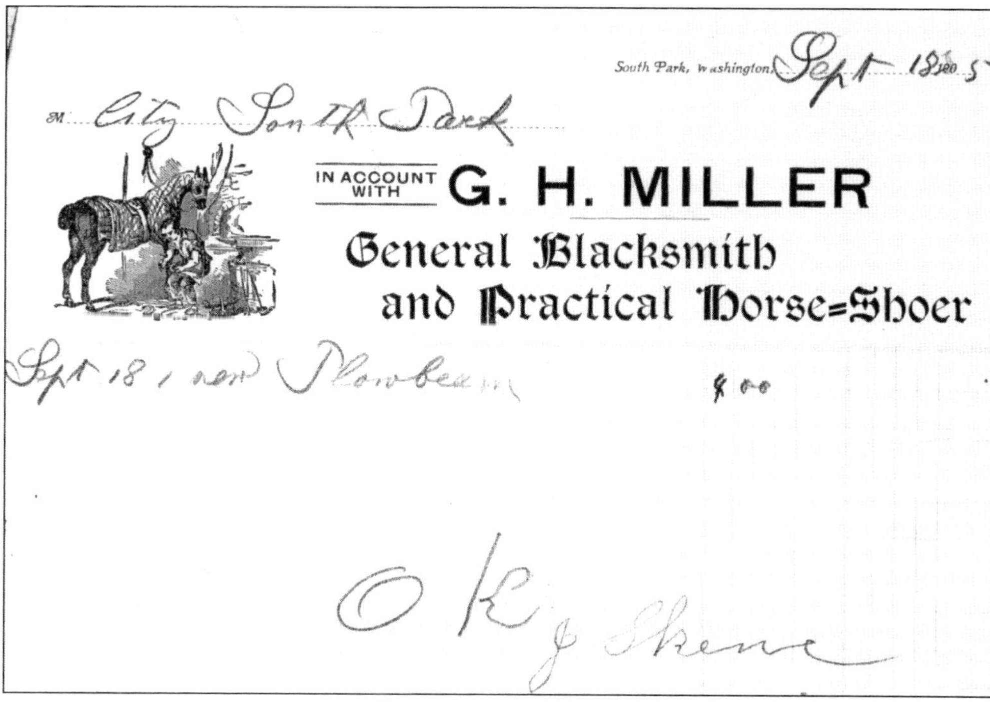

South Park, Washington, Sept 1905

M City South Park

IN ACCOUNT WITH G. H. MILLER

General Blacksmith and Practical Horse-Shoer

Sept 18 1 new Plowbeam 4 00

O K J Skene

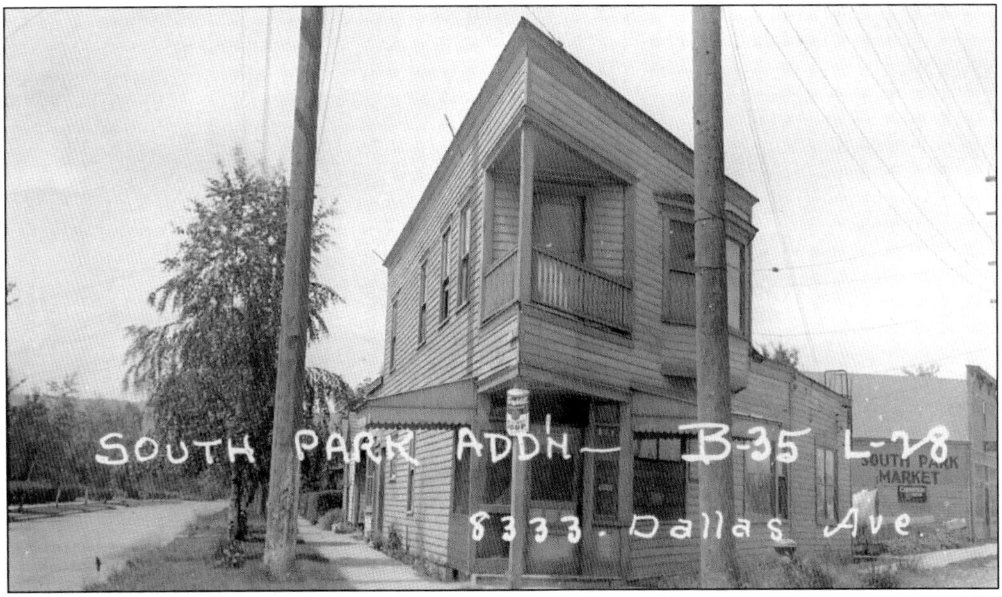

The building at 8333 Dallas Avenue South is a peculiar triangle structure that was owned by Robert Green in 1937, when it was a two-story building with a store on the bottom and two apartments on the top. This building was constructed in 1898 and remodeled in 1956 by Edward H. Allen when the store was removed and the apartments expanded. This structure still serves as an apartment building and looks nothing like it did in 1937, when this photograph was taken. (Courtesy of PSRA.)

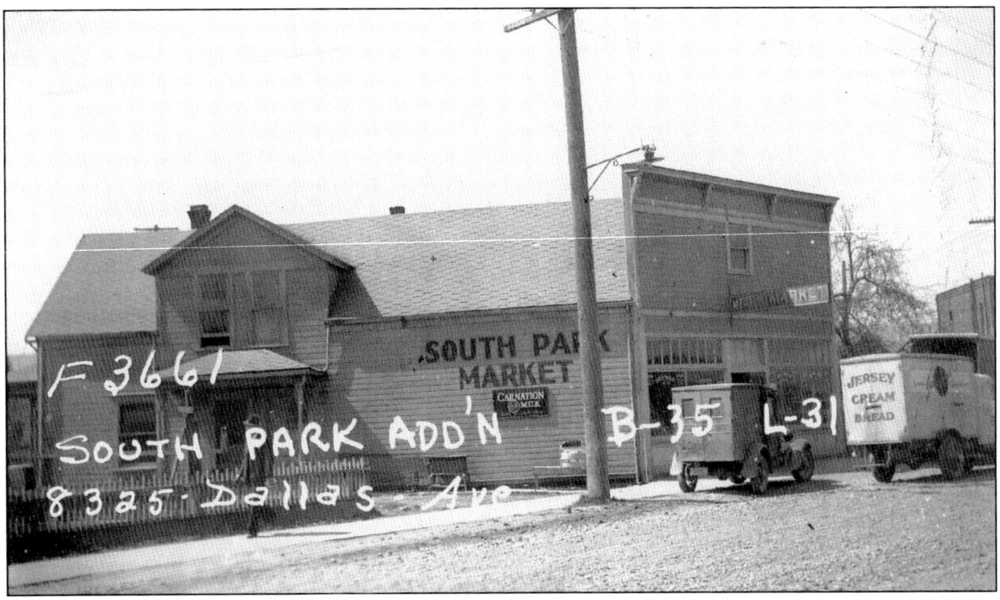

This building at 8325 Dallas Avenue South was constructed in 1904, during the early days of the Dallas Avenue commercial district development. Owned by Glen Jacobs in 1937, it had a store on the first floor and two apartments on the second floor. Today it is an apartment building. (Courtesy of PSRA.)

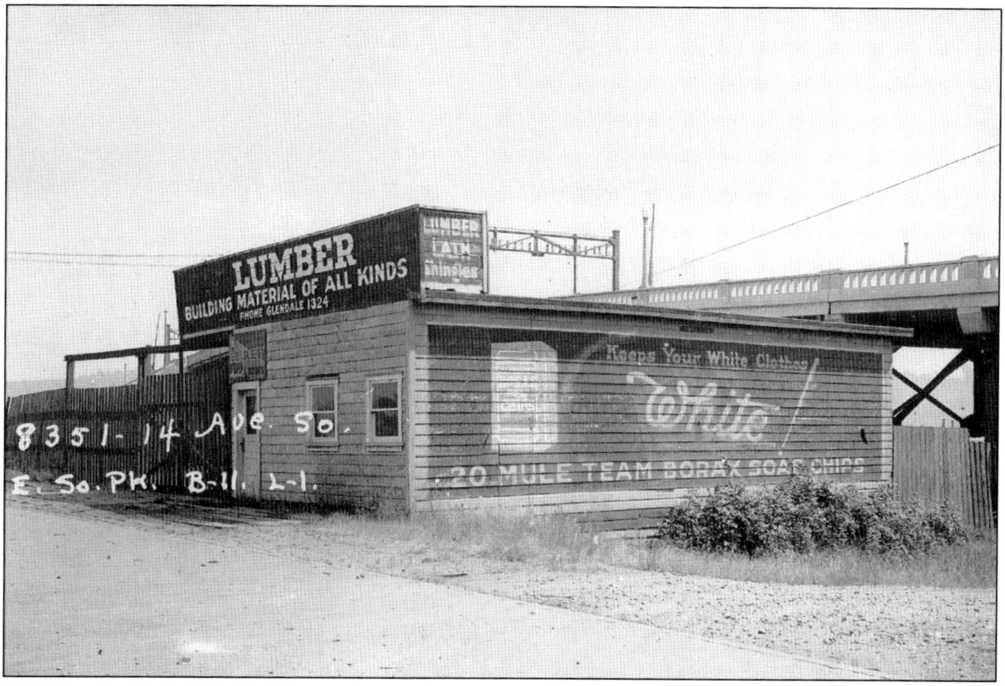

R. F. Burdic owned this lumber store, built in 1916, at 8351 Fourteenth Avenue South as well as the feed store across the street. One can see the brick pavers that are still present on this stretch of the old World War I memorial highway. There is no longer an 8351 Fourteenth Avenue South address. (Courtesy of PSRA.)

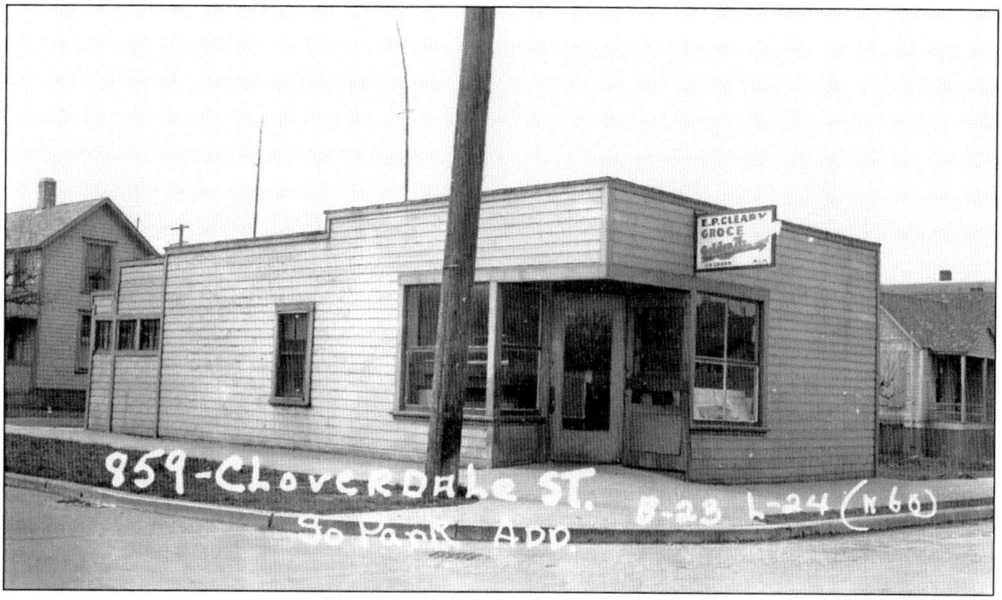

E. P. Cleary's grocery store used to occupy the building located at 849 South Cloverdale Street. It was torn down, and in 1979, a four-unit apartment was built in its place. Cloverdale Street was rezoned in the 1960s from single-family and neighborhood commercial buildings to high density. As properties along Cloverdale Street are bought, new owners capitalize on the high-density zoning. (Courtesy of PSRA.)

This is a 1906 letter from the New York booking office of the Third Avenue Theater inquiring if South Park was interested in an amphitheater for boxing matches. At one point, South Park was also considered as a potential site for a sports stadium. Instead, the Kingdome site was selected to keep the money closer to downtown Seattle. (Courtesy of the City of Seattle Municipal Archives.)

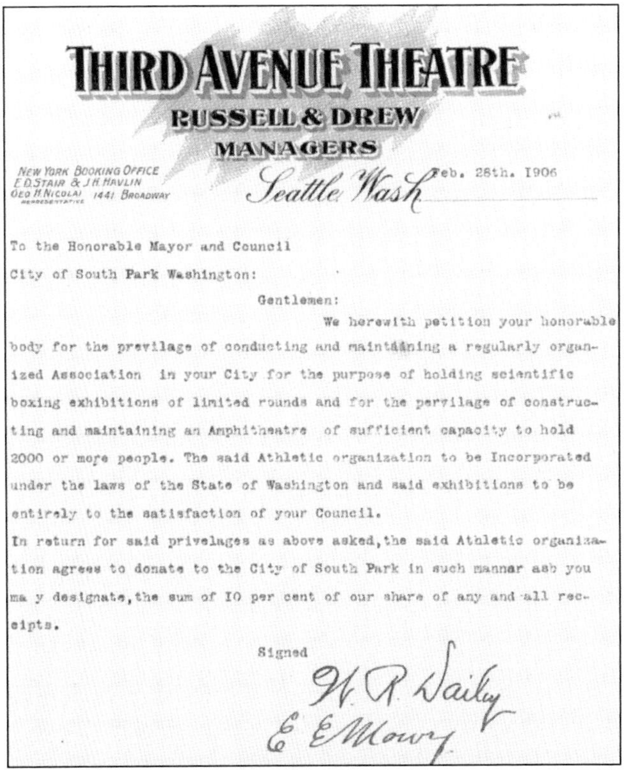

THIRD AVENUE THEATRE
RUSSELL & DREW
MANAGERS

NEW YORK BOOKING OFFICE
E.D.STAIR & J.H.HAVLIN
GEO.H.NICOLAI 1441 BROADWAY
REPRESENTATIVE

Seattle Wash Feb. 28th. 1906

To the Honorable Mayor and Council
City of South Park Washington:

Gentlemen:

We herewith petition your honorable body for the previlage of conducting and maintaining a regularly organized Association in your City for the purpose of holding scientific boxing exhibitions of limited rounds and for the pervilage of constructing and maintaining an Amphitheatre of sufficient capacity to hold 2000 or more people. The said Athletic organization to be Incorporated under the laws of the State of Washington and said exhibitions to be entirely to the satisfaction of your Council.

In return for said privelages as above asked, the said Athletic organization agrees to donate to the City of South Park in such manner asb you ma y designate, the sum of IO per cent of our share of any and all receipts.

Signed
W. R. Daily
E. E. Mowry

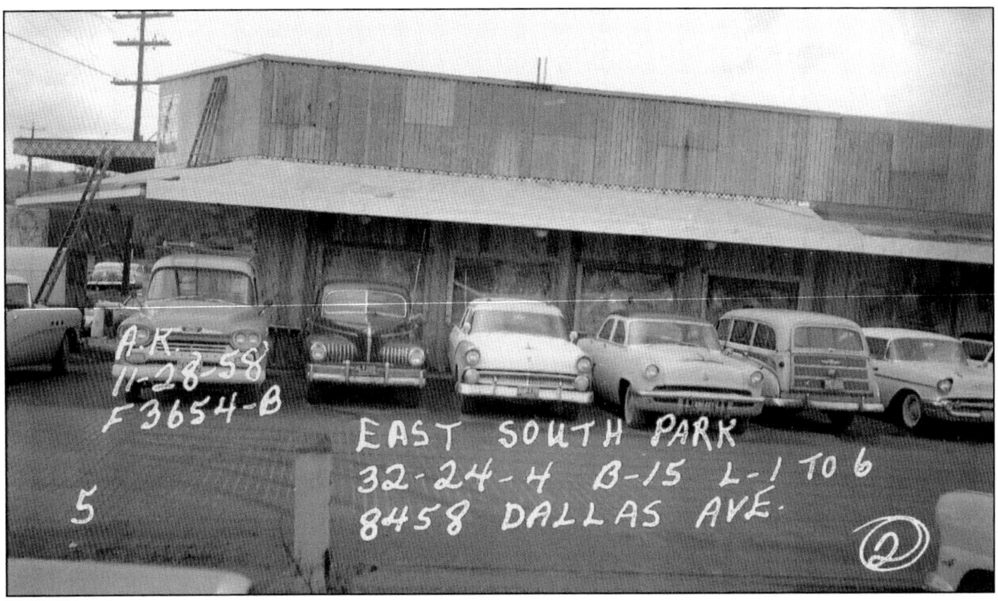

Built by R. F. Burdic in 1943, Burdic's Feed Store, pictured here in 1958, was located at 8458 Dallas Avenue South. Note that the parking lot is paved with bricks. This remnant marks the northern terminus and is all that remains of the landscaped memorial boulevard from the Duwamish River to Tacoma; one of the few surviving stretches of unpaved brick roadway remaining in King County. The memorial boulevard was constructed to commemorate the fallen soldiers of World War I. (The memorial route follows Des Moines Memorial Drive.) (Courtesy of PSRA.)

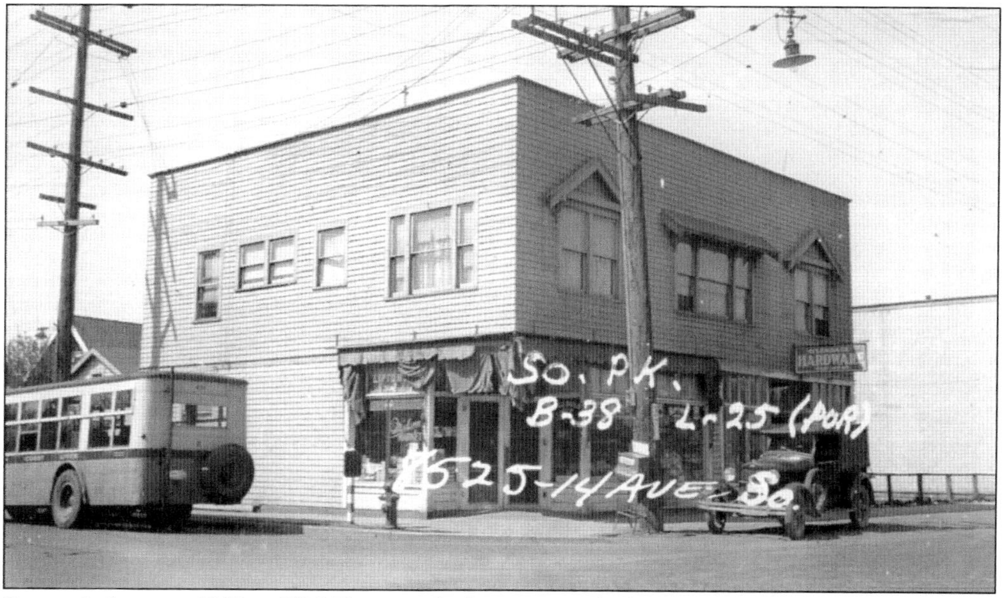

Pictured above in 1937 is 8525 Fourteenth Avenue South, located on the northwest corner of Fourteenth and Cloverdale Street. Over the years, a market and Glendale Hardware have occupied the building. (Courtesy of PSRA.)

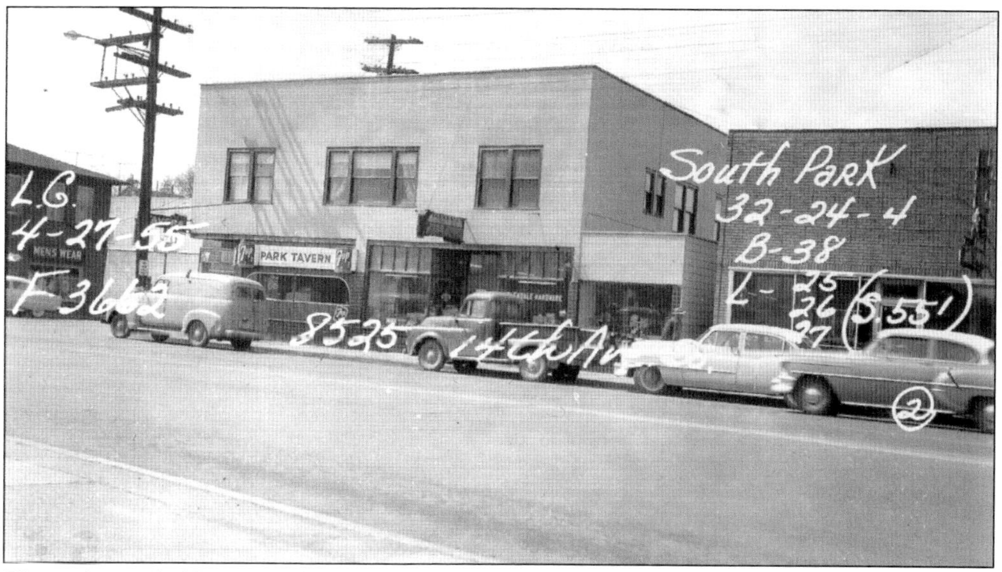

This is how 8525 Fourteenth Avenue South appeared in 1955. The South Park Tavern later became Murdoch's Tavern, which closed in 2001. Murdoch's front door had a sign that said "No Crybabies," meaning patrons needed to politely overlook anything suspicious or illegal in the bar or go somewhere else for a beer. The building currently is a Mexican Video Mar. (Courtesy of PSRA.)

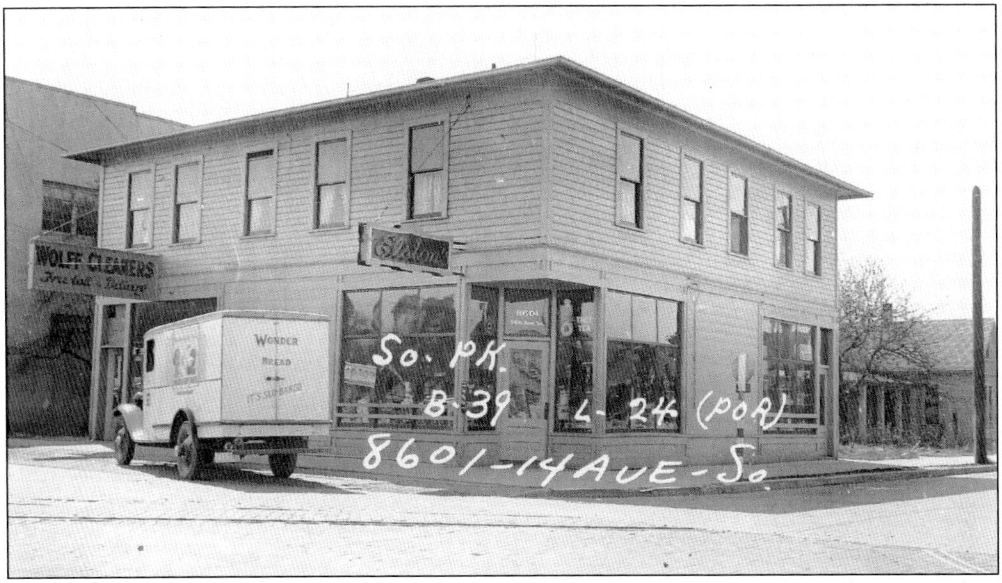

At the southwest corner of Fourteenth Avenue South and Cloverdale Street was Elston's Market, pictured here in 1937. Located at 8601 Fourteenth Avenue South, it became the major retail corner with the newly implemented South Park Bridge. (Courtesy of PSRA.)

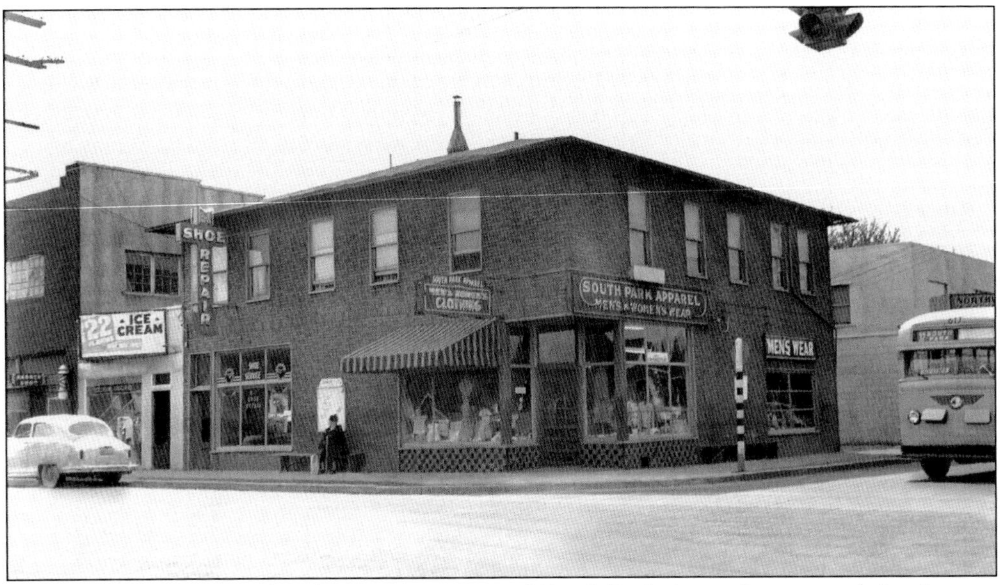

In 1949, an ice cream parlor, shoe repair store, and South Park Apparel comprised the shops at 8601 Fourteenth Avenue South, with an apartment unit on the second floor. Most recently, this was a Mexi Mart, owned and operated by Sal Hernandez. (Courtesy of PSRA.)

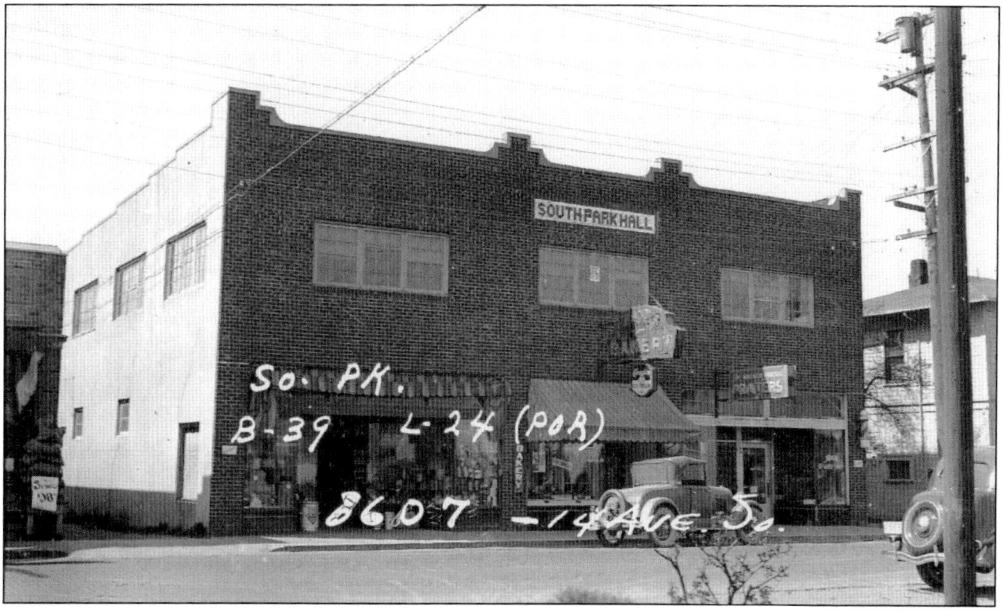

In 1937, this was the South Park Hall, located at 8607 Fourteenth Avenue South. This structure remains intact, and still hanging on the front of the building is the original South Park Hall sign. (Courtesy of PSRA.)

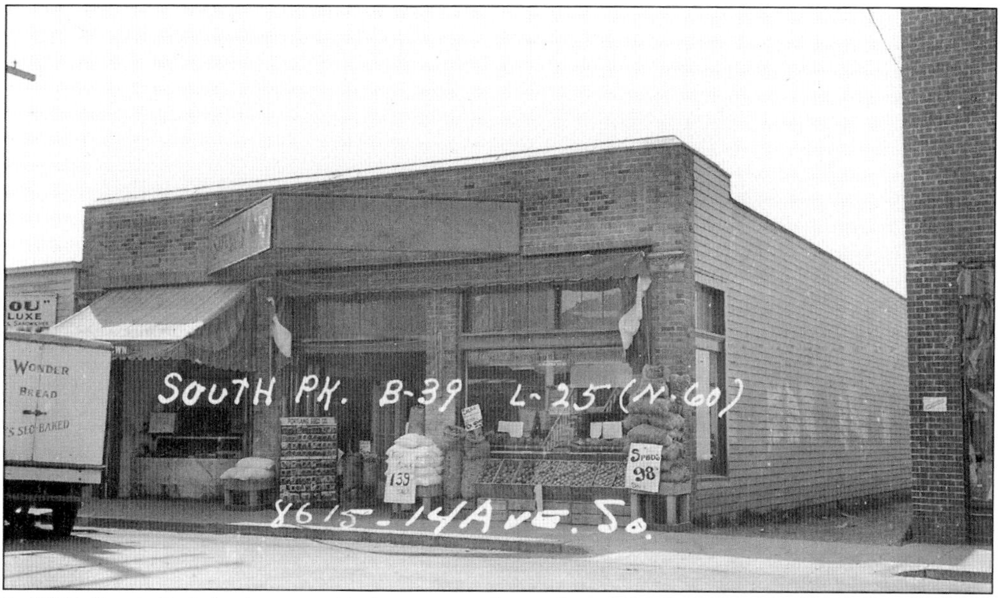

In 1937, South Park had its own Safeway store, located on 8615 Fourteenth Avenue South. This building remains, but Safeway has not been in the neighborhood for years. As more people started owning their own automobiles, small grocery stores faded throughout all of Seattle. (Courtesy of PSRA.)

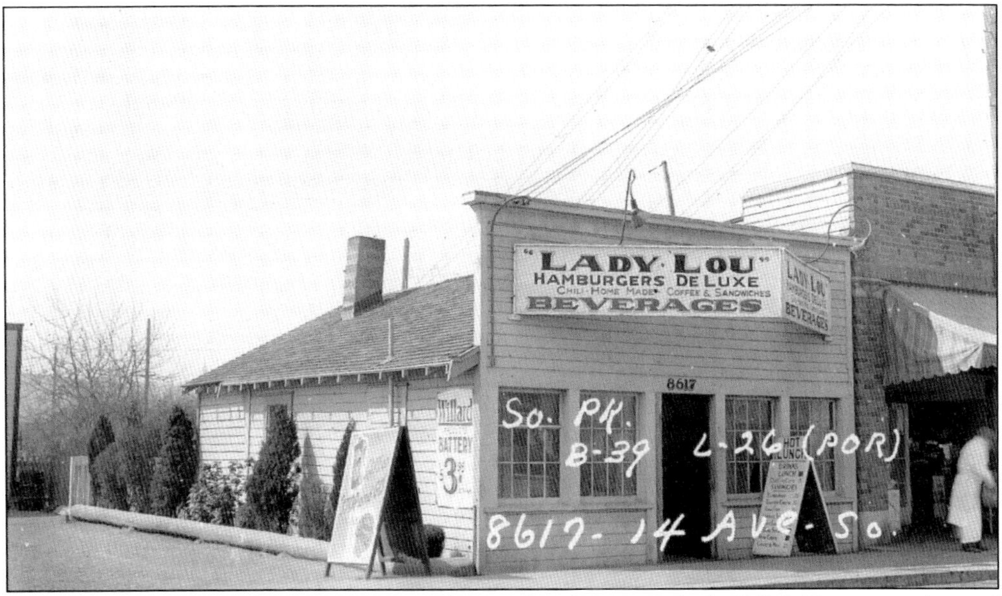

Pictured here in 1937 as burger restaurant, favorite local watering hole Kelly's Tavern was located at 8617 Fourteenth Avenue South for many years. The tavern closed in 2005; the building is vacant. (Courtesy of PSRA.)

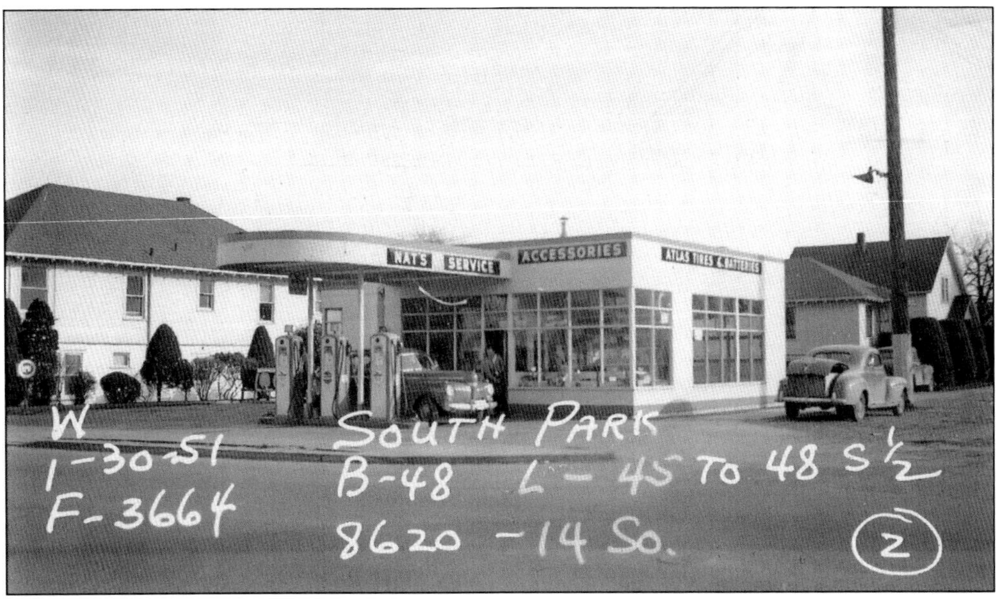

A service station was located on 8620 Fourteenth Avenue South in 1951. A new 76 station opened across the street, and the station located at this site closed. This building is currently a private residence but zoned for neighborhood commercial purposes. (Courtesy of PSRA.)

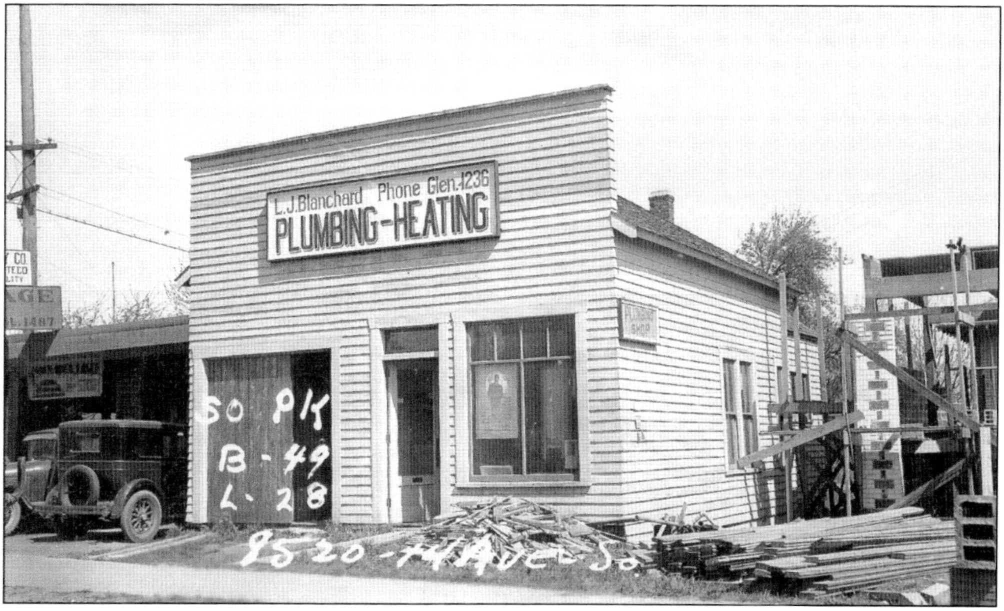

This building at 8520 Fourteenth Avenue South was a plumbing and heating contractor service in 1937. As large hardware chains sprung up in the 1940s and 1950s and consumers were attracted to larger franchises, small specialty shops such as this one went out of business. This building now houses a beauty salon catering to Latinos. (Courtesy of PSRA.)

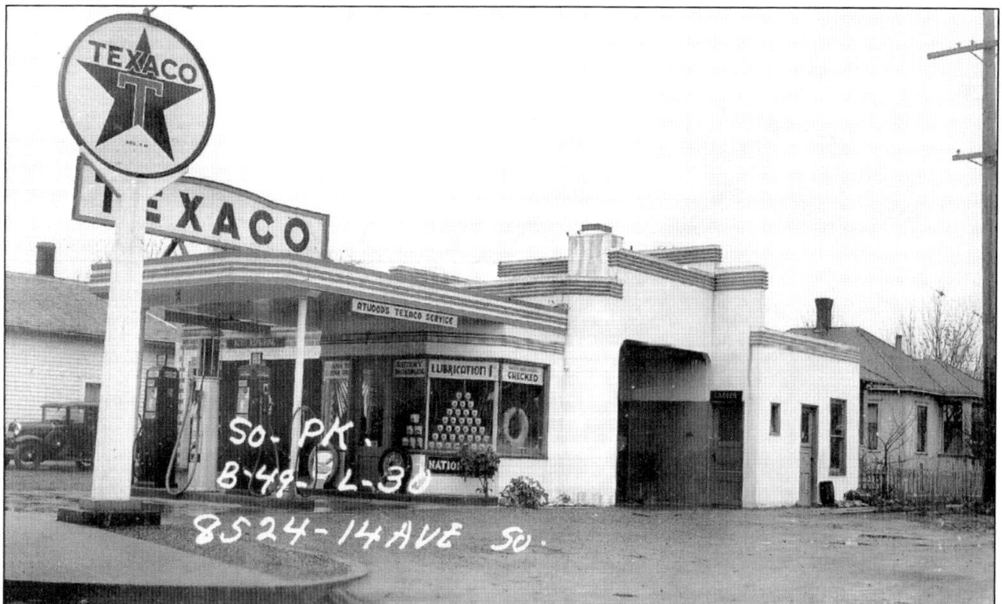

Now a vegetable market with an espresso stand in the parking lot, 8524 Fourteenth Avenue South, pictured here in 1937, was once a Texaco, one of South Park's primary gas stations. It later became a taxicab repair service. (Courtesy of PSRA.)

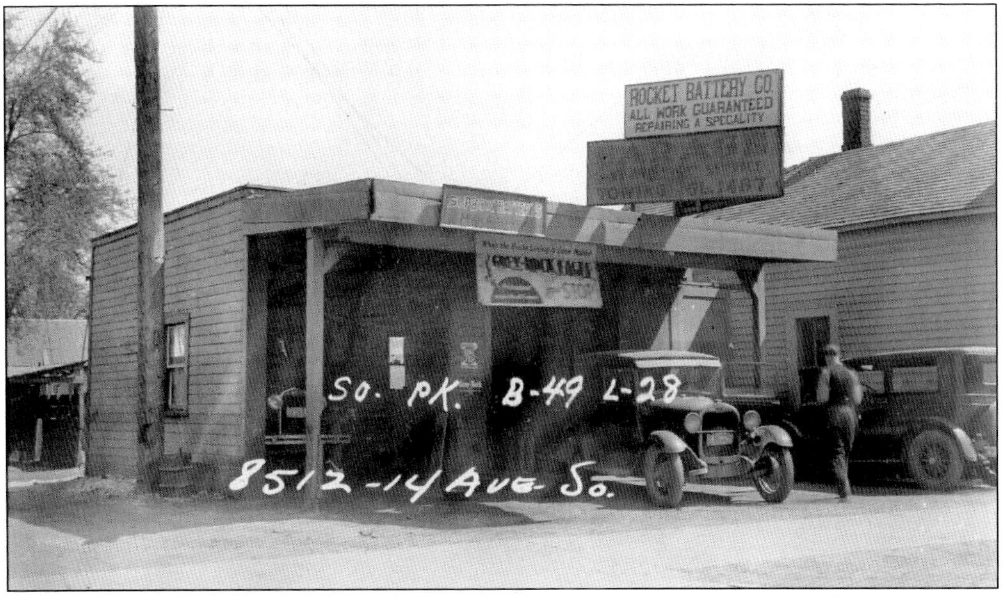

In 1937, this building, located at 8512 Fourteenth Avenue South, was an automobile repair shop. This is now a Latino money-wiring service. Next door was 8414 Fourteenth Avenue South, now a Latino travel agency. (Courtesy of PSRA.)

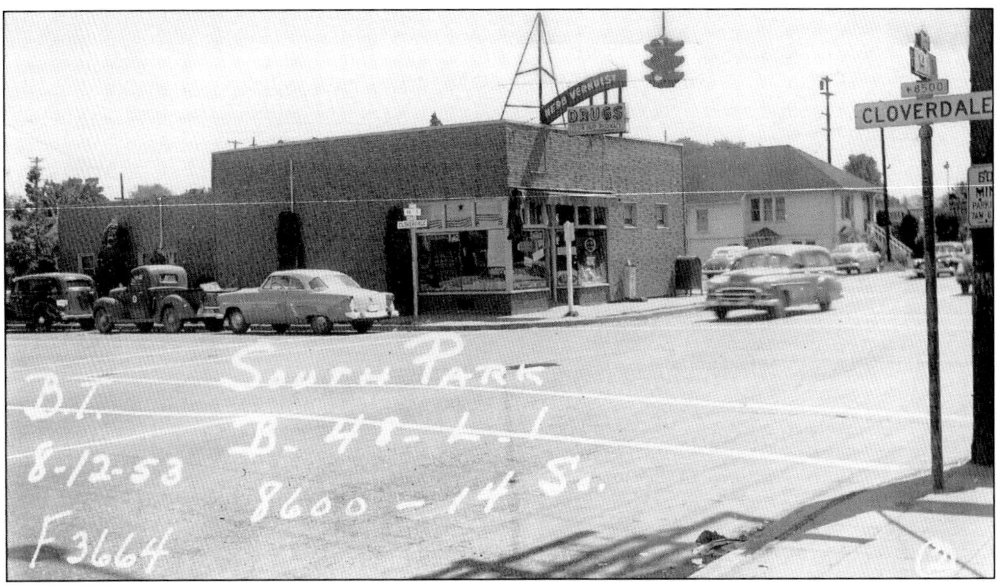

In 1953, the building at 8600 Fourteenth Avenue South was a pharmacy run by Herb Vernquist. It is now the Napoli restaurant, which serves pizza and hoagies to a busy lunch crowd from the area's industrial businesses. (Courtesy of PSRA.)

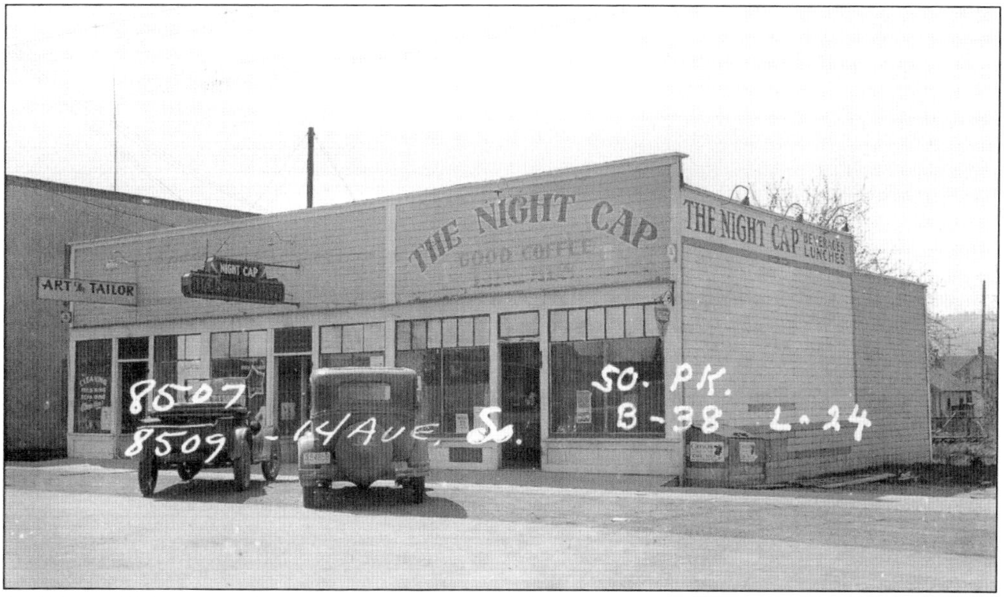

In 1937, 8509 Fourteenth Avenue South housed the Night Cap Tavern and Art the Tailor. A colorful mural on the north side of the building depicts South Park's current image of an industrial, culturally diverse, environmentally active community. This building currently has a dollar store, or Ken's Grocery. (Courtesy of PSRA.)

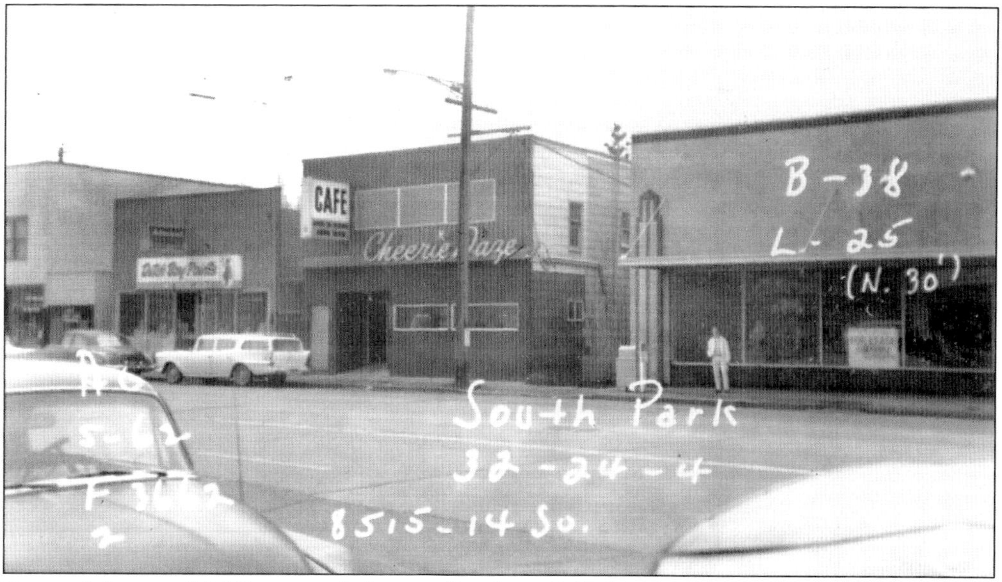

Pictured above is 8515 Fourteenth Avenue South in 1962. Also visible is a Dutch Boy Paint store located next to Cheerie Daze, a favorite neighborhood diner. Today these buildings house Jalisco Restaurant (which used to be the building located at 8522 Eighth Avenue South and was moved in 1946 to its current location) and Muy Macho. (Courtesy of PSRA.)

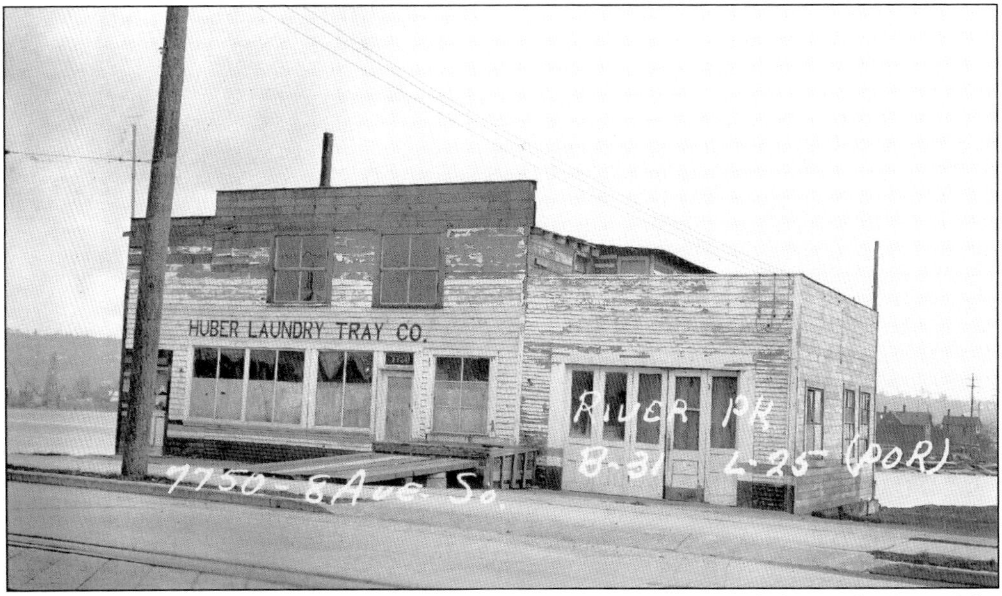

The Huber Laundry Tray Company at 7750 Eighth Avenue South, resided near the foot of the Eighth Avenue South Bridge. Trolley tracks are visible in this photograph taken in 1937. Today this is near the Graham Trucking parking lot. (Courtesy of PSRA.)

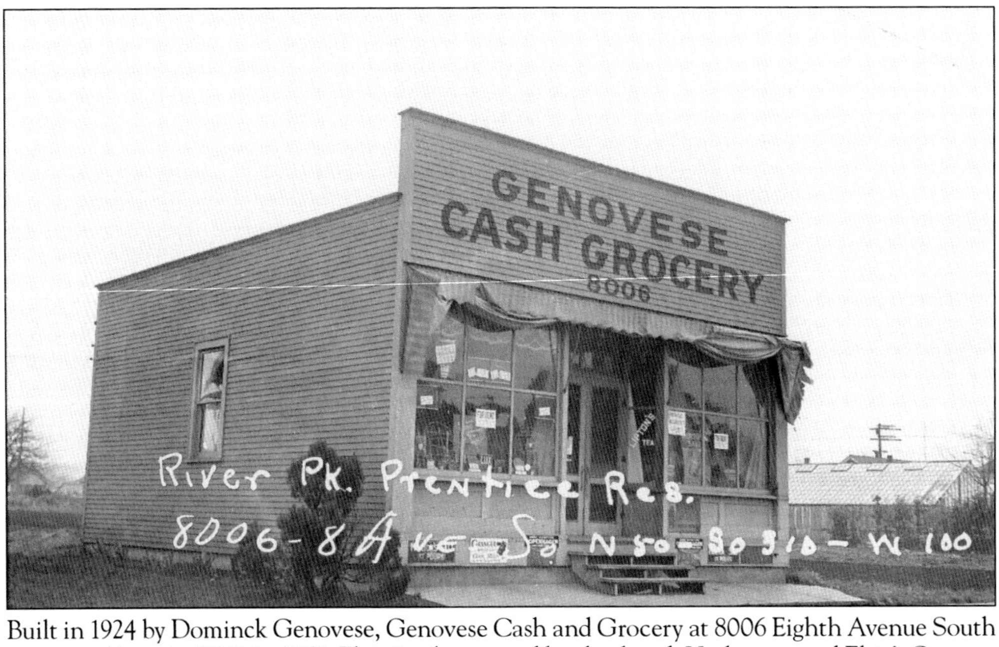

Built in 1924 by Dominck Genovese, Genovese Cash and Grocery at 8006 Eighth Avenue South is pictured here in 1937. In 1952, Elsie Leishman and her husband, Herb, operated Elsie's Grocery store here. Businessmen, who frequented Elsie's grocery regularly for ready-made sandwiches and clothing, accounted for the majority of her sales. This property is currently zoned industrial and is the Long Painting property. (Courtesy of PSRA.)

Nine

The Dilemma of Zoning

The story of South Park is the agonizing story of residents trying to respect the past in the face of urbanization.

The development of South Park into an industrial neighborhood results from early city planners looking to fully appreciate the possibility of developing a port. City planners studied the ports and harbors in Hamburg, Antwerp, Montreal, and the Manchester Canal.

> Seattle's greatest commercial asset is her harbor. Spacious and free from obstructions to navigation, it can be entered every day in the year; when Lake Washington canal is completed, the harbor will offer the most generous haven in the world, where ships may lie in either salt or fresh water. With no extremes of heat or cold, no ice in the harbor, no winds exceeding thirty-six miles an hour, Seattle is two days nearer to the Oriental ports than San Francisco, and four hundred seventy miles nearer to the Great Lakes at Duluth. (Municipal Plans Division, Seattle, 1911.)

Stimulated by the wartime economy, industry quickly encroached on South Park's fertile farmland. In 1956, the city council rezoned South Park as "transition to industrial."

In the mid-1960s, the city again threatened to rezone all of South Park as industrial. After more than 4,000 residents staged a protest at city hall, some of the existing residential neighborhood was zoned high-density residential. The integrity of the community remained threatened during the 1970s as the historic South Park church, Our Lady of Lourdes, was abandoned and demolished. To compound the neighborhood issues, construction of Highway 99 sliced the neighborhood in half.

The addition of the Duwamish Waterway Park at Tenth and Kenyon in 1978 began some positive changes in South Park. In 1989, the old South Park Field House was torn down and replaced with a new building. In 2000, Concord School was remodeled and reopened. In 2005, Cesar Chavez Park at Seventh and Cloverdale Street was dedicated. In 2005, the River City Skate Park on Cloverdale Street was started. A South Park branch of the Seattle Public Library is slated to open in August 2006 and a new riverfront park at Eighth and Portland is underway.

At the same time, South Park's affordable housing and proximity to downtown Seattle attracts new buyers. Some newcomers are surprised by the presence of industry around them, airplanes above them, the sense of community inside a square mile, and the dampness in their basements. That's just part of living in South Park.

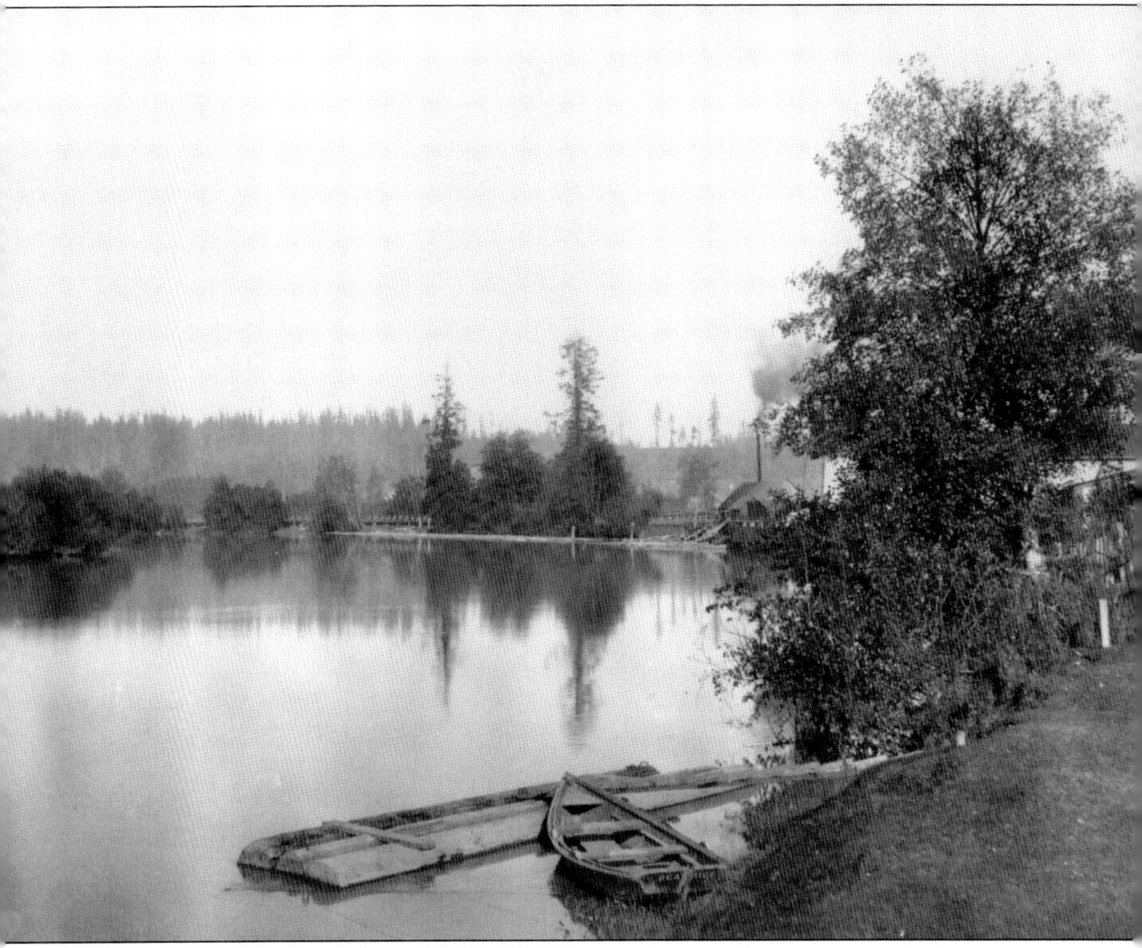

An early home is pictured on a bank of the Duwamish River, date unknown. Today it is unusual to see any small boats in the Duwamish River other than Muckleshoot fishermen. The river's straightened deep channel is not pleasure-boat friendly and is polluted from years of heavy industrial use. Public access to the river is scarce and discouraged due to heavy marine traffic. The community was once very marshy because of the river. To cross into Georgetown, residents would use small private boats (like the one pictured here) if they chose not to take the ferry. (Courtesy of University of Washington Libraries, Special Collections, UW26367.)

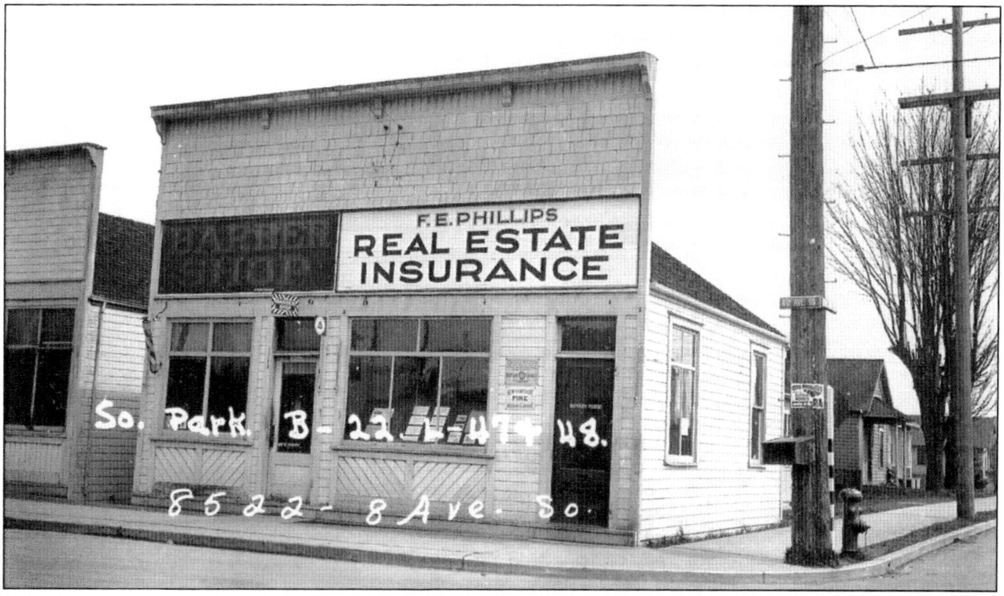

This barbershop and real estate insurance building at 8522 Eighth Avenue South, built in 1914, was moved in 1946 to its new and current location at 8517 Fourteenth Avenue South, which is now the Jalisco Mexican restaurant. The address next to it was 8520 Eighth Avenue South, which used to be a tailor shop but was removed to accommodate the present-day Fire Station No. 26. (Courtesy of PSRA.)

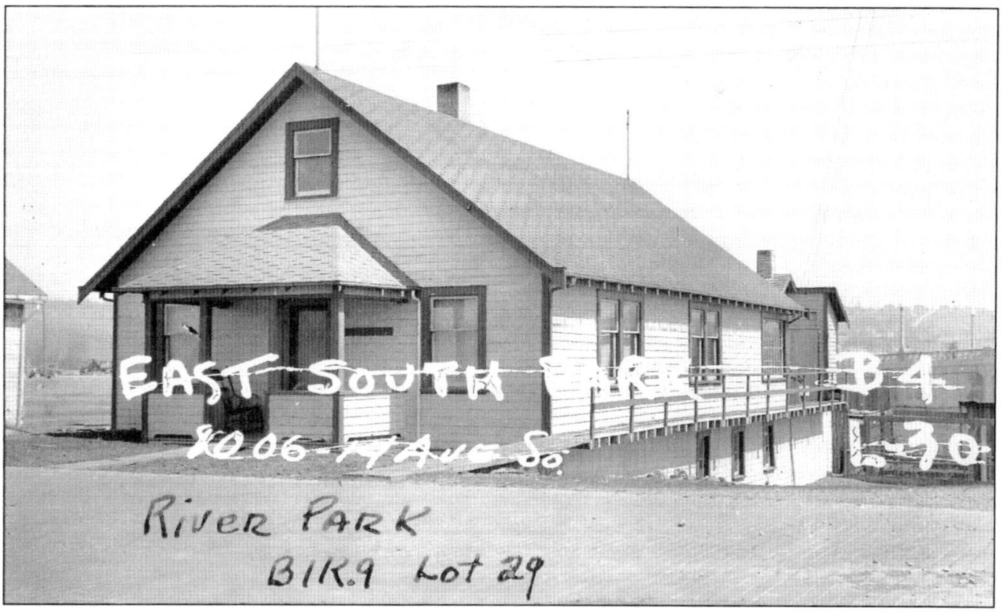

Pictured here in 1937 is 8006 Fourteenth Avenue South at the foot of the new South Park Bridge. The house was built in 1931 and was moved around 1953 to 704 Southern, when its new location was rezoned industrial. It is now part of Anthony Construction's lot. (Courtesy of PSRA.)

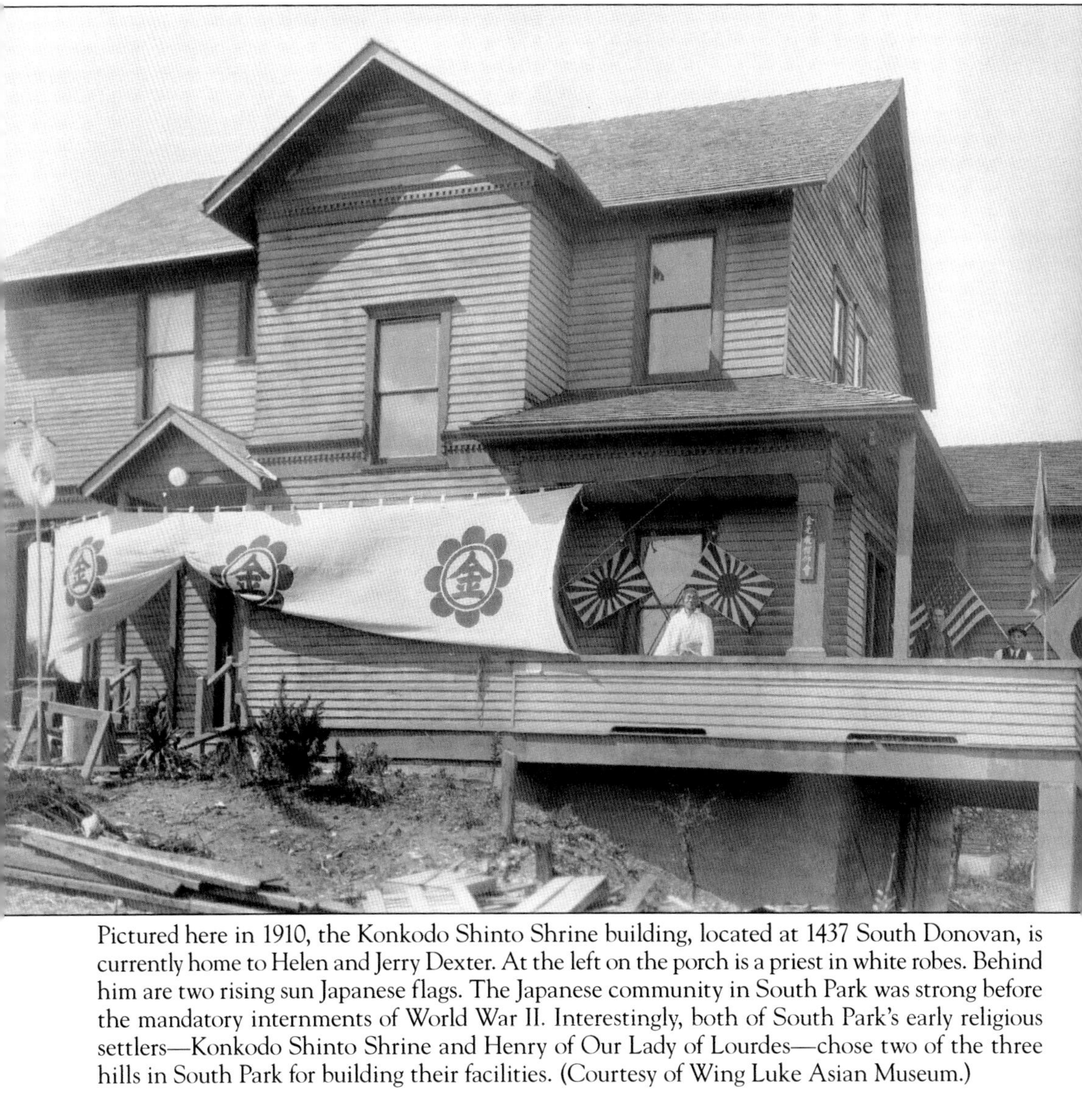

Pictured here in 1910, the Konkodo Shinto Shrine building, located at 1437 South Donovan, is currently home to Helen and Jerry Dexter. At the left on the porch is a priest in white robes. Behind him are two rising sun Japanese flags. The Japanese community in South Park was strong before the mandatory internments of World War II. Interestingly, both of South Park's early religious settlers—Konkodo Shinto Shrine and Henry of Our Lady of Lourdes—chose two of the three hills in South Park for building their facilities. (Courtesy of Wing Luke Asian Museum.)

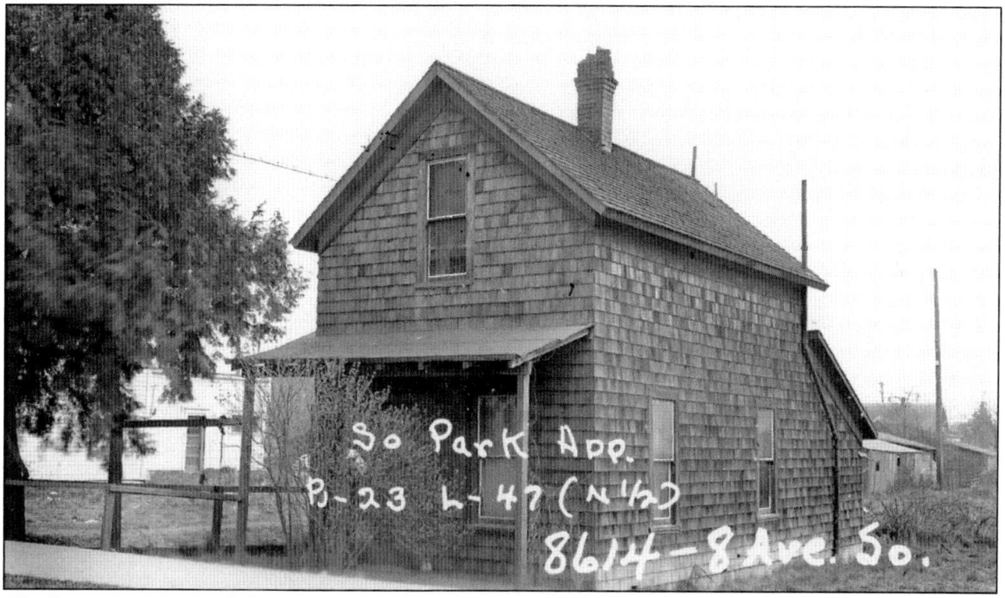

The house at 8614 Eighth Avenue South, built in 1909, is pictured here in 1937. It was demolished by Dwight Smith in 1954, although it is unclear if it was torn down in preparation for the freeway or if the shift in zoning along Eighth Avenue prompted more multifamily housing. (Courtesy of PSRA.)

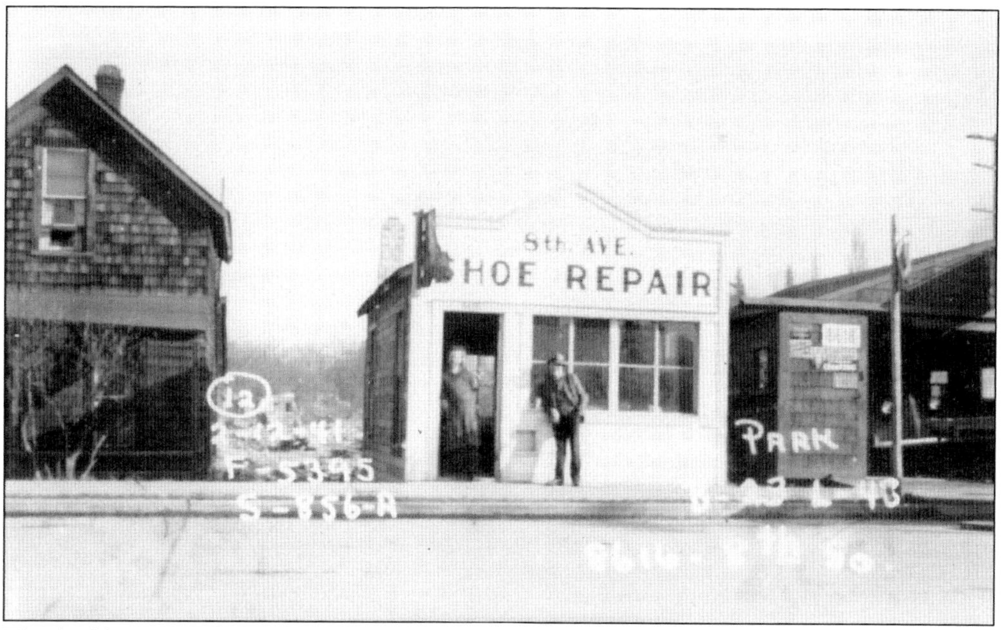

This building at 8616 Eighth Avenue South, pictured here in 1937, was built in 1903. The homes that occupied 8614–8624 Eighth Avenue South were torn down in 1961 to make way for the Donovan Apartments, whose mid-century architecture sticks out in an otherwise Old World block of turn-of-the-century homes. (Courtesy of PSRA.)

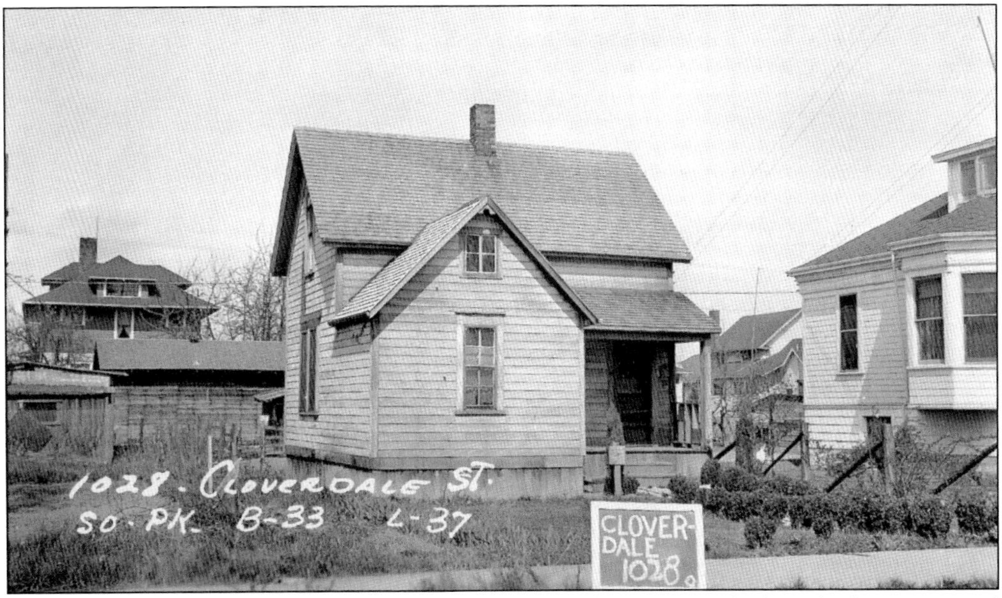

Pictured here in 1937, this house at 1028 South Cloverdale Street was built in the late 1800s and is still a home in the community. The only change is that the exterior is hidden underneath aluminum siding. It is believed that a siding salesman lived in South Park and convinced many homeowners to cover their beautiful but high-maintenance fir and cedar siding with economical, low maintenance aluminum or asbestos siding. (Courtesy of PSRA.)

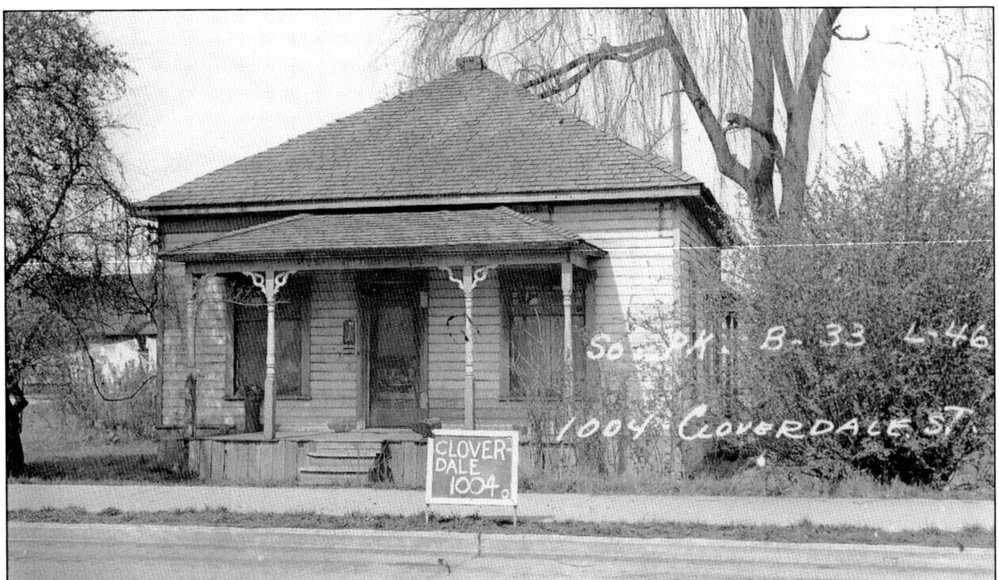

As a result of rezoning Cloverdale Street to high density in the 1960s, 1004 South Cloverdale Street, pictured here in 1937, is now home to an apartment building with over 35 apartments. The largest apartment building complex to ever be constructed in South Park was the South Park Courts, which housed over 250 families. (Courtesy of PSRA.)

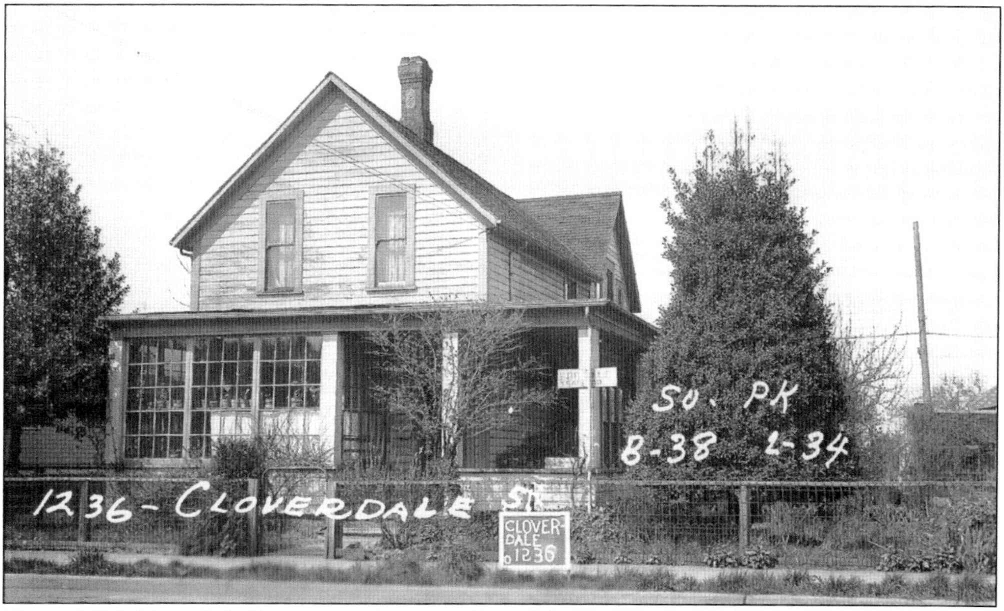

This is 1236 Cloverdale Street in 1937, when Cloverdale Street was zoned for single-family housing. The many houses with large lots along Cloverdale Street contributed to the sense that South Park was a small town. Many old homes on Cloverdale Street still survive despite the high-density zoning. (Courtesy of PSRA.)

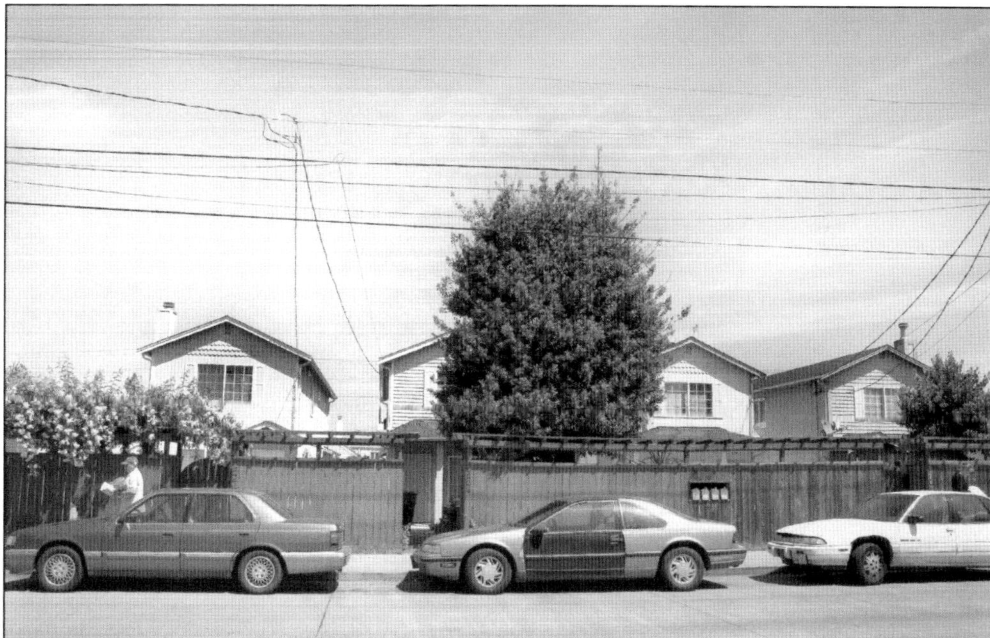

This is the same address, 1236 Cloverdale Street, in 2006, with "skinnies," which began appearing in the community due to parts of the neighborhood being rezoned to high density in the 1960s. As the old owners sold off their property, developers purchased the land and began putting up multiple tall, thin homes on the small lots. (Courtesy of the South Park Neighborhood Association.)

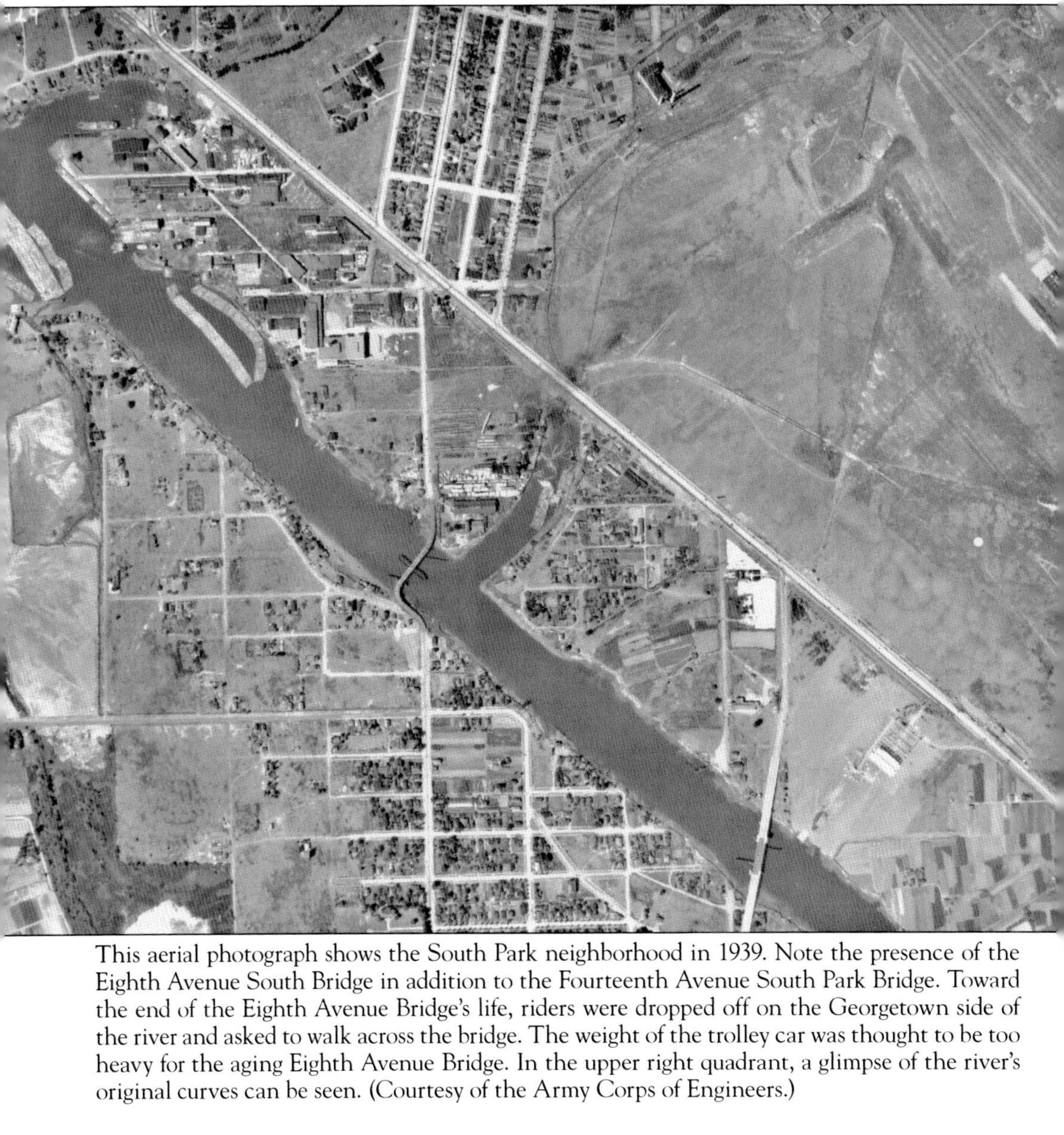

This aerial photograph shows the South Park neighborhood in 1939. Note the presence of the Eighth Avenue South Bridge in addition to the Fourteenth Avenue South Park Bridge. Toward the end of the Eighth Avenue Bridge's life, riders were dropped off on the Georgetown side of the river and asked to walk across the bridge. The weight of the trolley car was thought to be too heavy for the aging Eighth Avenue Bridge. In the upper right quadrant, a glimpse of the river's original curves can be seen. (Courtesy of the Army Corps of Engineers.)

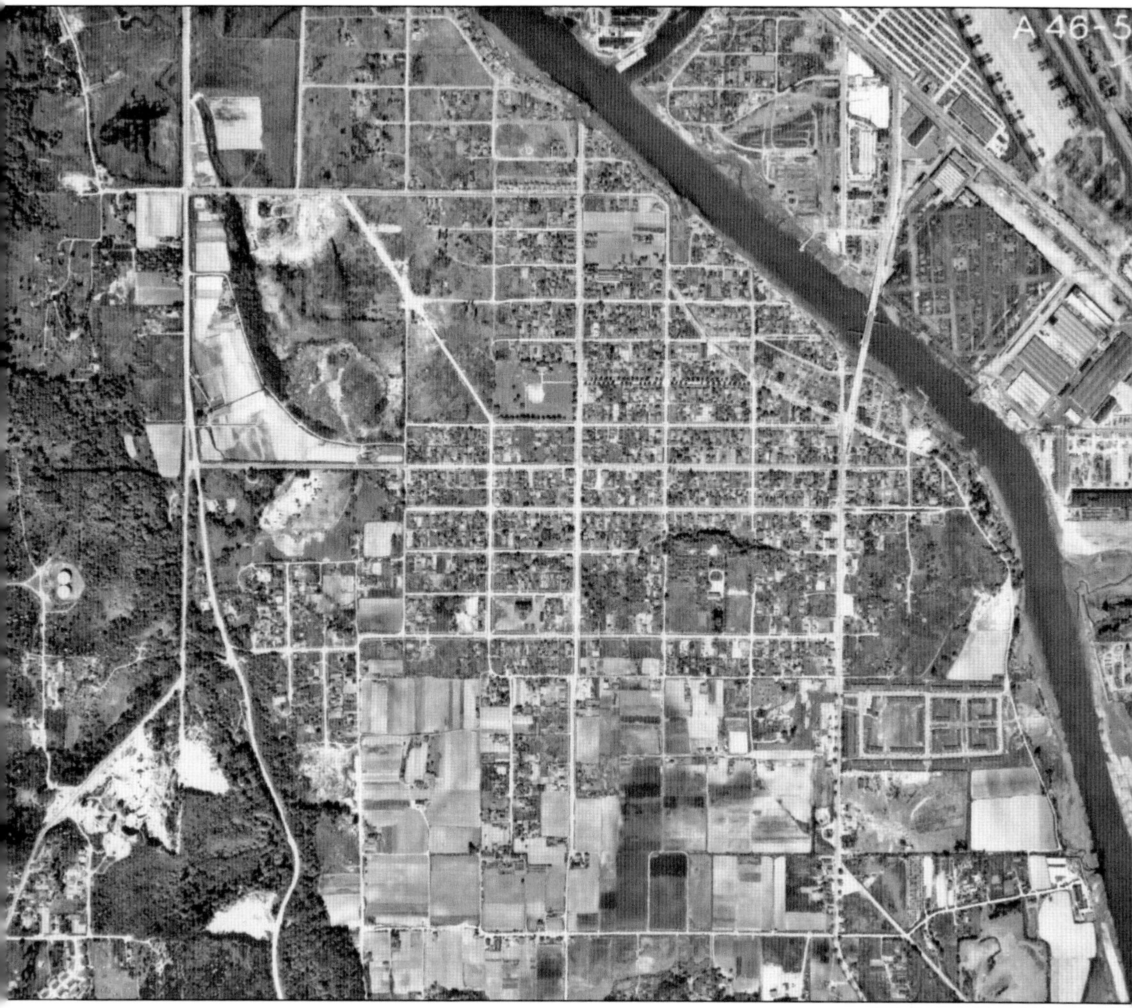

This 1946 aerial photograph reveals that the Eighth Avenue Bridge is gone, and Boeing field is no longer a grassy field but an airstrip prepping bombers for war. Boeing's growth during World War II greatly impacted South Park's housing development. (Courtesy of the Army Corps of Engineers.)

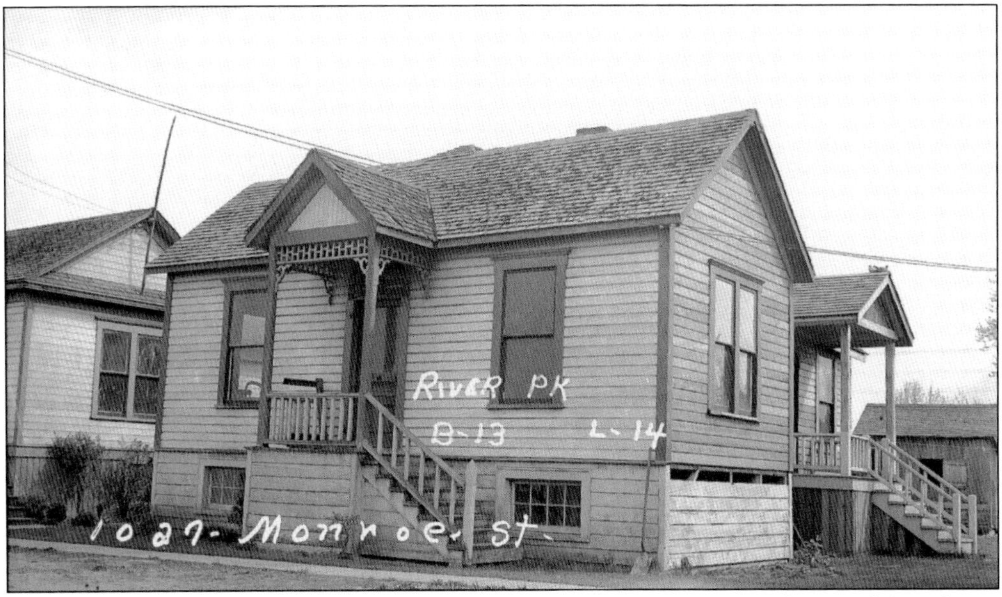

In 1937, this home sat at 1027 Monroe Street. This property was graciously spared from being zoned industrial, but the house was torn down in 1968 along with a few others on Monroe and Elmgrove Streets to create the Duwamish Waterway Park, one of the few places where residents can publicly access the river. (Courtesy of PSRA.)

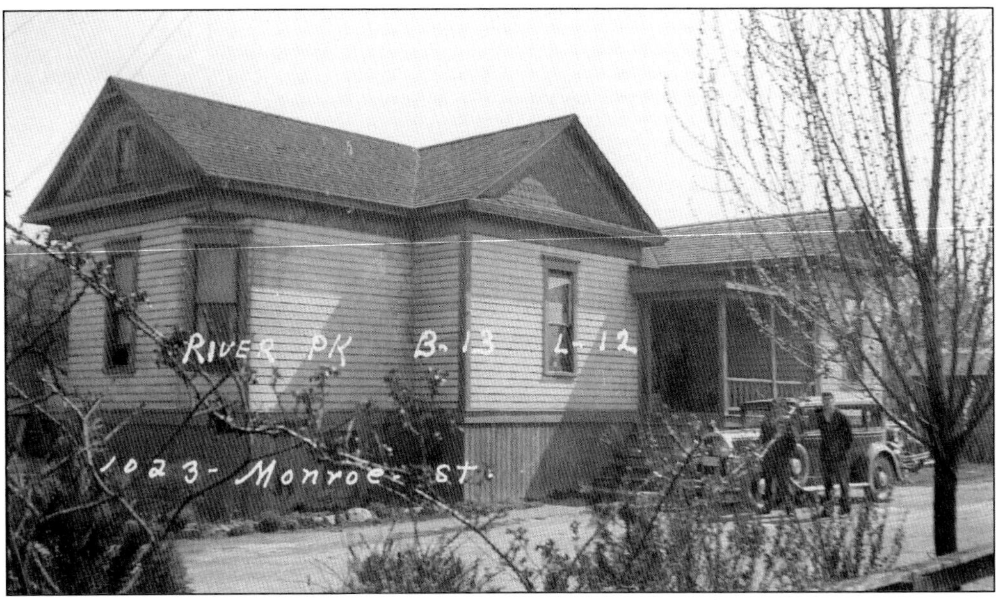

Monroe Street has seen a great deal of change over the years. In 1937, the property at 1023 Monroe Street was occupied by a home; however, this house was torn down in 1966. Monroe Street no longer has a street or houses on it. Duwamish Waterway Park and Long Painting now occupy this section of Monroe Street. (Courtesy of PSRA.)

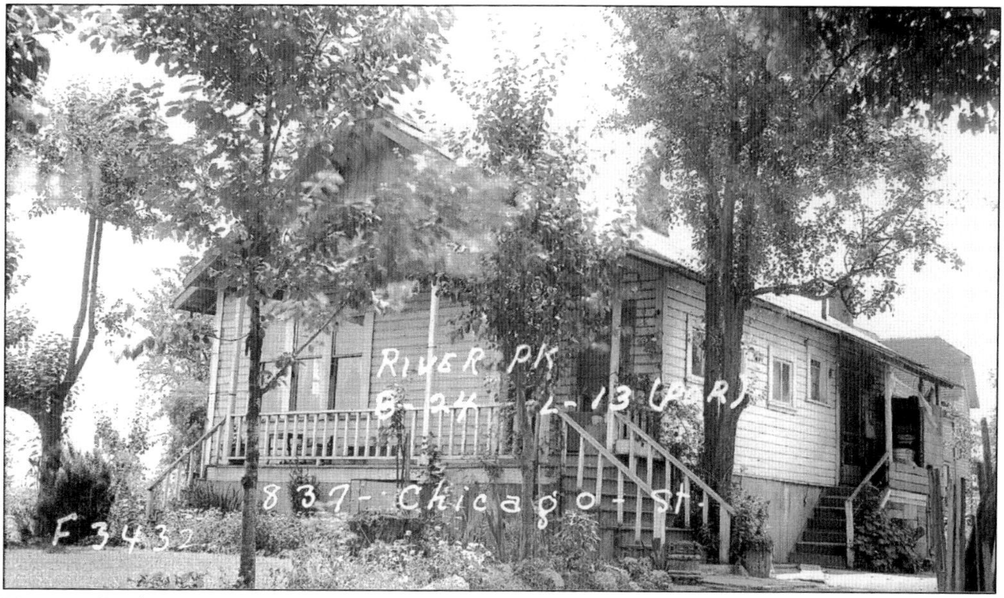

Here is 837 Chicago Street as it appeared in 1937. This part of South Park was known as the River Park Addition. The Duwamish River was moved closer to this house when it was straightened. The house was so close to the newly straightened river that its lot was rezoned industrial. (Courtesy of PSRA.)

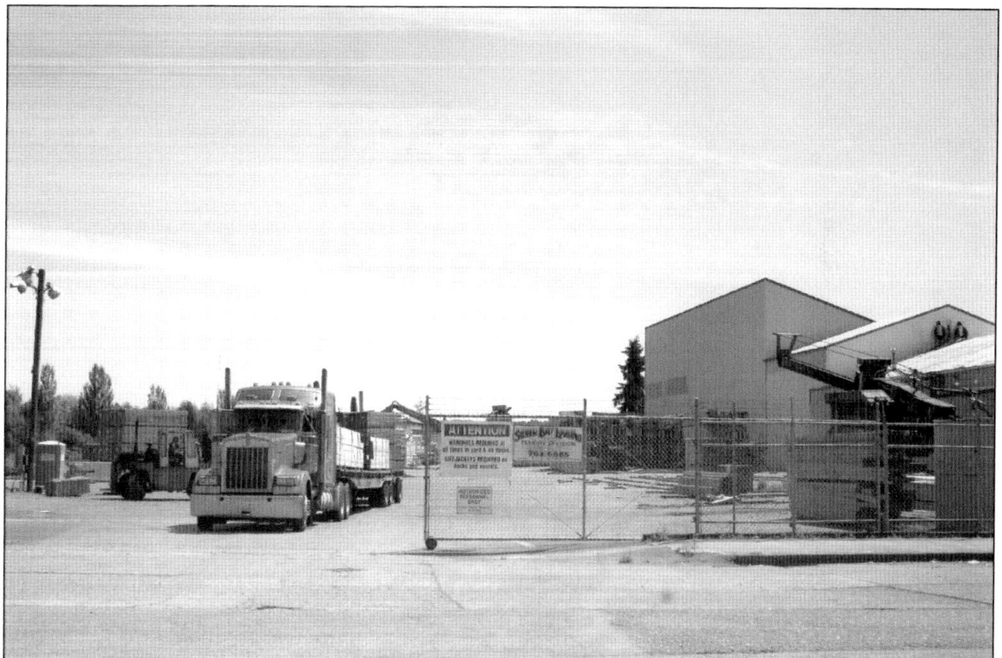

In 2006, 837 Chicago Street is part of Silver Bay Logging. The pile of wood on the right is about where the house at 837 Chicago Street once stood—a full two to three blocks from the original meandering river. The straightened waterway assists industries, like Silver Bay, in barging supplies to and from the site. (Courtesy of the South Park Neighborhood Association.)

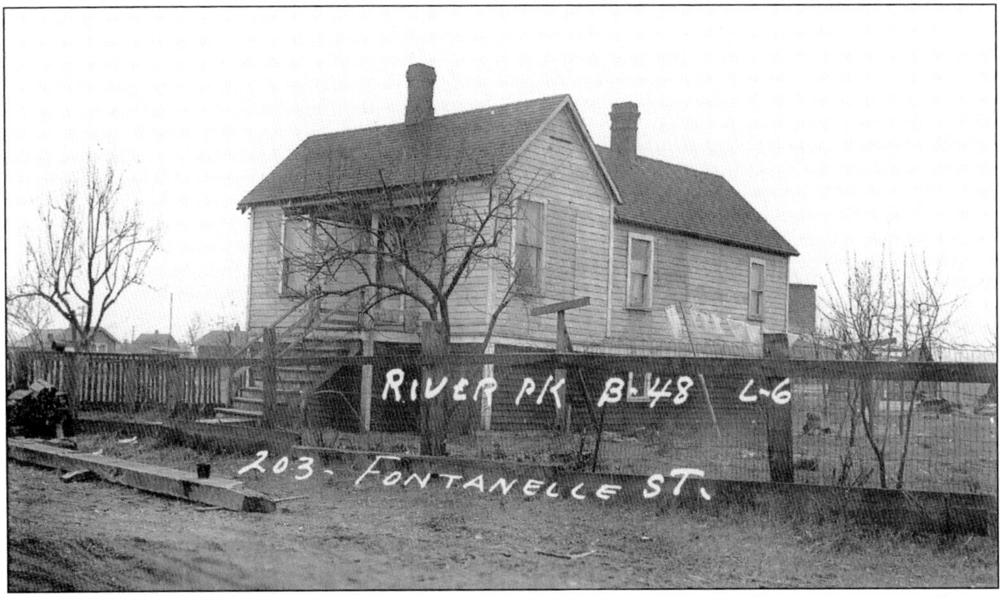

This home at 203 Fontanelle, pictured here in 1937, is now part of the Northwest Center warehouse and facility, which provides jobs to the developmentally delayed. (Courtesy of PSRA.)

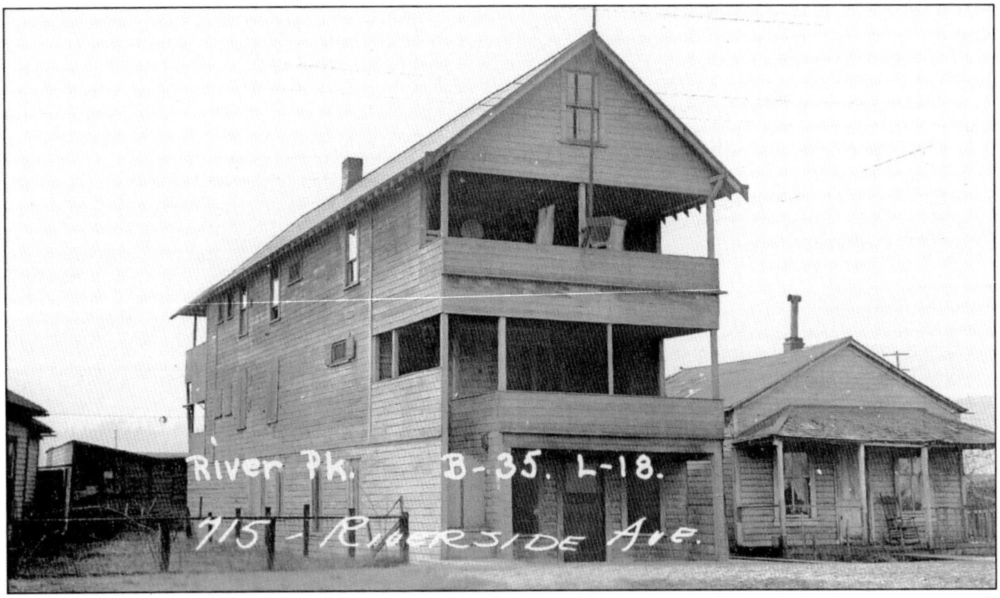

Riverside Drive was once entirely occupied by homes. Once parts of South Park were rezoned, however, the homes on Riverside Drive disappeared and were replaced by industrial businesses. This 1937 photograph shows 715 Riverside Drive (constructed in the early 1900s), now part of the warehouse of Lukas Machine, Inc. Resident Theresa Lytle recalls that during World War II, it served as a black market where one could purchase items that were hard to get during the war. Only about four residential homes remain on Riverside Drive. (Courtesy of PSRA.)

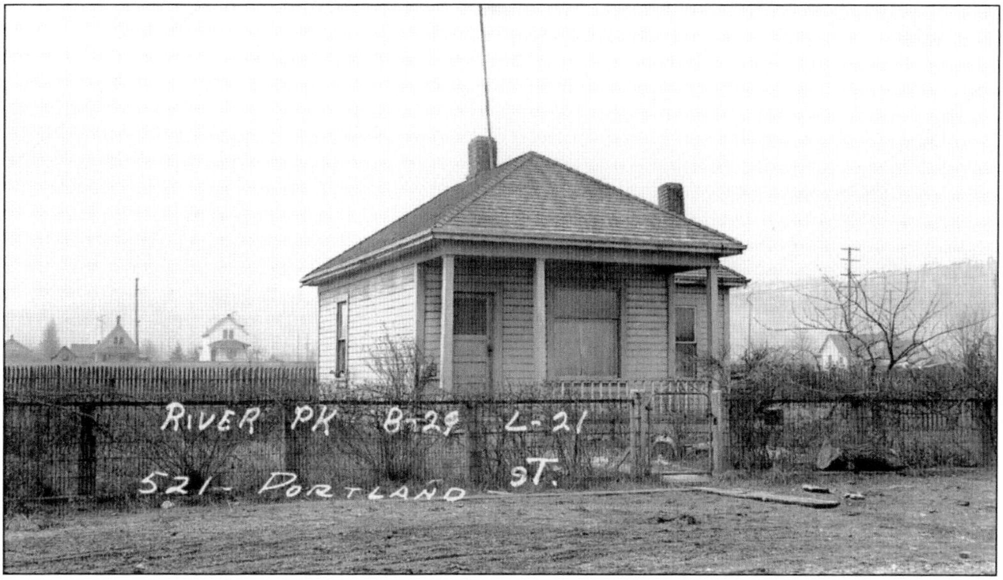

In 1937, 521 Portland was in a part of South Park known as River Park Addition, which was the northern part of the neighborhood that bordered the river before it was dredged. (Courtesy of PSRA.)

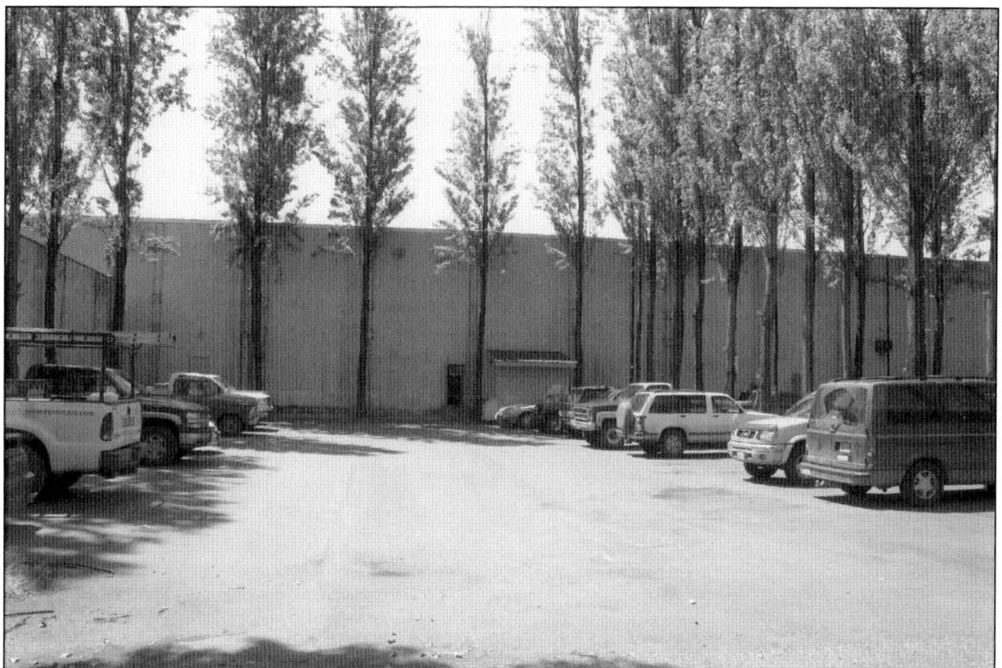

In 2006, 521 Portland is a parking lot for area industrial businesses and still in a part of South Park that is close to the new straight channel of the Duwamish River. (Courtesy of the South Park Neighborhood Association.)

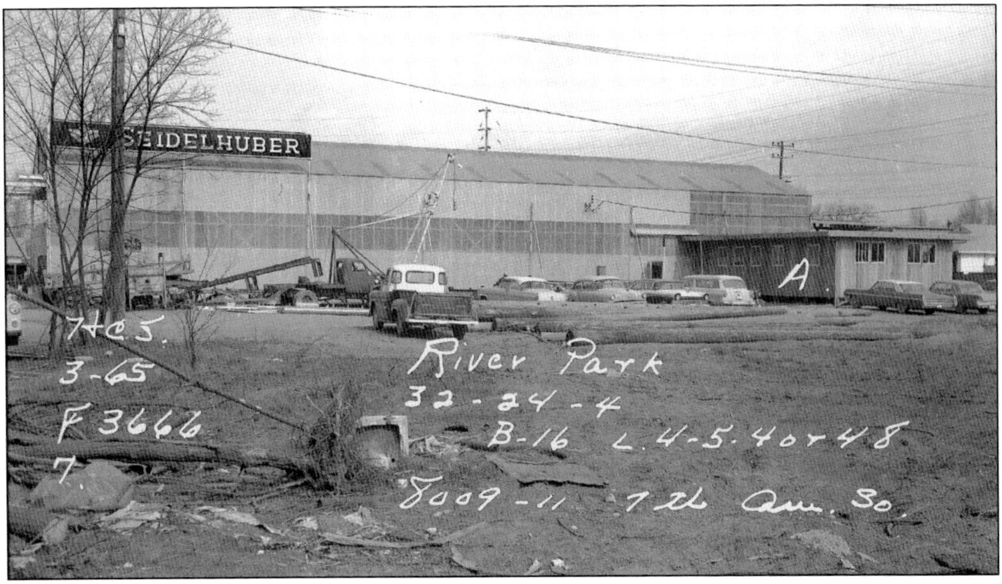

One of the oldest industrial companies in the South Park neighborhood is Seidelhuber Iron Works, pictured here in 1965. The company, located at 8009 Seventh Avenue South, is known for its work with the Historic Preservation Board on the Pioneer Square Pergola. (Courtesy of PSRA.)

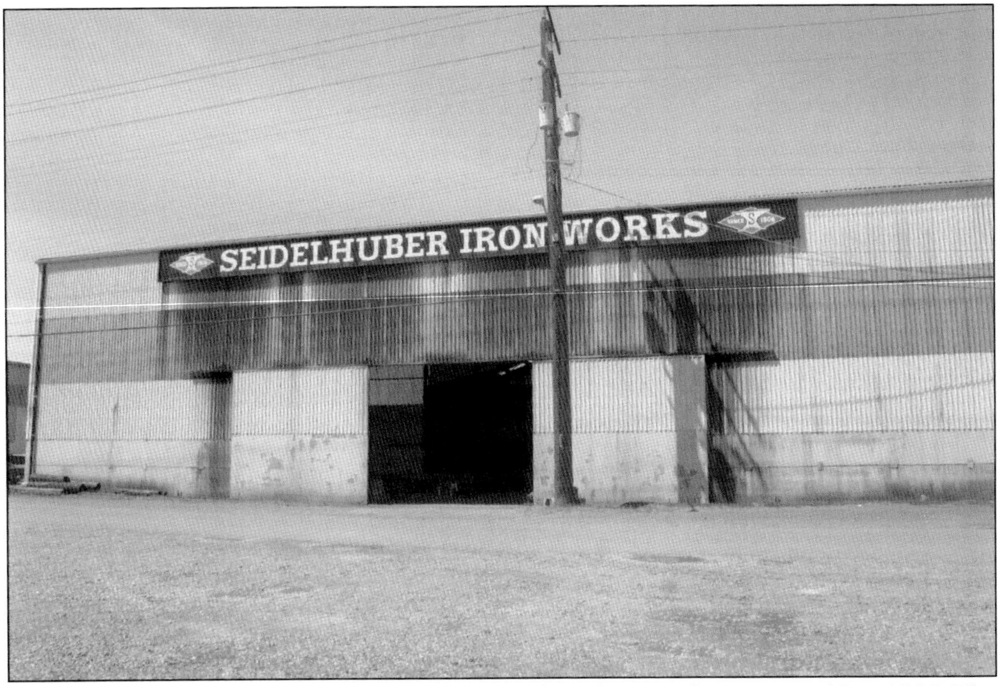

Seidelhuber Iron Works, open since 1906 in South Park, turned 100 years old in 2006. The owners are active in the community and find South Park's unique residential and industrial mix a great place to own a business. (Courtesy of the South Park Neighborhood Association.)

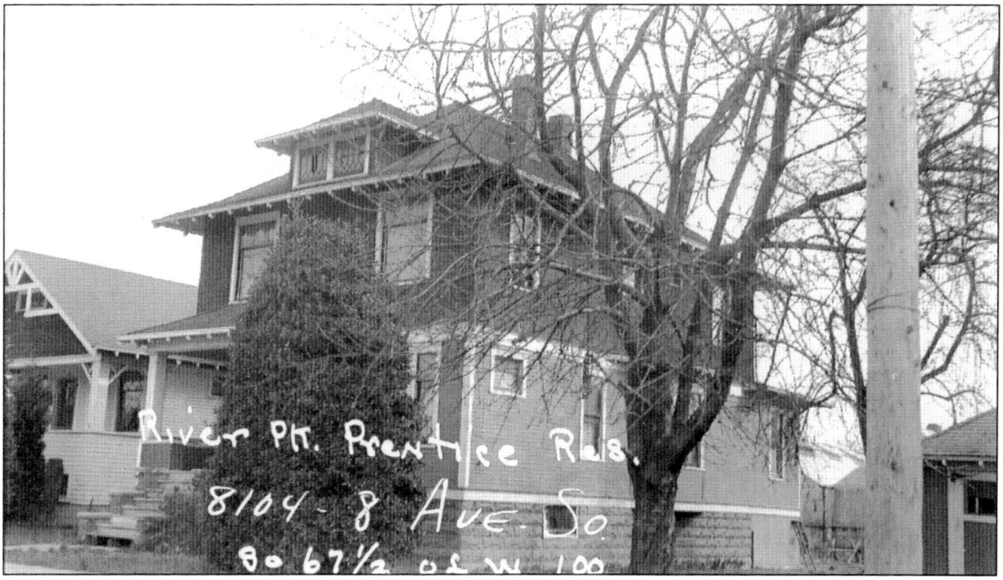

Once located at 8104 Eighth Avenue South, this home no longer exists. The original owner also owned several greenhouses on Elmgrove Street and ran a nursery business. When the river was straightened, this lot was rezoned industrial due to its proximity to the river. This photograph was taken in 1937. (Courtesy of PSRA.)

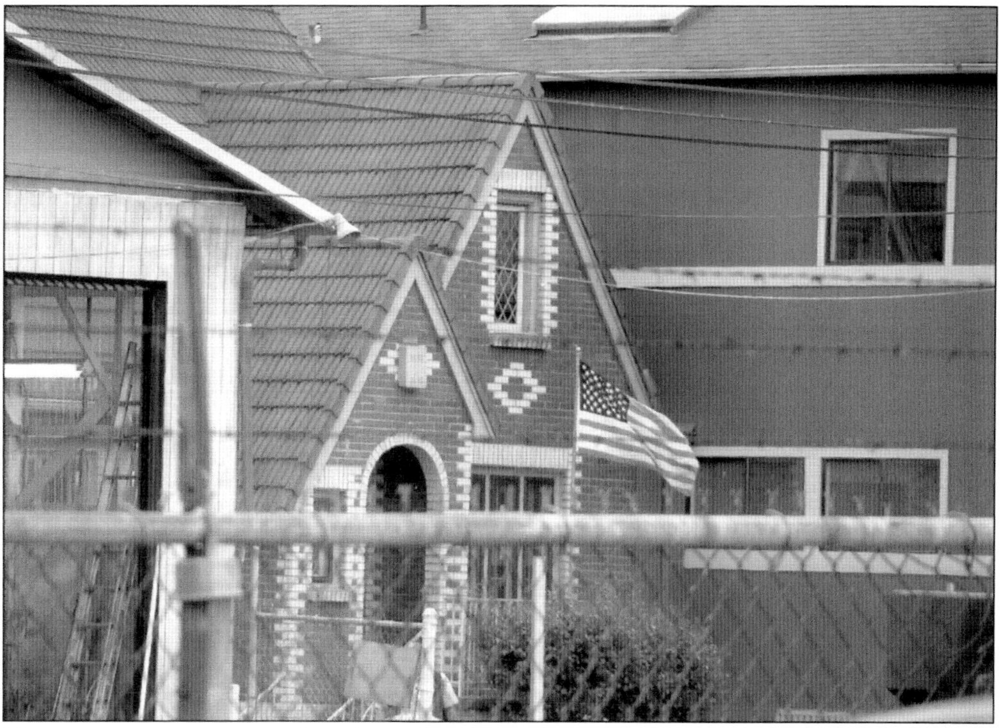

This property is now part of the large Long Painting Company property. Currently it is being leased to a transit company but is being used as an office building. Note the remaining brick Tudor in the middle of the property. The house was spared from being torn down and serves as an office. (Courtesy of the South Park Neighborhood Association.)

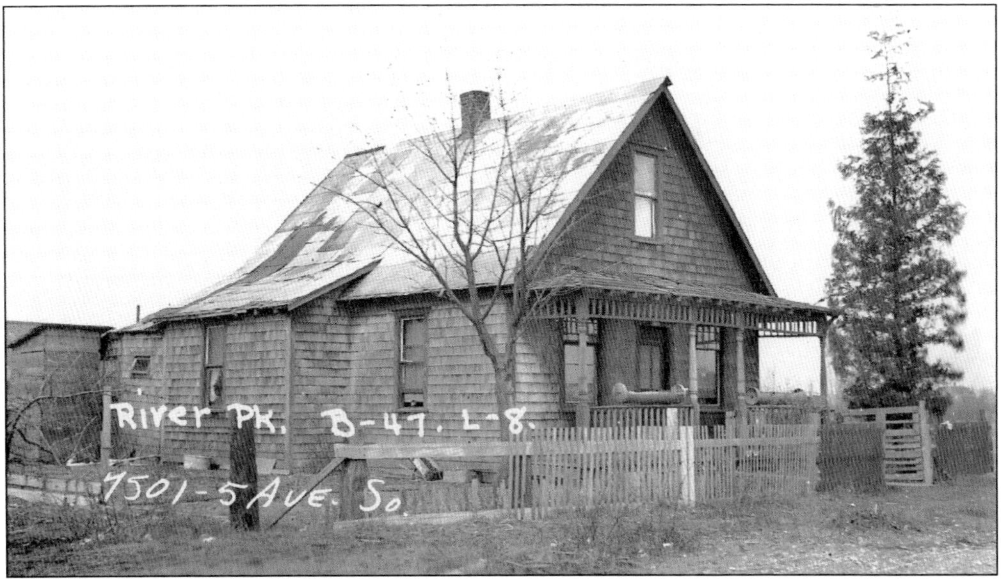

This was 7501 Fifth Avenue South in 1937 in the River Park Addition area of South Park. The excellent soil and abundant water supply fed the many farms and nurseries around this house. This is now a mattress warehouse and is surrounded by industrial properties. (Courtesy of PSRA.)

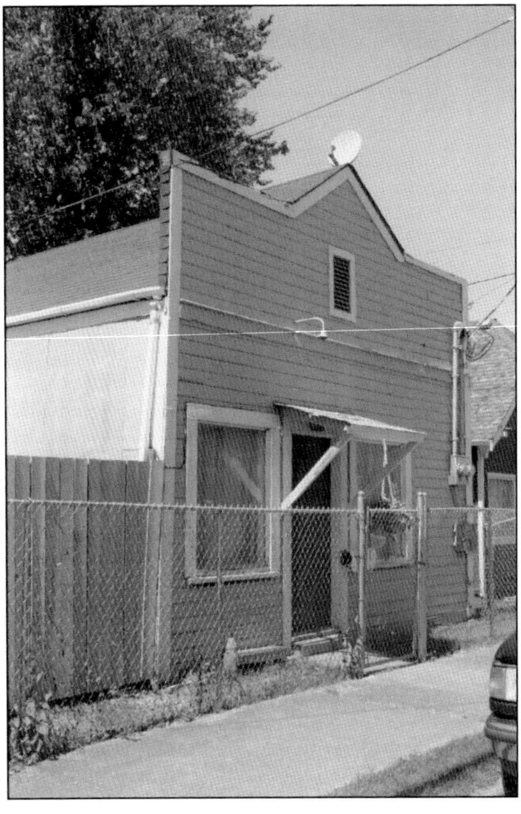

This used to be South Park Washing Machine Sales and Service on Eighth Avenue South, near La Cantina at the corner of Eighth and Cloverdale Street. It is now owned by the South Park Tongan Assembly of God and is used as a private residence, as it was remodeled from a store to a home. One can still see the obvious architecture that indicates it was once a storefront. (Courtesy of the South Park Neighborhood Association.)

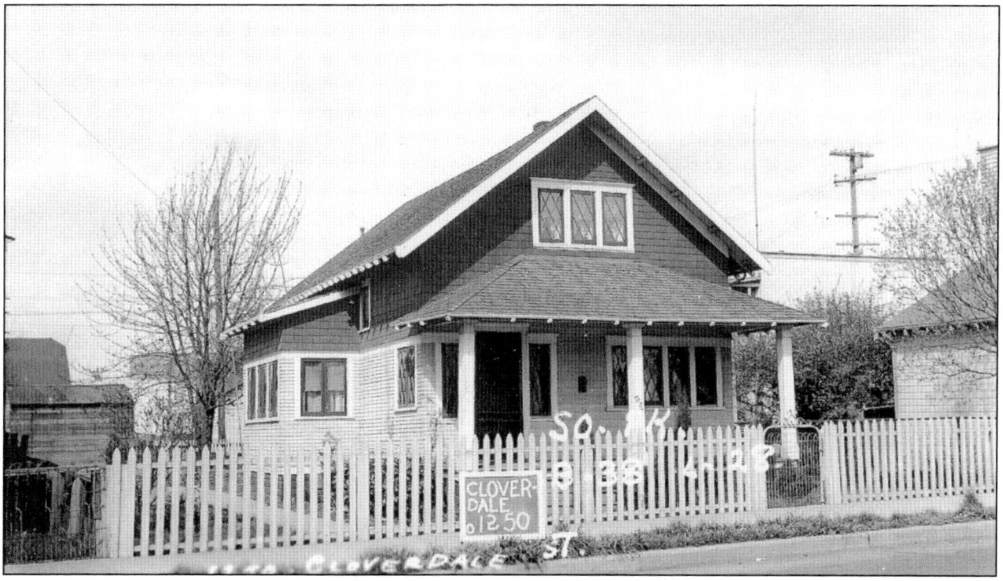

This 1937 photograph shows 1250 Cloverdale Street, now the parking lot for Muy Macho, Jalisco, and the Mexican Video Mar. As the retail core shifted from Eighth Avenue to Fourteenth Avenue, and as more people owned vehicles, parking along Fourteenth Avenue South was somewhat remedied when this house was removed. (Courtesy of PSRA.)

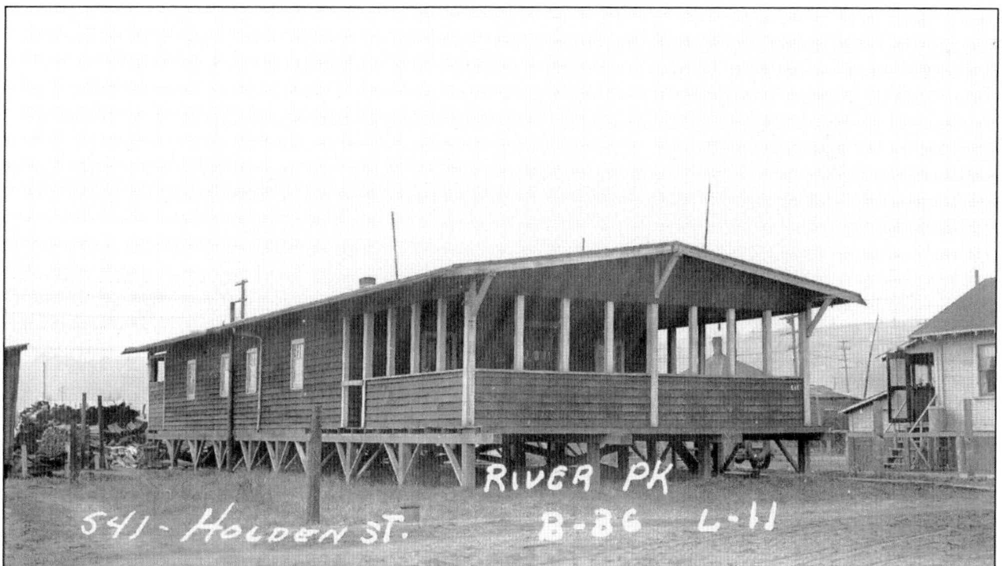

Pictured above in 1937 is 541 Holden Street in the River Park Addition portion of South Park. The proximity to the river probably required the post-and-pillar construction of this building to keep it above water and muck. The property is now the shipping and receiving storage yard for The Gear Works. (Courtesy of PSRA.)

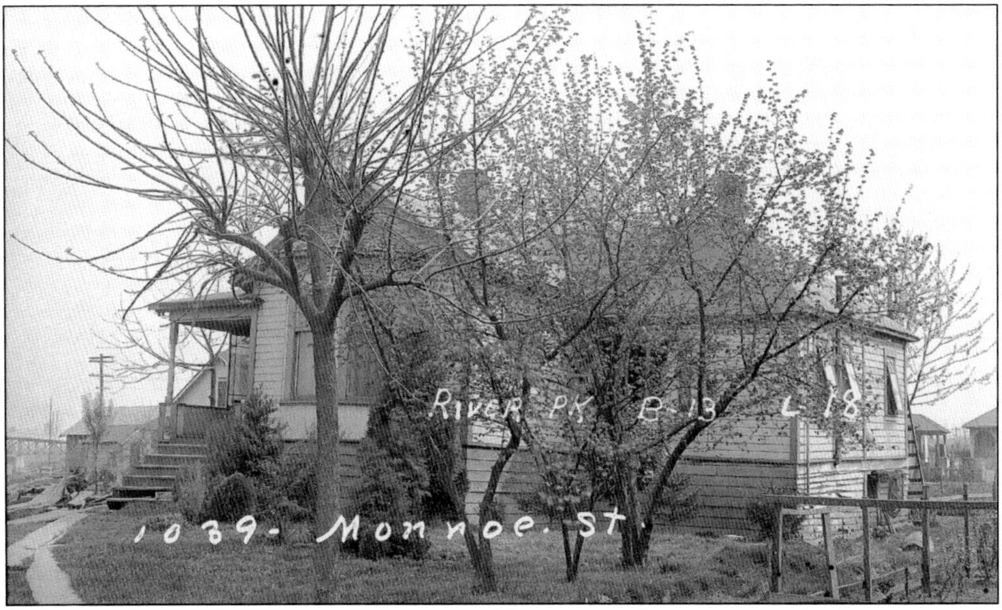

Here is 1039 Monroe Street in 1937. Now part of the Duwamish Waterway Park, the property was once part of a 10-acre truck and turkey farm. It was deeded as a gift to King County, but Seattle Parks and Recreation operate the current park. Note the South Park Bridge on the left side of the photograph. (Courtesy of PSRA.)

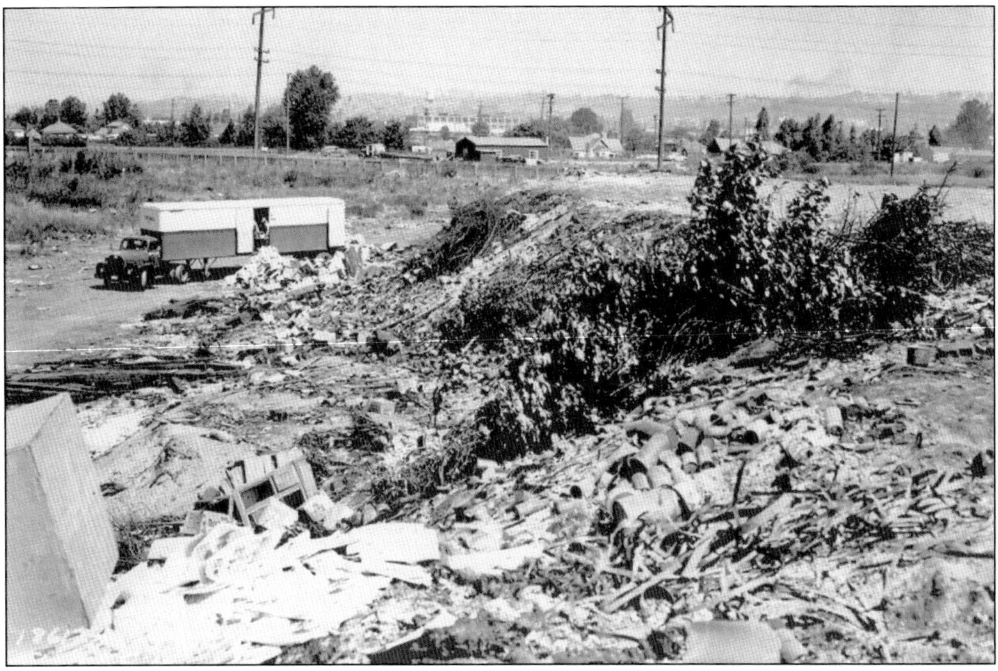
The South Park Landfill, located on Fifth Avenue South, is pictured here in 1955. Trash was burned openly, and eventually the neighborhood contested this practice. The current South Park transfer station resides just north of the old South Park Landfill site, which the city plans on cleaning up. They also plan to update the transfer facility. (Courtesy of the City of Seattle Municipal Archives.)

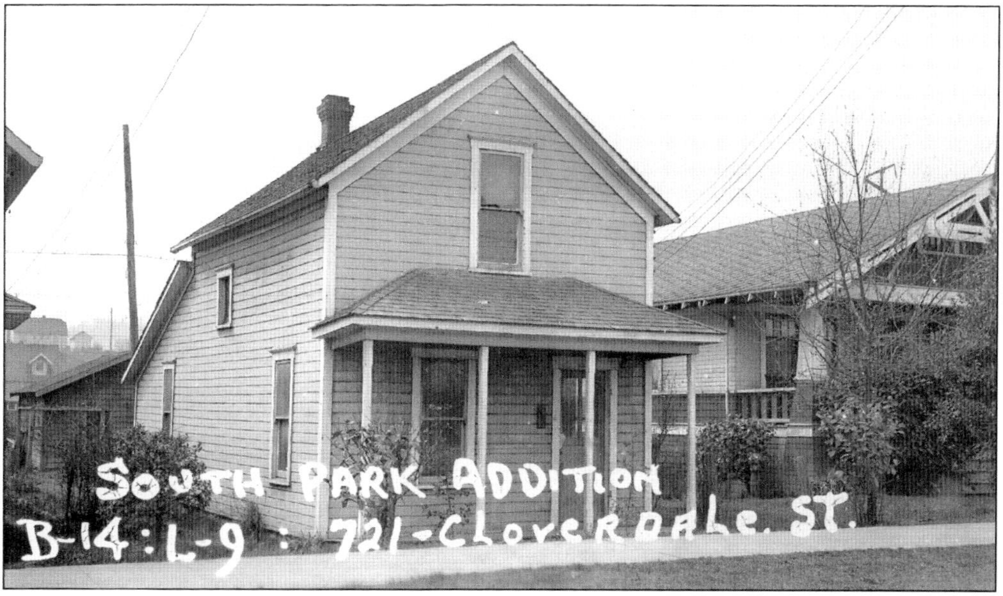

Built in 1910, this home at 721 South Cloverdale Street is pictured here in 1937 before it was removed for Highway 99 to be built. Some of the homes that had to be removed for the freeway were actually moved to other parts of South Park. The homes were in good condition, and it made no sense to the owners to tear them down. Today 721 South Cloverdale would be about where Cesar Chavez Park sits. (Courtesy of PSRA.)

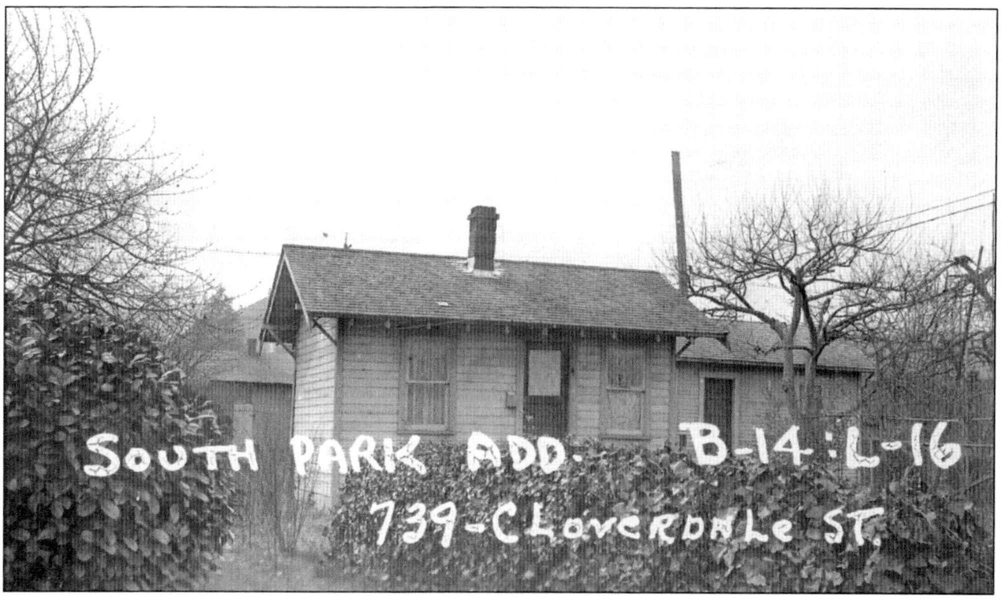

This is how 739 South Cloverdale Street appeared in 1937. The house was built in 1921 and owned by Henry H. Johnson. It was moved to 721 Director Street when Highway 99 forced its removal. Today 739 South Cloverdale is the entrance to Highway 99, which dissected the once unified neighborhood into two halves. Pedestrians and motorists had to figure out how to get from one side of South Park to the other, as the freeway created dozens of dead-end streets in South Park. (Courtesy of PSRA.)

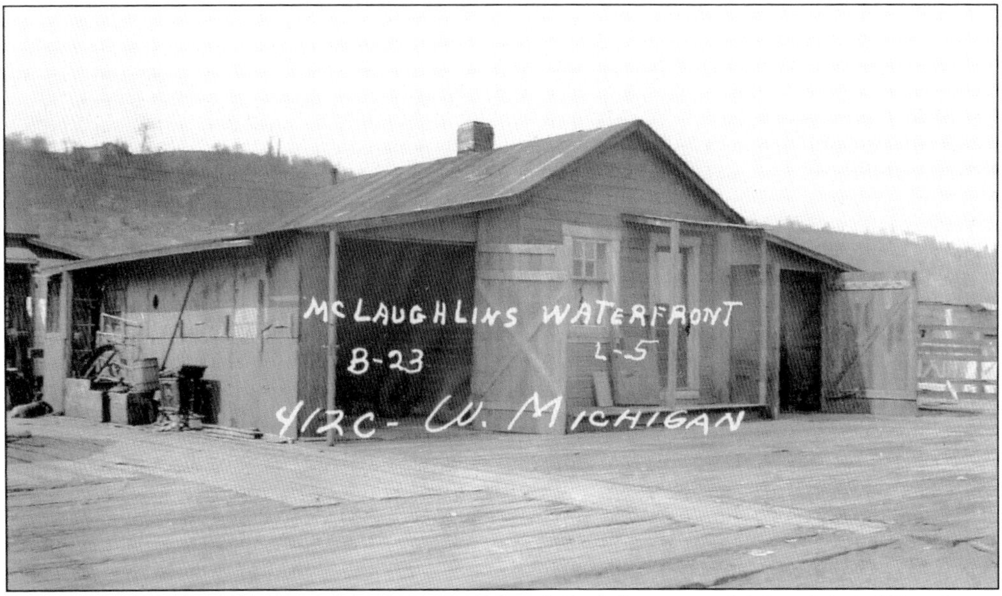

In 1937, 412 West Michigan was in an area of South Park known as McLaughlin's Waterfront. The First Avenue Bridge was not constructed until 1956, which left much of the Duwamish River shoreline to homes and businesses like this one. (Courtesy of PSRA.)

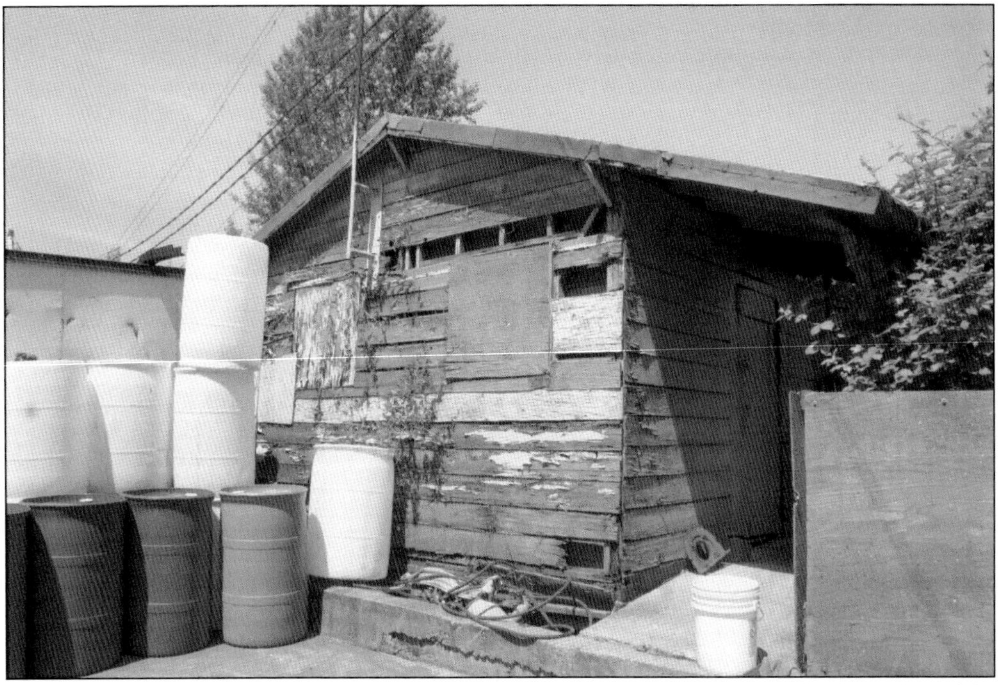

The address of 412 West Michigan is difficult to get to, as it is largely fenced off to keep the public safe from the heavy industry that takes place there now. Currently, Northwest Cooperage/Industrial Container Services and Alaska Marine Lines operate on this property, which is in the shadow of the First Avenue Bridge. They provide living-wage jobs and employ many new immigrants. (Courtesy of the South Park Neighborhood Association.)

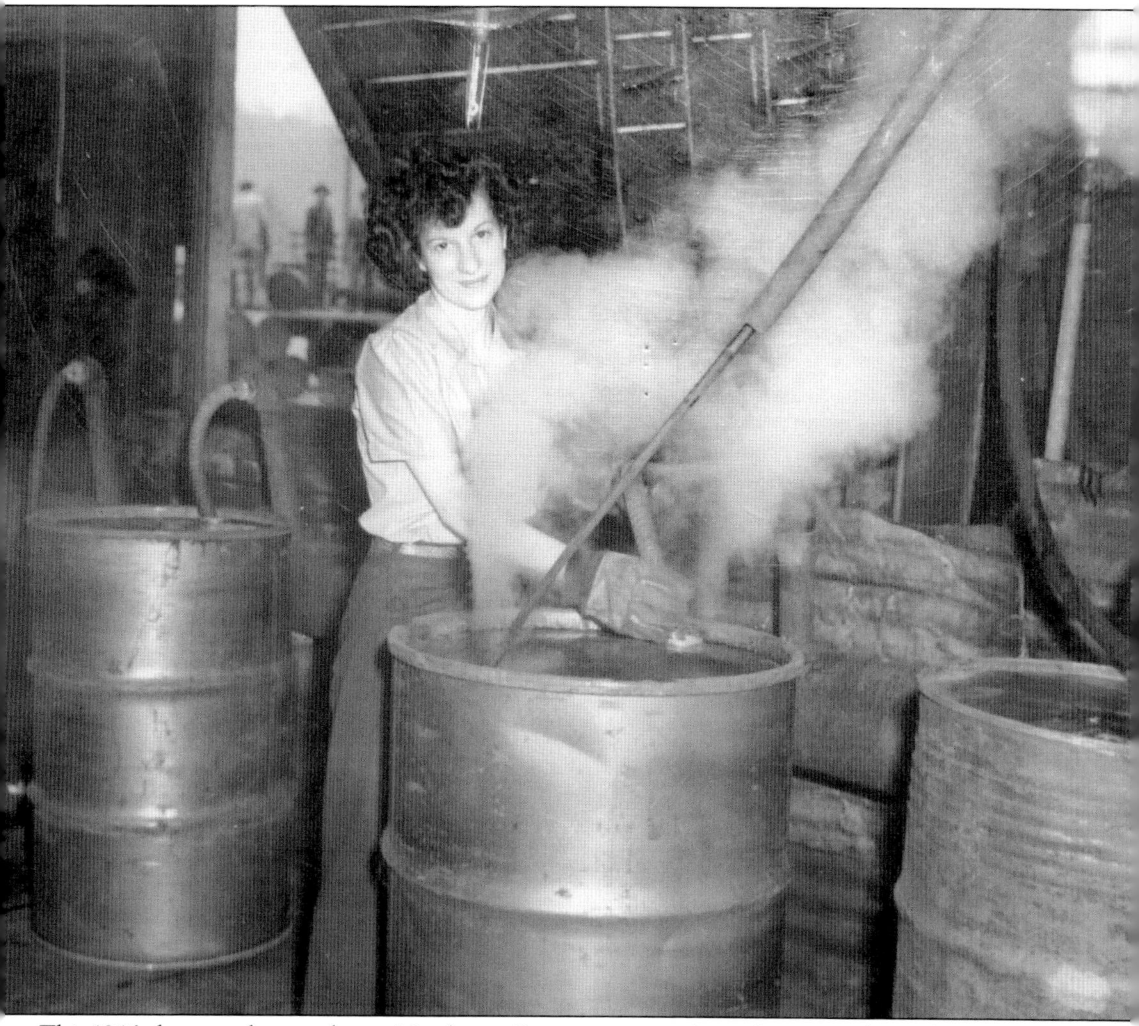

This 1946 photograph was taken at Northwest Cooperage, an industrial company located in South Park near West Marginal Way and the First Avenue Bridge. The photograph illustrates the type of industry that flourished in the area during the war years. During wartime, Northwest Cooperage cleaned more than 10,000 barrels a day. Many women, including those from South Park, joined the workforce to support the war effort. The company is now known as Industrial Container Services and cleans over 2,500 containers per day, as packaging has changed over the years and fewer barrels are used for industrial purposes. (Courtesy of Industrial Container Services.)

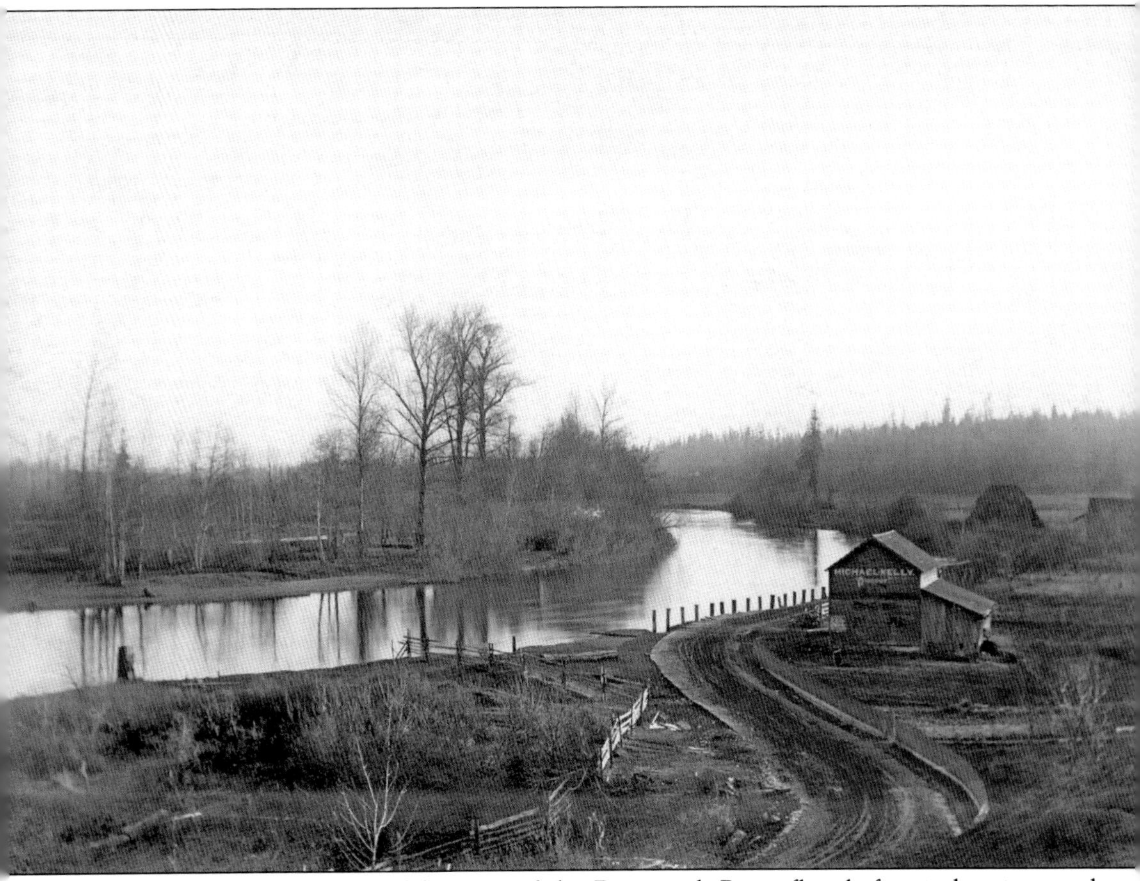

The peaceful and resourceful waters of the Duwamish River flow before industrious and entrepreneurial planners altered its graceful curves forever. The signage on the building says, "Michael Kelly, Pioneer." The early Town of South Park municipal archives reflect that Michael Kelly was involved in the neighborhood, as his signature is on 1906 petition to annex the town of South Park to the city of Seattle. This photograph is believed to be from the late 1800s. (Courtesy of MOHAI, No. 2002.50.87.)

TIMELINE

1800s The area surrounding present-day South Park was used extensively by the Duwamish tribe for fishing and farming.
1851 Eli Maple, one of the first settlers to the area, staked a claim that included most of present-day South Park.
1853 The first ferry license was obtained for passage over the Duwamish River.
1854 Henry Van Asselt became South Park's first naturalized citizen.
1871 Over eight families who had settled along the shores of the Duwamish River in the South Park neighborhood moved away because of a Native American attack scare.
1873 The people of South Park decided to construct their own railroad after the city of Seattle decided that the existing one would not be continued through the South Park area. The railroad took 13 years to complete.
1891 The Grant Street Electric Railway extended a trolley line from Seattle to South Park, crossing over the Duwamish River on a wooden drawbridge.
1910 The first firehouse in South Park was built. The building, however, would be outdated quickly and replaced by a new one in 1920.
1913 The U.S. Army Corps of Engineers re-channels the Duwamish River.
1915 The South Park neighborhood was completely crippled by a big snowstorm.
1920 The Boeing Airplane Company begins building airplanes for the U.S. military, creating a population increase in the South Park neighborhood.
1927 Cleveland High School opens, accepting students living as far away as Burien. Cleveland was where the majority of South Park students attended school.
1931 Several of the streets and sidewalks of South Park were paved and maple trees were planted.
1955 The Washington State Pollution Control Commission investigates the pollution in the "green" Duwamish River.
1956 South Park is rezoned as "transitioning the area to complete industrial use."
1972 The federal Clean Water Act was established as a law for the Duwamish River Waterway.
1974 A cracked transformer case released 255 gallons of 100 percent PCB transformer oil into the Duwamish Waterway. Final cleanup of sediment took place in March 1976 and achieved approximately 92 percent removal of the PCBs. This focused in on the need for a major Duwamish cleanup.
1989 The City of Seattle removes and rebuilds the South Park Community Center.
1991 Federal consent establishes the Elliot Bay and Duwamish River Restoration Program. The city of Seattle and King County will spend approximately $24 million on a habitat restoration, sediment cleanup, and source control projects.
2001 The EPA places the lower Duwamish Waterway on its National Priorities List.
2004 King County removes 66,000 cubic yards of contaminated sediments from the Duwamish.